The Law of Emergencies

The Law of Emergencies
Public Health and Disaster Management

Nan D. Hunter

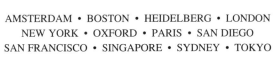

AMSTERDAM • BOSTON • HEIDELBERG • LONDON
NEW YORK • OXFORD • PARIS • SAN DIEGO
SAN FRANCISCO • SINGAPORE • SYDNEY • TOKYO

ELSEVIER

Butterworth-Heinemann is an imprint of Elsevier

Butterworth-Heinemann is an imprint of Elsevier
30 Corporate Drive, Suite 400, Burlington, MA 01803, USA
Linacre House, Jordan Hill, Oxford OX2 8DP, UK

Library of Congress Cataloging-in-Publication Data
Hunter, Nan D.
  The law of emergencies: public health and disaster management / Nan D. Hunter.
    p. cm.
  ISBN 978-1-85617-547-0
1. Medical emergencies—United States. 2. Emergency management—United States.
3. Public health—Law and Legislation—United States. I. Title.
[DNLM: 1. Disaster Planning—legislation & jurisprudence—United States.
2. Emergencies—United States. 3. Public Health—legislation & jurisprudence—
United States. WA 33 AA1 H946L 2009]
  RC86.7.H86 2009
  616.02'5—dc22

                                                                    2009017008

British Library Cataloguing-in-Publication Data

ISBN: 978-1-85617-547-0

For information on all Butterworth–Heinemann publications
visit our Web site at www.elsevierdirect.com

Printed in the United States of America

09 10 11 12 10 9 8 7 6 5 4 3 2 1

Table of Contents

Preface

The origins of this book lay somewhere between happenstance and inevitability. I have been a teacher and student of public health law since AIDS first engaged my attention in the 1980s. Like many others, I was introduced to the law of emergencies in the period following the attacks of September 11. My own path was charted by my work as legal consultant to the Redefining Readiness Project of the New York Academy of Medicine. The purpose of that project was to study how community-based emergency preparedness planning could help mitigate the effects of a wide range of disasters, including both natural events and hostile attacks. The legal research and analysis that I developed for the Academy led me to expand my public health law course into one that covered emergency preparedness as well. Thus began the effort of compiling legal documents and developing the structure of what has become this book.

Since September 11 and the anthrax attacks that quickly followed, the lens of "emergency" has had a major impact on our culture and law. Before the enhanced apprehension of bioterrorism and the potential created by increased global travel for accelerating the spread of new infectious diseases, many citizens and officials alike probably assumed that vaccines and other medications would form the first, and probably the only necessary, line of defense against mass communicable illness. Quarantines were a relic of the distant past. Ironically, however, in the 21st century, we have had to reconsider the use of measures such as isolation and quarantine because adequate pharmacologic treatments do not exist for some of the biggest threats to public health.

Similarly, a heightened concern has emerged in recent years regarding natural disasters, driven in part no doubt by the tragedy of Hurricane Katrina and its aftermath (which continues) and in part by the greater media attention that attaches to each approaching storm. The field of emergency management has become increasingly professionalized and increasingly melded into an all-hazards model using quasi-military command structures.

This book seeks to provide a comprehensive introduction to the legal issues associated with both fields. It begins with fundamental legal doctrines, such as the separation of powers, that are necessary to understand the deeper issues behind the legal debates. Throughout, the text uses cases and examples drawn from public health or emergency response contexts to illustrate wider themes.

The first four chapters lay the foundation, by introducing the reader to the basic constitutional structures underlying the three branches of government, the principles of law upon which protection of individual liberty is based, and the questions raised by the application of executive power through the domestic use of military troops.

The second cluster of four chapters addresses public health law issues, first analyzing the powers (and limits on power) of the federal government and then examining the state and local laws that form the primary guidance for most first responders. Another chapter provides insights into contemporary questions in the field, such as rationing of medications in an emergency or the role of the World Health Organization. The final chapter in this segment probes the role of employers, hospitals, and other private sector institutions in a public health emergency.

Then begins a series of chapters on disaster management. Again, the progression is from federal to state law. The third chapter in this cluster – Who Does What? – focuses on the incident command system that applies to all forms of disaster management. It also illustrates how the many agencies of government can work together in a real-time context. Three additional chapters address specific legal issues: searches, seizures, and evacuations; sovereign immunity and government liability; and the risk of individual liability.

The book closes with two chapters that constitute extended hypothetical problem exercises, one involving a dirty bomb explosion in Washington, D.C., and the other, a pandemic influenza outbreak in New Jersey. Finally, there is an appendix documenting the response to a health emergency that unfolded just as the book was going to press: the swine flu outbreak of spring 2009. The appendix provides a real-world review of much of what is in the text.

A word about the audience – this book is designed for graduate and undergraduate courses throughout the university as well as for practicing professionals. Although not styled in a traditional casebook fashion, the book can also be used in law schools.

No book is the work of only one person, and this is no exception. Several law students worked as research assistants on this project. Clara Altman and Devin Cain performed essential work; Virginia Anderson, Lynsey Heffernan, Rachel Seevers, and Carrie Zoubul also were extremely helpful. Dr. Roz Lasker, the principal investigator of the Redefining Readiness Project, proved a marvelous colleague, as did the other members of the coordinating committee and the many wonderful people who joined the Redefining Readiness Project in the pilot communities. My gratitude goes to all who contributed.

Nan D. Hunter
Washington, D.C.

Foreword

On any given day across our nation, an individual, a family, a community, a State, or a region is liable to experience a disaster. In this context, we use the term *liable* to mean that there is a probability or a likelihood of a disaster. If we apply a legal perspective, that gives the word *liable* a completely different meaning. Disasters and emergencies are human events that cause individuals and institutions to respond, react, and eventually recover, but they also involve complex legal issues that reflect the very essence of our democratic government: separation of powers, individual liberties, states' rights versus federal responsibilities, obligations on the private sector, and initiatives by individuals who voluntarily act as good Samaritans.

Real-life examples of the confluence of legal and personal issues abound. When a Category 5 hurricane is heading toward the mainland of Florida, who has the authority to tell citizens that they must evacuate? How do evacuated citizens know that there will be resources made available to rebuild when they return to find a devastated community? In the context of natural hazards, there are established legal precedents that guide and facilitate governmental and community action although they are not well understood. In the post–September 11 environment, concerns over possible bioterrorism incidents have raised concerns over the responsibility and authority for policies almost unknown in recent decades, such as mass inoculations and quarantines.

As recently as April 2009, the potential for a worldwide pandemic was made evident by the outbreak of swine flu that originated in Mexico but was quickly carried to countries across the globe. The Mexican government responded by closing schools and limiting public gatherings to minimize the spread of the flu. Other countries where cases were discovered took different types of action, and in some cases possibly overreacted, but what this event illustrated is that of all types of disasters short of nuclear war, in public health emergencies, the role of government and of its coercive powers remains both unclear and controversial. Understanding the legal framework under which the various levels of government and the private sector would operate in a public health emergency is of critical importance to all individuals, disciplines, and professions that would be impacted by a public health emergency.

As Chief of Staff of the Federal Emergency Management Agency (FEMA), from 1994 to 2001, I was responsible for response and recovery in a myriad of disasters in over 3,000 counties throughout the United States.

These disasters included Hurricanes Floyd and Fran, the Oklahoma City bombing, the Northridge, California earthquake, the Midwest floods in 1993, and the repeat flood in 1995, hundreds of devastating tornadoes, ice storms, wild land fires and urban interface fires in California and Florida, hazardous materials incidents, and leaking from underground storage tanks. We successfully evacuated three million people on the East Coast during Hurricane Floyd. We relocated and then returned the entire population of Grand Forks, Minnesota after their devastating floods. We built temporary malls for businesses to relocate after the Northridge earthquake.

All these actions were taken pursuant to an elaborate legal structure of statutes, regulations, and case law. However, throughout my tenure at FEMA, one of our biggest concerns was how we would manage a major public health emergency. Luckily for me, I was never faced with answering questions about what the role of FEMA would be in an unprecedented infectious disease epidemic, and whether and how the Stafford Act would be invoked. Those concerns have only intensified since I was at FEMA. Increased globalization and the potential threats from both bioterrorism and the nonmalicious spread of virulent strains of flu present enormous challenges to our governmental, emergency, and private sector systems.

As evidenced by the H1N1 Mexican flu incident, it is critical to understand the legal, organizational, and statutory background, and issues that govern this new frontier of public health emergencies. In this volume, Professor Hunter has provided just that understanding. She has identified the critical players at the federal, state, local, and private sector levels, and the laws that govern their actions and limitations. This book provides a comprehensive discussion of federal and state law, and how these laws will be implemented in any kind of emergency. It also explores the contemporary public debates that arise when government must take extraordinary actions, as well as the implications for government liability and individual liability. These concepts and principles are illustrated and reinforced by the inclusion of two chapters that offer practical exercises in the form of pandemic flu and dirty bomb scenarios.

To me, the most important aspect of this book is the approach and language the author used in writing this text. Professor Hunter has made it accessible to all students and disciplines responsible for or potentially impacted by a public health emergency or other kind of disaster. Yes, it is a legal volume, but it should be considered essential reading for public health officials, emergency managers, health care providers, federal, state, and local government administrators, students of public policy, and other interested individuals. In this book, Professor Hunter has removed the mystery and confusion that often surround an emergency by setting forth the legal responsibilities of government entities that are involved when disaster strikes and the legal rights of American citizens.

I believe this book is essential reading for anyone who may be involved in emergency response. It will provoke thought, discussion, and most importantly, action to help enhance our capability as individuals, professionals, communities, and institutions to make a difference in the myriad of emergencies that we will face in the future.

Jane Bullock
Chief of Staff
Federal Emergency Management Agency (1994–2001)
Washington, D.C.

PART

I

The Legal Framework

# 1

Our Constitutional Structure of Government

What You Will Learn

- How the provisions of the U.S. Constitution created a government based on separation of powers
- The criteria by which courts analyze what actions the President may take in an emergency
- Why legal scholars are debating an "emergency constitution"
- How federalism affects public health law

Introduction

This chapter will introduce you to the basic components of American constitutional law insofar as it determines the structure of our government and allocates power among the three branches of government and between the federal and state governments. Both separation of powers and federalism are key concepts in understanding the law of emergencies.

The Structure of the Constitution

We begin this book with the Constitution, which provides both the structure and the boundaries of our government and laws. Since its ratification in 1788, the U.S. Constitution has been the supreme law of our land; no law and no governmental action may violate its provisions. It is essential to understand the constitutional structure of our government to understand the law of emergencies, or any other area of law.

The Constitution establishes a national government with three branches – legislative, executive, and judicial – and states the respective powers of each. The powers of these branches are both fluid and fixed: the Constitution establishes certain limits beyond which each branch must not reach, but allows the specific meaning of those limits to change over time and to be determined through a process of interaction and negotiation among the three branches.

Often this interbranch interaction occurs in the context of litigation, when plaintiffs challenge the lawfulness of actions taken by Congress or the Executive Branch, and the Supreme Court rules on whether the actions are permitted. After such rulings, either the Congress or the Executive Branch or both may revisit the questions at issue in the litigation, seeking to formulate laws that will pass muster under judicial review. And then the process of challenge and decision may begin again. The Constitution creates the framework for how these three branches of government interact.

Although all three branches are bound to enforce and to uphold the Constitution, each fulfills a distinct role within the legal system – the legislature (Congress) enacts statutes, the executive carries out laws through orders and regulations, and the judiciary interprets both statutes and the terms of the Constitution itself through decisions in cases (called "case law"). Thus, when we speak of "the law" we refer to several types of legal authority, each associated primarily with one branch of the government and resulting from the legal process unique to that branch.

There are three aspects of the structure of our Constitution with which we will be concerned in this book:

- Separation of powers
- Federalism
- Individual rights and liberties

We will address the first two in this chapter. Individual rights and liberties will be the subject of Chapter 2 and will also be addressed in several other chapters.

Separation of Powers

The first three articles of the Constitution list the powers and authorities of the different branches of the federal government. The framers began with congressional power in Article I, addressed executive branch power in Article II, and established the contours of the federal judiciary in Article III. They wrote in broad strokes, leaving a great deal of room for interpretation as to how much power each branch would have vis-à-vis the others. In emergency situations, as we shall see, the vagueness of the Constitution's language can become frustrating.

In Article I, Section 8, the Constitution lists, or enumerates, the powers of Congress. In addition to the power to declare war, raise taxes, and provide for military appropriations, this section includes broad powers "to provide for the common defense and general welfare of the United States," "to regulate commerce among the states," and "to make all laws which shall be necessary and proper for carrying into execution the foregoing powers." Unless there is *some* basis in the Constitution for Congress to legislate on a particular matter, it lacks the power to do so. Although these clauses have been interpreted broadly, their scope is not limitless. For example, the small number of business activities that have no connection whatsoever with interstate commerce are beyond the reach of Congress' power to regulate through legislation.

Article II sets out the powers of the President and the Executive Branch. It describes the President's role as commander in chief of the Armed Forces and as the person who nominates judges, cabinet officers, and ambassadors. In addition, Section 3 declares that the President shall propose legislation to the Congress "as he shall judge necessary and expedient," and "shall take care that the laws be faithfully executed." As with Congress, these powers have been interpreted broadly, but are not limitless, as we shall see in the *Youngstown* case below.

Article III establishes the U.S. Supreme Court and declares that Congress shall have the power to authorize lower level federal courts. Congress set up two tiers of federal courts below the Supreme Court level: trial courts (called district courts) and courts of appeal. For our purposes, one of the most important aspects of the federal court system is a principle established in a critical case decided early in the history of the nation: judicial review.

The courts can review laws in two important ways. In *Marbury v. Madison* in 1803, the Supreme Court ruled that the courts have the power to declare whether acts of Congress violate the Constitution and therefore are invalid and cannot be enforced. The courts also have the power to interpret the meaning of statutes enacted by Congress when there is ambiguity. If the Supreme Court finds that a statute has a particular meaning and Congress does not agree with that interpretation, Congress can remove the ambiguity by amending the law to clarify its meaning. Assuming that ambiguity was the only problem with the statute, Congress has the last word. If, however, the Supreme Court finds that a statute is unconstitutional, Congress' only option is to enact a new statute in line with the criteria set out by the Court, because the Supreme Court has the last word on the meaning of the Constitution.

■ ■ ■ ▬▬▬▬▬▬▬▬▬▬▬▬▬▬▬▬▬▬▬▬▬▬▬▬▬▬▬▬▬

How Do We Define "Emergency"?

There is no one accepted definition of emergency, but in analyzing emergency-related laws, the Congressional Research Service discerned four characteristics. I have adapted them as follows:

1. Temporal – sudden, possibly unforeseen, and with consequences of unknown duration
2. Gravity – potentially posing a severe threat to life and property
3. Exigency – requiring immediate action in response
4. Collectivity – affecting a large number of persons and necessitating a response by government

▬▬▬▬▬▬▬▬▬▬▬▬▬▬▬▬▬▬▬▬▬▬▬▬▬▬ ■ ■ ■

The *Youngstown* Case

One of the most important cases in American history addressing the scope of separation of powers arose during an emergency. In 1952, the United States was embroiled in the Korean War. The production of steel for military arms and vehicles was essential to the war effort. At the same time, workers at the Youngstown steel mills were demanding higher wages. The owners resisted, and the steelworkers' union threatened to strike.

During World War II, Congress had enacted a law granting to the Executive Branch the power to set wages and other terms of employment in war-related industries, to insure that production was kept at maximum capacity. That law expired in 1946, however, and Congress did not enact a new law granting the same power to the President for the Korean War.

President Truman, however, felt that he needed to act to prevent a strike from occurring at the Youngstown steel factory. So he issued an order declaring that the government would take over operation of the factory for such time as was necessary for the owners and the union to negotiate a new contract. In the meantime, no strikes would be allowed and the government would set the hourly wage rates for employees. The company challenged President Truman's order, and the case went to the Supreme Court.

Youngstown Sheet & Tube Co. v. Sawyer
U.S. Supreme Court, 1952

We are asked to decide whether the President was acting within his constitutional power when he issued an order directing the Secretary of Commerce to take possession of and operate most of the Nation's steel mills. The mill owners argue that the President's order amounts to lawmaking, a legislative function which the Constitution has expressly confided to the Congress and not to the President. The Government's position is that the order was made on findings of the President that his action was necessary to avert a national catastrophe which would inevitably result from a stoppage of steel production, and that in meeting this grave emergency the President was acting within the aggregate of his constitutional powers as the Nation's Chief Executive and the Commander in Chief of the Armed Forces of the United States. ...

The President's power, if any, to issue the order must stem either from an act of Congress or from the Constitution itself. There is no statute that expressly authorizes the President to take possession of property as he did here. Nor is there any act of Congress to which our attention has been directed from which such a power can fairly be implied. Indeed, we do not understand the Government to rely on statutory authorization for this seizure. ...

It is clear that if the President had authority to issue the order he did, it must be found in some provisions of the Constitution. And it is not claimed that express constitutional language grants this power to the President. The contention is that presidential power should be implied from the aggregate of his powers under the Constitution. Particular reliance is placed on provisions in Article II which say that "the executive Power shall be vested in a President ..."; that "he shall take Care that the Laws be faithfully executed"; and that he "shall be Commander in Chief of the Army and Navy of the United States."

The order cannot properly be sustained as an exercise of the President's military power as Commander in Chief of the

Armed Forces. The Government attempts to do so by citing a number of cases upholding broad powers in military commanders engaged in day-to-day fighting in a theater of war. Such cases need not concern us here. Even though 'theater of war' be an expanding concept, we cannot with faithfulness to our constitutional system hold that the Commander in Chief of the Armed Forces has the ultimate power as such to take possession of private property in order to keep labor disputes from stopping production. This is a job for the Nation's lawmakers, not for its military authorities.

Nor can the seizure order be sustained because of the several constitutional provisions that grant executive power to the President. In the framework of our Constitution, the President's power to see that the laws are faithfully executed refutes the idea that he is to be a lawmaker. The Constitution limits his functions in the lawmaking process to the recommending of laws he thinks wise and the vetoing of laws he thinks bad. And the Constitution is neither silent nor equivocal about who shall make laws which the President is to execute. The first section of the first article says that "All legislative Powers herein granted shall be vested in a Congress of the United States. ..." After granting many powers to the Congress, Article I goes on to provide that Congress may "make all Laws which shall be necessary and proper for carrying into Execution the foregoing Powers and all other Powers vested by this Constitution in the Government of the United States, or in any Department or Officer thereof."

The President's order does not direct that a congressional policy be executed in a manner prescribed by Congress-it directs that a presidential policy be executed in a manner prescribed by the President. The preamble of the order itself, like that of many statutes, sets out reasons why the President believes certain policies should be adopted, proclaims these policies as rules of conduct to be followed, and again, like a statute, authorizes a government official to promulgate additional rules and regulations consistent with the policy proclaimed and needed to carry that policy into execution. The power of Congress to adopt such public policies as those proclaimed by the order is beyond question. It can authorize the taking of private property for public use. It can make laws regulating the relationships between employers and employees, prescribing rules designed to settle labor disputes, and fixing wages and working conditions in certain fields of our economy. The Constitution did not subject this law-making power of Congress to presidential or military supervision or control. ...

Mr. Justice Jackson, concurring in the judgment and opinion of the Court.

... The actual art of governing under our Constitution does not and cannot conform to judicial definitions of the power of any of its branches based on isolated clauses or even single Articles torn from context. While the Constitution diffuses power the better to secure liberty, it also contemplates that practice will integrate the dispersed powers into a workable government. It enjoins upon its branches separateness but interdependence, autonomy but reciprocity. Presidential powers are not fixed but fluctuate, depending upon their disjunction or conjunction with those of Congress. We may well begin by a somewhat over-simplified grouping of practical situations in which a President may doubt, or others may challenge, his powers, and by distinguishing roughly the legal consequences of this factor of relativity.

1. When the President acts pursuant to an express or implied authorization of Congress, his authority is at its maximum, for it includes all that he possesses in his own right plus all that Congress can delegate. In these circumstances, and in these only, may he be said (for what it may be worth), to personify the federal sovereignty. If his act is held unconstitutional under these circumstances, it usually means that the Federal Government as an undivided whole lacks power. A seizure executed by the President pursuant to an Act of Congress would be supported by the strongest of presumptions and the widest latitude of judicial interpretation, and the burden of persuasion would rest heavily upon any who might attack it.

2. When the President acts in absence of either a congressional grant or denial of authority, he can only rely upon his own independent powers, but there is a zone of twilight in which he and Congress may have concurrent authority, or in which its distribution is uncertain. Therefore, congressional inertia, indifference or quiescence may sometimes, at least as a practical matter, enable, if not invite, measures on independent presidential responsibility. In this area, any actual test of power is likely to depend on the imperatives of events and contemporary imponderables rather than on abstract theories of law.

3. When the President takes measures incompatible with the expressed or implied will of Congress, his power is at its lowest ebb, for then he can rely only upon his own constitutional powers minus any constitutional powers of Congress over the matter. Courts can sustain exclusive Presidential control in such a case only by disabling the Congress from acting upon the subject. Presidential claim to a power at once so conclusive and preclusive must be scrutinized with caution, for what is at stake is the equilibrium established by our constitutional system.

Into which of these classifications does this executive seizure of the steel industry fit? It is eliminated from the first by admission, for it is conceded that no congressional authorization exists for this seizure. ...

Can it then be defended under flexible tests available to the second category? It seems clearly eliminated from that class because Congress has not left seizure of private property an open field but has covered it by three statutory policies inconsistent with this seizure. ...

This leaves the current seizure to be justified only by the severe tests under the third grouping, where it can be supported only by any remainder of executive power after subtraction of such powers as Congress may have over the subject. In short, we can sustain the President only by holding that seizure of such strike-bound industries is within his domain and beyond control by Congress. Thus, this Court's first review of such seizures occurs under circumstances which leave Presidential power most vulnerable to attack and in the least favorable of possible constitutional postures. ...

The clause on which the Government ... relies is that "The President shall be Commander in Chief of the Army and Navy of the United States ... ." These cryptic words have given rise to some of the most persistent controversies in our constitutional history. Of course, they imply something more than an empty title. But just what authority goes with the name has plagued Presidential advisers who would not waive or narrow it by nonassertion yet cannot say where it begins or ends. It undoubtedly puts the Nation's armed forces under Presidential command. Hence, this loose appellation is sometimes advanced as support for any presidential action, internal or external, involving use of force, the idea being that it vests power to do anything, anywhere, that can be done with an army or navy.

That seems to be the logic of an argument tendered at our bar – that the President having, on his own responsibility, sent American troops abroad derives from that act 'affirmative power' to seize the means of producing a supply of steel for them. To quote, "Perhaps the most forceful illustrations of the scope of Presidential power in this connection is the fact that American troops in Korea, whose safety and effectiveness are so directly involved here, were sent to the field by an exercise of the President's constitutional powers." Thus, it is said, he has invested himself with 'war powers.'

I cannot foresee all that it might entail if the Court should indorse this argument. Nothing in our Constitution is plainer than that declaration of a war is entrusted only to Congress. Of course, a state of war may in fact exist without a formal declaration. But no doctrine that the Court could promulgate would seem to me more sinister and alarming than that a President whose conduct of foreign affairs is so largely uncontrolled, and often even is unknown, can vastly enlarge his mastery over the internal affairs of the country by his own commitment of the Nation's armed forces to some foreign venture. I do not, however, find it necessary or appropriate to consider the legal status of the Korean enterprise to discountenance argument based on it.

Assuming that we are in a war de facto, whether it is or is not a war de jure, does that empower the Commander in Chief to seize industries he thinks necessary to supply our army? The Constitution expressly places in Congress power 'to raise and support Armies' and "to provide and maintain a Navy." This certainly lays upon Congress primary responsibility for supplying the armed forces. Congress alone controls the raising of revenues and their appropriation and may determine in what manner and by what means they shall be spent for military and naval procurement. I suppose no one would doubt that Congress can take over war supply as a Government enterprise. On the other hand, if Congress sees fit to rely on free private enterprise collectively bargaining with free labor for support and maintenance of our armed forces can the Executive because of lawful disagreements incidental to that process, seize the facility for operation upon Government-imposed terms?

There are indications that the Constitution did not contemplate that the title Commander in Chief of the Army and Navy will constitute him also Commander in Chief of the country, its industries and its inhabitants. He has no monopoly of 'war powers,' whatever they are. While Congress cannot deprive the President of the command of the army and navy, only Congress can provide him an army or navy to command. ...

We should not use this occasion to circumscribe, much less to contract, the lawful role of the President as Commander in Chief. I should indulge the widest latitude of interpretation to sustain his exclusive function to command the instruments of national force, at least when turned against the outside world for the security of our society. But, when it is turned inward, not because of rebellion but because of a lawful economic struggle between industry and labor, it should have no such indulgence. His command power is not such an absolute as might be implied from that office in a militaristic system but is subject to limitations consistent with a constitutional Republic whose law and policy-making branch is a representative Congress. ...

[Another] clause in which the Solicitor General [the attorney representing the President] finds seizure powers is that "he shall take Care that the Laws be faithfully executed ... ." That authority must be matched against words of the Fifth Amendment that "No person shall be ... deprived of life, liberty, or property, without due process of law ... ." One gives a governmental authority that reaches so far as there is law, the other gives a private right that authority shall go no farther. These signify about all there is of the principle that ours is a government of laws, not of men, and that we submit ourselves to rulers only if under rules.

The Solicitor General lastly grounds support of the seizure upon nebulous, inherent powers never expressly granted but said to have accrued to the office from the customs and claims of preceding administrations. The plea is for a resulting power to deal with a crisis or an emergency according to the necessities of the case, the unarticulated assumption being that necessity knows no law.

Loose and irresponsible use of adjectives colors all non-legal and much legal discussion of presidential powers. "Inherent" powers, "implied" powers, "incidental" powers, "plenary" powers, "war" powers and "emergency" powers are used, often interchangeably and without fixed or ascertainable meanings.

The vagueness and generality of the clauses that set forth presidential powers afford a plausible basis for pressures within and without an administration for presidential action beyond that supported by those whose responsibility it is to defend his actions in court. The claim of inherent and unrestricted presidential powers has long been a persuasive dialectical weapon in political controversy. While it is not surprising that counsel should grasp support from such unadjudicated claims of power, a judge cannot accept self-serving press statements of the attorney for one of the interested parties as authority in answering a constitutional question ...

In the practical working of our Government we already have evolved a technique within the framework of the Constitution by which normal executive powers may be considerably expanded to meet an emergency. Congress may and has granted extraordinary authorities which lie dormant in normal times but may be called into play by the Executive in war or upon proclamation of a national emergency. ...

... I have no illusion that any decision by this Court can keep power in the hands of Congress if it is not wise and timely in meeting its problems. A crisis that challenges the President equally, or perhaps primarily, challenges Congress. ... We may say that power to legislate for emergencies belongs in the hands of Congress, but only Congress itself can prevent power from slipping through its fingers.

... We do not know today what powers over labor or property would be claimed to flow from Government possession if we should legalize it, what rights to compensation would be claimed or recognized, or on what contingency it would end. With all its defects, delays and inconveniences, men have discovered no technique for long preserving free government except that the Executive be under the law, and that the law be made by parliamentary deliberations.

Such institutions may be destined to pass away. But it is the duty of the Court to be last, not first, to give them up. ...

■ ■ Critical Thinking ■

If you were a member of Congress and believed that the President should have greater powers in a time of emergency, what would you do? As you will see in Chapter 3, there was no serious systemization of statutes establishing emergency powers until the 1970s. Today there are a number of statutes that seek to better specify presidential power. One, the War Powers Act, provides a framework of checks and balances for the deployment of armed forces.

The War Powers Act

In the absence of a declaration of war, in any case in which United States Armed Forces are introduced –

(1) into hostilities or into situations where imminent involvement in hostilities is clearly indicated by the circumstances;

(2) into the territory, airspace or waters of a foreign nation, while equipped for combat, except for deployments which relate solely to supply, replacement, repair, or training of such forces; or

(3) in numbers which substantially enlarge United States Armed Forces equipped for combat already located in a foreign nation;

the President shall submit within 48 hours to the Speaker of the House of Representatives and to the President pro tempore of the Senate a report, in writing, setting forth –

(A) the circumstances necessitating the introduction of United States Armed Forces;

(B) the constitutional and legislative authority under which such introduction took place; and

(C) the estimated scope and duration of the hostilities or involvement. …

Within sixty calendar days after a report is submitted or is required to be submitted … whichever is earlier, the President shall terminate any use of United States Armed Forces with respect to which such report was submitted (or required to be submitted), unless the Congress –

(1) has declared war or has enacted a specific authorization for such use of United States Armed Forces

(2) has extended by law such sixty-day period or

(3) is physically unable to meet as a result of an armed attack upon the United States. Such sixty-day period shall be extended for not more than an additional thirty days if the President determines and certifies to the Congress in writing that unavoidable military necessity respecting the safety of United States Armed Forces requires the continued use of such armed forces in the course of bringing about a prompt removal of such forces.

Notwithstanding [the previous section], at any time that United States Armed Forces are engaged in hostilities outside the territory of the United States, its possessions and territories without a declaration of war or specific statutory authorization, such forces shall be removed by the President if the Congress so directs by concurrent resolution.

An "Emergency Constitution"?

The issues in *Youngstown* remain controversial today, all the more so since September 11. Should Congress take more steps to provide for both expansion and limitations on presidential power in an emergency? What do you think of the following proposal?

Terrorism and the Constitutional Order
Bruce Ackerman

> We panicked the last time terrorists struck, and we will panic the next time. September 11 was merely a pinprick compared

to the devastation of a suitcase A-bomb or an anthrax epidemic. The next major attack may kill tens of thousands of
innocents, dwarfing the personal anguish of those who lost
family and friends on 9/11. The political tidal wave threatens
to leave behind a mass of repressive legislation far more drastic than anything imagined by the USA PATRIOT Act.

A downward cycle threatens: After each successful attack,
politicians will come up with a new raft of repressive laws
that ease our anxiety by promising greater security – only to
find that a different terrorist band manages to strike a few
years later. This new disaster, in turn, will create a demand
for more repression, and on and on. Even if the next half-
century sees only three or four attacks on a scale that dwarfs
September 11, the pathological political cycle will prove devastating to civil liberties by 2050.

The root of the problem is democracy itself. A Stalinist
regime might respond to an attack by a travel blockade and
a media blackout, leaving most of the country in the dark,
going on as if everything were normal.

This cannot happen here. The shock waves will ripple through
the populace with blinding speed. Competitive elections will
tempt politicians to exploit the spreading panic to partisan
advantage, challenging their rivals as insufficiently "tough on
terrorism," and depicting civil libertarians as softies who are
virtually laying out the welcome mat for our enemies. And so
the cycle of repression moves relentlessly forward, with the
blessing of our duly elected representatives.

Our traditional defense against such pathologies has been the
courts. No matter how large the event, no matter how great
the panic, they will protect our basic rights against our baser
impulses.

Or so we tell ourselves – but it just is not true. The courts have
not protected us sufficiently in the past, and they will not do
better in the future. We need a strong and independent judiciary, but we need something more. We require an "emergency
constitution" that allows for effective short-term measures that
will do everything plausible to stop a second strike – but which
firmly draws the line against permanent restrictions. Above all

else, we must prevent politicians from exploiting momentary panic to impose long-lasting limitations on liberty. Given the clear and present danger, it makes sense to tie ourselves to the mast as a precaution against deadly enticements.

In speaking of an emergency constitution, I do not mean to be taken too literally. Almost nothing I propose will require formal constitutional amendment – the emergency constitution can be enacted by Congress as a framework statute governing responses to terrorist attacks. ... My emergency constitution adapts our inherited system to meet the distinctive challenges of the twenty-first century.

First and foremost, it imposes strict limits on unilateral presidential power. Presidents will not be authorized to declare an emergency on their own authority, except for a week or two while Congress is considering the matter. Emergency powers should then lapse unless a majority of both houses votes to continue them – but even this vote is valid for only two months. The President must then return to Congress for reauthorization, and this time a supermajority of sixty percent is required; after two months more, the supermajority will be set at seventy percent; and then eighty percent for every subsequent two-month extension. Except for the worst terrorist onslaughts, this "super-majoritarian escalator" will terminate the use of emergency powers within a relatively short period. It will also force the President to think twice before requesting additional extensions, unless he can make a compelling case to the broader public.

Defining the scope of emergency power is a serious and sensitive business. But at its core, it involves the short-term detention of suspected terrorists to prevent a second strike. Nobody will be detained for more than forty-five days, and then only on reasonable suspicion. Once the forty-five days have lapsed, the government must satisfy the higher evidentiary standards that apply in ordinary criminal prosecutions. And even during the period of preventive detention, judges will be authorized to intervene to protect against torture and other abuses. ...

We are at a distinctive moment in modern history: The state is losing its monopoly over the means of mass destruction.

And once a harmful technology escapes into the black market, it is almost impossible for government to suppress the lucrative trade completely. Think of drugs and guns. Even the most puritanical regimes learn to live with vice on the fringe. But when a fringe group obtains a technology of mass destruction, it will not stay on the fringe for long. ...

The emergency constitution is predicated on [this] description of [the emergency]: We are reeling in the wake of a surprise attack, and we do not know whether the terrorists were just plain lucky, whether they have the capacity to organize a rapid second strike, or whether they are in it for the long haul. So let us do what is necessary in the short term, and buy some time to figure out what is appropriate in the longer run.

The short-term problem is the second strike. Though the government may be deeply embarrassed by the initial attack, it is the only government we have. The terrorist strike will predictably generate bureaucratic chaos, but we should grant the security services the extraordinary powers needed to preempt the second strike that may (or may not) be coming. This is the real danger at the moment, and we should focus all our collective energies on preventing it from happening, rather than launching a never-ending war on terrorism.

This is the point of the "super-majoritarian escalator." While the country might go on emergency alert for two months, or even six, the escalator assures a return to normalcy if the security services manage to disrupt the conspiracy, or the terrorists prove to be a passing threat. Without a suitable constitutional framework, Presidents will predictably respond by calling on us to sacrifice more and more of our freedom if we ever hope to win this "war." But with an emergency constitution in place, collective anxiety can be channeled into more constructive forms. ...

The Priority of Morality: The Emergency Constitution's Blind Spot
David Cole

Ackerman's attempt to impose a meaningful but flexible time constraint on emergency powers is laudable: Undoubtedly *one* problem with "states of emergency" and their attendant powers is that they have a way of dragging on far longer than the actual emergency does. His insight that political process safeguards are critically important in checking emergency powers is perceptive and important, as is his sense that we should think about emergency powers *now*, before the next attack sends us into panic mode again. His solution is creative and, if adopted, might even work: The "super-majoritarian escalator" might actually succeed in putting an end to states of emergency in a timely manner. But time limits are only *one* problem with emergency powers, and a solution to the durational issue leaves unanswered the more difficult question of precisely what substantive powers ought to be assigned to the government for the duration of the emergency.

… Preventive detention is one possible response to the emergency posed by a terrorist attack, but there are many others. In the wake of September 11, for example, we have seen in the United States, to name just a few measures: increased reliance on surveillance and identification regimes; increased cooperation among foreign intelligence and domestic law enforcement agencies; efforts to limit access to potential targets; development of human intelligence sources; data mining; ethnic profiling; expanded criminal sanctions; the use of administrative measures to combat financing of terrorist groups; and increased use of the military to capture, hold, and try the "enemy." Each of these initiatives raises distinct normative issues regarding the tradeoff between security and liberty, and few of those issues would be resolved by a "super-majoritarian escalator." Rather, each initiative requires a direct assessment of distinct substantive value judgments. Like many process scholars before him, Ackerman seeks a magic bullet where there is none.

… He would eliminate contemporaneous individualized judicial review of the need for any given instance of preventive detention … Instead, he would substitute an ill-conceived compensation scheme, whereby "innocent detainees" would not be released, but would be paid for being locked up. Yet this solution fails to reconcile a fundamental contradiction in his proposal: Ackerman wants to authorize detention *without suspicion*, but at the same time wants to deter detention of innocent persons. The problem is that if detention without suspicion is expressly authorized, there is nothing illegal about detaining innocent persons. And by the same token, if it is wrong to detain innocent persons, as Ackerman's compensation scheme seems to imply, why dispose of the threshold requirement of suspicion in the first place?

Ackerman's rationale appears to be that preventive detention does a public service (regardless of who is detained) by "reassuring" the public in times of "panic." Ackerman's "reassurance rationale" justifies preventive detention as a means of conveying the message that the state has matters "under control." It is quite possible, as a purely descriptive matter, that preventive detention is reassuring in this way, especially when those being incarcerated are seen as different from the majority – say, communists, aliens, Japanese, or Arabs and Muslims. The public may well have been reassured by the Justice Department's frequent announcements of how many hundreds of "suspected terrorists" it had apprehended in the weeks after September 11. But as [various historical examples] demonstrate, such reassurance is a fiction paid for by innocents.

At bottom, what is most troubling about Ackerman's proposal is that in his fascination with the idea of the "super-majoritarian escalator," he never addresses the fundamental normative question presented by his proposal. As a normative matter, it is one thing to say, as the framers did, that in response to a "rebellion" or "invasion," habeas corpus may be suspended when "the public safety may require it"; it is another thing entirely to argue, as Ackerman does, that we should empower the Executive to incarcerate individuals for up to two months without suspicion, even in the absence of any threat to the nation's existence, merely to "reassure" a public in "panic." Putting innocent people who pose no danger behind bars to reassure a panicked public is normatively unacceptable, no matter what "super-majoritarian escalator" has been put in place, and no matter how much we "compensate" them after the fact. ... While a political process check may be an important *supplement* to a regime of limited emergency powers, it is no *substitute* for the hard work of striking an appropriate normative balance between liberty and security. ...

■ ■ ■

Article I of the Constitution

Section 1

All legislative Powers herein granted shall be vested in a Congress of the United States, which shall consist of a Senate and House of Representatives. …

Section 8

The Congress shall have Power To lay and collect Taxes, Duties, Imposts and Excises, to pay the Debts and provide for the common Defence and general Welfare of the United States; but all Duties, Imposts and Excises shall be uniform throughout the United States;

To borrow Money on the credit of the United States;

To regulate Commerce with foreign Nations, and among the several States, and with the Indian Tribes;

To constitute Tribunals inferior to the supreme Court;

To define and punish Piracies and Felonies committed on the high Seas, and Offences against the Law of Nations;

To declare War, grant Letters of Marque and Reprisal, and make Rules concerning Captures on Land and Water;

To raise and support Armies, but no Appropriation of Money to that Use shall be for a longer Term than two Years;

To provide and maintain a Navy;

To make Rules for the Government and Regulation of the land and naval Forces;

To provide for calling forth the Militia to execute the Laws of the Union, suppress Insurrections and repel Invasions;

To provide for organizing, arming, and disciplining, the Militia, and for governing such Part of them as may be employed in the Service of the United States, reserving to the States respectively, the Appointment of the Officers, and the Authority of training the Militia according to the discipline prescribed by Congress; ... – And

To make all Laws which shall be necessary and proper for carrying into Execution the foregoing Powers and all other Powers vested by this Constitution in the Government of the United States, or in any Department or Officer thereof.

Section 9
... The Privilege of the Writ of Habeas Corpus shall not be suspended, unless when in Cases of Rebellion or Invasion the public Safety may require it. ...

Section 10
No State shall enter into any Treaty, Alliance, or Confederation; ...

No State shall, without the Consent of Congress, ... keep Troops, or Ships of War in time of Peace, enter into any Agreement or Compact with another State, or with a foreign Power, or engage in War, unless actually invaded, or in such imminent Danger as will not admit of delay.

Article II of the Constitution
Section 1
The executive Power shall be vested in a President of the United States of America. ...

Section 2
The President shall be Commander in Chief of the Army and Navy of the United States, and of the Militia of the several States, when called into the actual Service of the United States; ...

Section 3
He shall ... take Care that the Laws be faithfully executed, and shall Commission all the Officers of the United States.

Federalism

The American constitutional system is one of separated powers between the branches of government – a sort of horizontal concept of power – and it is also federalist – a more vertical concept of power. Federalism refers to the division of authority between the national government (which we often call the federal government) and the states. Each state has its own constitution, and each state has replicated the three branches of the federal government: legislative, executive, and judicial.

Again, the starting point for understanding federalism is the Constitution. Part of Article I lists specific acts that are forbidden to the states, such as signing separate treaties with foreign governments or printing currency. The Tenth Amendment provides that "the powers not delegated to the United States by the Constitution, nor prohibited by it to the States, are reserved to the States respectively, or to the people ..."

What happens when a federal law and a state law are directly contradictory? As long as the subject matter is within the scope of federal authority – for example, if the law pertains to activities that have a connection with interstate commerce – then the federal law trumps. The framers of the Constitution included a Supremacy Clause in Article VI stating that "this Constitution and the laws of the United States ... shall be the supreme Law of the Land, and the Judges in every State shall be bound thereby, any Thing in the Constitution or Laws of any State to the Contrary notwithstanding."

One way of thinking of the federalist dimension of American government is the concept of dual sovereignty: within their respective realms, both the national government and state governments have the sovereign, that is, dominant, authority to regulate conduct. In the beginning of our nation, the scope of state government sovereignty was broader than that of the national government; today the reverse is true. However, there are still some areas of law that remain primarily under the control of the states. Disputes continue to arise about where the line should be drawn on particular issues.

The *Jacobson* Case

The following case, one of the most important in the history of public health law, also arose during an emergency, but one of a very different sort than the background for the Youngstown steel case. At the turn of the twentieth century, infectious disease was the leading cause of death in the United States. Between 1901 and 1903, a smallpox outbreak in

Boston killed 276 people of the almost 1,600 who became ill. In 1902, the board of health in Cambridge, a town adjacent to Boston, passed a resolution requiring every resident of the town to be vaccinated for smallpox. One resident, Henning Jacobson, refused, and eventually his case reached the Supreme Court.

■ ■ ■ ━━━━━━━━━━━━━━━━━━━━━━━━━━━━━━

What Is Smallpox?

Smallpox is a highly contagious viral disease characterized by fever and an eruption of vesicles and pustules, which kills 5 to 30 percent of infected persons. It is spread through close contact when infected persons cough out particles of the virus (variola major) from sores in their mouths and lungs. These particles can be inhaled, but are more commonly picked up as tiny dried droplets in the environment and inadvertently ingested or rubbed into the eyes.

The period during which an infected person can spread the infection is about three weeks, from just prior to the appearance of the rash until the last scab disappears. About half of those exposed to the virus develop the infection. There is an incubation period of 7 to 19 days (mean: 12 days) during which the infected person exhibits no symptoms. Once infected, a person always goes on to develop symptoms, but the severity of the cases varies from mild illness to rapid death.

━━━━━━━━━━━━━━━━━━━━━━━━━━━━━━ ■ ■ ■

Jacobson v. Commonwealth of Massachusetts
U.S. Supreme Court, 1905

Mr. Justice Harlan delivered the opinion of the court:

> *This case involves the validity, under the Constitution of the United States, of certain provisions in the statutes of Massachusetts relating to vaccination.*
>
> *The [statutes] of that commonwealth provide that 'the board of health of a city or town, if, in its opinion, it is necessary for the public health or safety, shall require and enforce the vaccination and revaccination of all the inhabitants thereof, and shall provide them with the means of free vaccina-*

tion. Whoever, being over twenty-one years of age and not under guardianship, refuses or neglects to comply with such requirement shall forfeit $5.'

An exception is made in favor of 'children who present a certificate, signed by a registered physician, that they are unfit subjects for vaccination.'

Proceeding under the above statutes, the board of health of the city of Cambridge, Massachusetts, on the 27th day of February, 1902, adopted the following regulation: 'Whereas, smallpox has been prevalent to some extent in the city of Cambridge, and still continues to increase; and whereas, it is necessary for the speedy extermination of the disease that all persons not protected by vaccination should be vaccinated; and whereas, in the opinion of the board, the public health and safety require the vaccination or revaccination of all the inhabitants of Cambridge; be it ordered, that all the inhabitants of the city who have not been successfully vaccinated since March 1st, 1897, be vaccinated or revaccinated.'

The above regulations being in force, ... Jacobson, was proceeded against by a criminal complaint ... The complaint charged that on the 17th day of July, 1902, the board of health of Cambridge, being of the opinion that it was necessary for the public health and safety, required the vaccination and revaccination of all the inhabitants ..., and provided them with the means of free vaccination; and that the defendant ... refused and neglected to comply with such requirement. ...

The authority of the state to enact this statute is to be referred to what is commonly called the police power – a power which the state did not surrender when becoming a member of the Union under the Constitution. Although this court has refrained from any attempt to define the limits of that power, yet it has distinctly recognized the authority of a state to enact quarantine laws and 'health laws of every description' indeed, all laws that relate to matters completely within its territory and which do not by their necessary operation affect the people of other states.

According to settled principles, the police power of a state must be held to embrace, at least, such reasonable regulations established directly by legislative enactment as will protect the public health and the public safety. It is equally true that the state may invest local bodies called into existence for purposes of local administration with authority in some appropriate way to safeguard the public health and the public safety. The mode or manner in which those results are to be accomplished is within the discretion of the state, subject, of course, so far as Federal power is concerned, only to the condition that no rule prescribed by a state, nor any regulation adopted by a local governmental agency acting under the sanction of state legislation, shall contravene the Constitution of the United States, nor infringe any right granted or secured by that instrument. ...

... The defendant insists that his liberty is invaded when the state subjects him to fine or imprisonment for neglecting or refusing to submit to vaccination; that a compulsory vaccination law is unreasonable, arbitrary, and oppressive, and, therefore, hostile to the inherent right of every freeman to care for his own body and health in such way as to him seems best; and that the execution of such a law against one who objects to vaccination, no matter for what reason, is nothing short of an assault upon his person.

But the liberty secured by the Constitution of the United States to every person within its jurisdiction does not import an absolute right in each person to be, at all times and in all circumstances, wholly freed from restraint. There are manifold restraints to which every person is necessarily subject for the common good. On any other basis organized society could not exist with safety to its members. Society based on the rule that each one is a law unto himself would soon be confronted with disorder and anarchy. Real liberty for all could not exist under the operation of a principle which recognizes the right of each individual person to use his own, whether in respect of his person or his property, regardless of the injury that may be done to others.

This court has more than once recognized it as a fundamental principle that "persons and property are subjected to all kinds of restraints and burdens in order to secure the general comfort, health, and prosperity of the state; of the perfect right of the legislature to do which no question ever was, or upon acknowledged general principles ever can be, made, so far as natural persons are concerned." In [a prior decision], we said: 'the possession and enjoyment of all rights are subject to such reasonable conditions as may be deemed by the governing authority of the country essential to the safety, health, peace, good order, and morals of the community. Even liberty itself, the greatest of all rights, is not unrestricted license to act according to one's own will. It is only freedom from restraint under conditions essential to the equal enjoyment of the same right by others. It is, then, liberty regulated by law.'

In the Constitution of Massachusetts adopted in 1780 it was laid down as a fundamental principle of the social compact that the whole people covenants with each citizen, and each citizen with the whole people, that all shall be governed by certain laws for 'the common good,' and that government is instituted 'for the common good, for the protection, safety, prosperity, and happiness of the people, and not for the profit, honor, or private interests of any one man, family, or class of men.' The good and welfare of the commonwealth, of which the legislature is primarily the judge, is the basis on which the police power rests in Massachusetts. ...

[W]hen the regulation in question was adopted smallpox ... was prevalent to some extent in the city of Cambridge, and the disease was increasing. If such was the situation, ... it cannot be adjudged that the present regulation of the board of health was not necessary in order to protect the public health and secure the public safety. Smallpox being prevalent and increasing at Cambridge, the court would usurp the functions of another branch of government if it adjudged, ... that the [vaccination order] was arbitrary, and not justified by the necessities of th[is] case. We say necessities of the case, because it might be that an acknowledged power of a local community to protect itself against an epidemic ... might be exercised in particular circumstances and in reference to particular persons in such an arbitrary, unreasonable manner, or might go so far beyond what was reasonably required for the safety of the public, as to

authorize or compel the courts to interfere for the protection of such persons. ...

There is, of course, a sphere within which the individual may assert the supremacy of his own will, and rightfully dispute the authority of any human government – especially of any free government existing under a written constitution, to interfere with the exercise of that will. But it is equally true that in every well-ordered society charged with the duty of conserving the safety of its members the rights of the individual in respect of his liberty may at times, under the pressure of great dangers, be subjected to such restraint, to be enforced by reasonable regulations, as the safety of the general public may demand. An American citizen arriving at an American port on a vessel in which, during the voyage, there had been cases of yellow fever or Asiatic cholera, he, although apparently free from disease himself, may yet, in some circumstances, be held in quarantine against his will on board of such vessel or in a quarantine station, until it be ascertained by inspection, conducted with due diligence, that the danger of the spread of the disease among the community at large has disappeared.

The liberty secured by the 14th Amendment, this court has said, consists, in part, in the right of a person 'to live and work where he will'; and yet he may be compelled, by force if need be, against his will and without regard to his personal wishes or his pecuniary interests, or even his religious or political convictions, to take his place in the ranks of the army of his country, and risk the chance of being shot down in its defense. It is not, therefore, true that the power of the public to guard itself against imminent danger depends in every case involving the control of one's body upon his willingness to submit to reasonable regulations established by the constituted authorities, under the sanction of the state, for the purpose of protecting the public collectively against such danger. ...

[T]he defendant refused to submit to vaccination for the reason that he had, 'when a child,' been caused great and extreme suffering for a long period by a disease produced by vaccination; and that he had witnessed a similar result of vaccination, not only in the case of his son, but in the cases of others. ...

Was defendant exempted from the operation of the statute simply because of his dread of the same evil results experienced by him when a child, and which he had observed in the cases of his son and other children? Could he reasonably claim such an exemption because 'quite often,' or 'occasionally,' injury had resulted from vaccination, or because it was impossible, in the opinion of some, by any practical test, to determine with absolute certainty whether a particular person could be safely vaccinated?

It seems to the court that an affirmative answer to these questions would practically strip the legislative department of its function to care for the public health and the public safety when endangered by epidemics of disease. Such an answer would mean that compulsory vaccination could not, in any conceivable case, be legally enforced in a community, even at the command of the legislature, however widespread the epidemic of smallpox, and however deep and universal was the belief of the community and of its medical advisers that a system of general vaccination was vital to the safety of all. ...

[We nonetheless observe] that the police power of a state ... may be exerted in such circumstances, or by regulations so arbitrary and oppressive in particular cases, as to justify the interference of the courts to prevent wrong and oppression. ... It is easy, for instance, to suppose the case of an adult who is embraced by the mere words of the act, but yet to subject whom to vaccination in a particular condition of his health or body would be cruel and inhuman in the last degree. We are not to be understood as holding that the statute was intended to be applied to such a case, or, if it was so intended, that the judiciary would not ... interfere and protect the health and life of the individual concerned. ...

[W]e are not inclined to hold that the statute establishes the absolute rule that an adult must be vaccinated if it be apparent or can be shown with reasonable certainty that he is not at the time a fit subject of vaccination, or that vaccination, by reason of his then condition, would seriously impair his health, or probably cause his death. No such case is here presented. It is the cause of an adult who, for aught that appears, was himself in perfect health and a fit subject of vaccination, and yet,

while remaining in the community, refused to obey the statute and the regulation adopted in execution of its provisions for the protection of the public health and the public safety, confessedly endangered by the presence of a dangerous disease.

We now decide only that the statute covers the present case, and that nothing clearly appears that would justify this court in holding it to be unconstitutional and inoperative in its application to the plaintiff.

■ ■ Critical Thinking ■

Jacobson is the most frequently cited case in American public health law. What is more, when there is a constitutional challenge to a public health statute, it is often cited by both plaintiff and defendant, even though the Supreme Court upheld the Massachusetts law that Jacobson refused to obey. What are the principles in *Jacobson* that would lead both sides in a modern case to cite it? What aspects of the decision, if any, are outdated?

Important Terms

- Federalism
- Enumerated powers
- Inherent powers
- Judicial review
- Police powers
- Political branches of government
- Preventive detention
- Separation of powers
- Social compact
- Super-majoritarian escalator
- Supremacy Clause
- War Powers Act

Review Questions

1. What are the provisions through which the Constitution established a system of separation of powers?
2. What are the different responsibilities and powers of each of the three branches of government?

3. How does ongoing interaction among the branches "make law"?
4. What powers does the U. S. Supreme Court have under the doctrine of judicial review?
5. What important principles of law emerged from the *Youngstown* case?
6. Make a list of the arguments for and against adoption of an "emergency constitution." Which position do you agree with?
7. After *Jacobson*, could there ever be a successful challenge to a vaccination law? If so, on what grounds? because the Supreme Court has the last word on the meaning of the Constitution.

2

The Constitution and Individual Rights

What You Will Learn

- The scope of the individual rights protected by the Constitution, and also their limitations
- The essential procedural criteria that a government action limiting a person's rights must have in order to be constitutional
- The standards set for protection of liberty and equality in constitutional law
- What habeas corpus means and how it is used in emergencies

Introduction

Our Constitution is not only a charter of government, as we saw in Chapter 1, but also a repository of individual rights and liberties. Many rights, such as free speech and the right not to incriminate oneself, have become staples of popular culture through TV references and movie characters. Somewhat less well known, but just as important, is the language of the Fourteenth Amendment, which will be our touchstone for most of this chapter. The Fourteenth Amendment commands that no state shall "deprive any person of life, liberty, or property, without due process of law; nor deny to any person within its jurisdiction the equal protection of the laws."

The Concept of Negative Liberty

The U.S. Constitution is often referred to as a promise of "negative liberty." What does that mean? "Negative liberty" embodies two related concepts. Both are included in the following description by the Supreme Court:

> *The [Due Process] Clause is phrased as a limitation on the State's power to act, not as a guarantee of certain minimal levels of safety and security. It forbids the State itself to deprive*

individuals of life, liberty or property without 'due process of law,' but its language cannot fairly be extended to impose an affirmative obligation on the State to ensure that those interests do not come to harm through other means. ... Its purpose was to protect the people from the State, not to ensure that the State protected them from each other. The framers were content to leave the extent of governmental obligation in the latter area to the democratic political processes.

DeShaney v. Winnebago County (1989)

First, the phrase "negative liberty" reflects the distinction between freedom from (negative), as opposed to freedom to (positive). The Constitution does not require the government to provide even basic necessities to the people, as constitutions in some other countries do. There is no constitutional right to health care or shelter, for example.

Second, the Constitution seeks to protect individuals from actions by government, not all actions. The overriding concern of the framers was that the powers of government could overwhelm and suppress the liberty of individuals. For that reason, the Constitution has been interpreted to protect individuals only from actions taken by some arm of government – federal, state, or local.

This does not mean that *no* laws restrict the actions of private individuals or entities such as corporations. Congress has the power to enact, and frequently has enacted, statutes that regulate myriad forms of private conduct – such as antitrust laws or environmental protection laws – and that provide selected benefits – such as medical insurance for persons over 65 or food stamps for the poor. Because it is elected, Congress acts as an arm of "the democratic political processes" that the Court was referring to in the quote above. As we saw in Chapter 1, however, statutes must fall within the scope of the powers allocated to Congress in Article I of the Constitution.

This chapter discusses only constitutional rights, not rights created by statutes passed by Congress, which will come up in many of the later chapters. Using primarily examples drawn from health or emergency contexts, we will see how courts have given life to such majestic, but vague, concepts as "due process of law."

We examine three kinds of rights embedded in the Fourteenth Amendment:

- Procedural due process
- Substantive due process
- Equal protection of the law

We also explore habeas corpus, the mechanism by which persons who are incarcerated or confined by any means (for example, quarantine) can challenge their confinement.

Constitutional principles will always be important in the law of emergencies because government agencies are the primary actors in the response to an emergency. When government action is involved, the Constitution must be adhered to.

Procedural Due Process

The concept of procedural due process is fairly self-evident: what process rights must a person be accorded if the government is acting to deprive her of life, liberty, or property. Most cases have centered on certain core protections, such as advance notice of the impending government action, the right to a hearing, and an impartial decision-maker. Courts have also made clear that the more important the interest at stake, the more painstaking must be the procedures that government has to follow.

One common scenario implicating procedural due process issues is that person might be confined, for example, through a quarantine order. Physical confinement amounts to a literal deprivation of physical liberty, and courts traditionally have held that this is the kind of situation in which government must act most carefully. In the two cases that follow, both dealing with persons who have infectious tuberculosis, you will see how one court perceives the need to step in to strengthen procedural due process protections while the second court finds that the procedures established by the health code were sufficient.

Greene v. Edwards
Supreme Court of West Virginia, 1980

> *William Arthur Greene, [who brought] this habeas corpus proceeding, is involuntarily confined in Pinecrest Hospital under an order of the Circuit Court of McDowell County entered pursuant to the West Virginia Tuberculosis Control Act. He alleges, among other points, that the Tuberculosis Control Act does not afford procedural due process because: (1) it fails to guarantee the alleged tubercular person the right to counsel; (2) it fails to insure that he may cross-examine, confront and present witnesses; and (3) it fails to require*

that he be committed only upon clear, cogent and convincing proof. We agree.

A petition alleging that Mr. Greene was suffering from active communicable tuberculosis was filed with the Circuit Court of McDowell County on October 3, 1979. After receiving the petition, the court, in accordance with the terms of [the Tuberculosis Control Act], fixed a hearing in the matter for October 10, 1979. The court also caused a copy of the petition and a notice of the hearing to be served upon Mr. Greene. The papers served did not notify Mr. Greene that he was entitled to be represented by counsel at the hearing.

After commencement of the October 10, 1979 hearing, the court, upon learning that Mr. Greene was not represented, appointed an attorney for him. The court then, without taking a recess so that Mr. Greene and his attorney could consult privately, proceeded to take evidence and to order Mr. Greene's commitment. [The court's actions were in conformity with the statute.]

It is evident from an examination of this statute that its purpose is to prevent a person suffering from active communicable tuberculosis from becoming a danger to others. A like rationale underlies our statute governing the involuntary commitment of a mentally ill person.

In [an earlier case], we examined the procedural safeguards which must be extended to persons charged under our statute governing the involuntary hospitalization of the mentally ill. We noted that [a finding of insanity results in a partial deprivation of liberty, through the process of commitment].

We concluded that due process required that persons [for whom involuntary commitment is sought] must be afforded: (1) an adequate written notice detailing the grounds and underlying facts on which commitment is sought; (2) the right to counsel; (3) the right to be present, cross-examine, confront and present witnesses; (4) the standard of proof to warrant commitment to be by clear, cogent and convincing evidence; and (5) the right to a verbatim transcript of the proceeding for purposes of appeal.

Because the Tuberculosis Control Act and the Act for the Involuntary Hospitalization of the Mentally Ill have like rationales, and because involuntary commitment for having communicable tuberculosis impinges upon the right to "liberty, full and complete liberty" no less than involuntary commitment for being mentally ill, we conclude that the procedural safeguards [required for commitment proceedings] must, and do, extend to persons charged under [the Tuberculosis Control Act]. Specifically, persons charged under the act must be afforded: (1) an adequate written notice detailing the grounds and underlying facts on which commitment is sought; (2) the right to counsel and, if indigent, the right to appointed counsel; (3) the right to be present, to cross-examine, to confront and to present witnesses; (4) the standard of proof to be by clear, cogent and convincing evidence; and (5) the right to a verbatim transcript of the proceedings for purposes of appeal.

[A]ppointment of counsel immediately prior to a trial in a criminal case is impermissible since it denies the defendant effective assistance of counsel. It is obvious that timely appointment and reasonable opportunity for adequate preparation are prerequisites for fulfillment of appointed counsel's constitutionally assigned role in representing persons charged ... with having communicable tuberculosis.

In the case before us, counsel was not appointed for Mr. Greene until after the commencement of the commitment hearing. Under the circumstances, counsel could not have been properly prepared to defend Mr. Greene. For this reason, Mr. Greene's writ [of habeas corpus] must be awarded and he must be accorded a new hearing. ...

In re Antoinette R.
Queens County, N.Y. Supreme Court, 1995

... [M]ulti-drug resistant strains of TB stay infectious and active over longer periods of time and therefore require long-term treatment with more toxic drugs. By comparison, the standard treatment for non-resistant TB consists of administering two drugs, isoniazid and rifampin, for approximately six months until the patient is cured. The cure rate for those completing this treatment is considered 100%. Multi-drug resistant tuberculosis, on the other hand, is resistant to these

drugs and to as many as seven other antibiotics. To obtain a cure rate of 60% or less, toxic drugs must be maintained over a minimum period of eighteen to twenty-four months. The most critical characteristic of these multi-drug resistant strains is that they are capable of being transmitted directly to others during the infectious stage. ...

On November 30, 1993 the respondent, a thirty-three year old female, was admitted to the Queens Hospital Center with pneumonia under the name of Marie C. exhibiting shortness of breath. A chest x-ray determined that she was suffering from inflammation in the upper right lobe, a classic indicator of tuberculosis. A sputum smear confirmed that she had an active, infectious case of TB. When the patient was interviewed, it was discovered that she had children who lived with her mother. She herself lived with them on occasion but also resided with various friends. She was informed of the consequences of tuberculosis and necessity of completing the appropriate medication to control the disease. Finally, she was recommended by the Department of Health to be a participant in Directly Observed Therapy, a program which involves the Department sending personnel to a patient's residence to observe and verify the patient's compliance with medication treatment. On December 4, however, the respondent left the hospital against medical advice prior to being rendered non-infectious. From December through February of 1994, she could not be contacted through her last known address. Moreover, despite several contacts with the respondent's mother, the mother did not know of her daughter's whereabouts, and was thus unable to provide any help in securing the proper medication for her daughter. In May, after numerous failed attempts at trying to contact the patient, the Department closed her case labeling the file, "Unable to Locate."

On May 31, 1994, the respondent checked into the Emergency Room at the Queens Hospital Center with breathing difficulties but checked out against medical advice. On June 6, 1994, she was readmitted with fever and chills under the name of Antoinette R. A sputum smear indicated a heavily positive tuberculosis infection. A chest x-ray of the right upper lobe of her lung showed cavitation present, which suggested a worsening of her condition. As a patient, the respondent was informed about tuberculosis pathology and control, she responded to the instructions in an uncooperative manner. In spite of efforts to conceal her identity, it was eventually discovered that the patient, Antoinette R., was the same person who had been unsuccessfully treated under the name of Marie C. She was then issued an order by the Commissioner of Health requiring her detention on June 11, 1994. On July 13, 1994, she was served with a Commissioner's Order to participate in Directly Observed Therapy which commenced upon release from the hospital on July 18.

Thereafter, between July 19 and July 31, she kept five of her eight scheduled appointments but kept no appointments after that date. On the occasions of Directly Observed Therapy, the respondent threw out medicine in the presence of the Public Health Advisor assigned to her case. She was subsequently non-compliant and lost to medical follow up despite numerous attempts to locate her at shelters and her last known address. Five months after her release from the hospital, her case file was again closed as "Unable to Locate."

On January 31, 1995 the respondent was readmitted to the hospital under the name of Chasity C. Her physical examination indicated a worsening of condition with extensive cavitary infiltrates in the right upper lobe with what appeared to be bronchogenic spread into the right middle and lower lobe on the right and left lungs. These findings were consistent with a reactivation of tuberculosis with bronchogenic spread. A sputum smear was collected which confirmed the diagnosis of infectious tuberculosis. A Public Health Advisor again explained the importance of taking and completing medication and discussed the possibility of participating in Directly Observed Therapy. The respondent agreed to participate and gave her mother's residence as a place of contact but refused to provide a phone contact. On March 8, however, once again it was discovered that the patient was the same person who under different identities refused to participate in outpatient treatment. The order of detention, currently before the court, was subsequently issued on March 9 by the Commissioner of Health. The respondent is presently diagnosed as having active tuberculosis which has been rendered non-infectious. Since it is not of the drug resistant type, the estimated date of completion of treatment is in October, 1995, seven months from now.

The mother of the respondent lives in a private home with four of her grandchildren and a newborn great-grandson, the grandchild of the respondent. The mother is willing to take the respondent into her home and provide cooperation should she be released from the hospital. Over the past two months the mother has visited her daughter on several occasions and talked with her over the phone on a daily basis. The mother has noticed a change in attitude in the respondent, that is, she is not as hostile. The mother attributes this change to the respondent's acceptance of religion. The respondent also contends that her attitude has been transformed and credits religion as her motivation. Since being detained at the hospital, she has joined various outpatient programs and attended parenting meetings. A nurse's aide and the head nurse, who attend to the medical needs of the respondent, both verify that there has been an improvement in the respondent's demeanor. She is now cooperative while taking her medicines and on occasions has independently approached the nursing staff to request her medicines. Relying on her "change in attitude," the respondent opposes the order of detention and again requests the option of participating in Directly Observed Therapy to be conducted at her mother's place of residence.

The petitioner's request for enforcement of the order of the Commissioner is granted. The petitioner has demonstrated through clear and convincing evidence the respondent's inability to comply with a prescribed course of medication in a less restrictive environment. The respondent has repeatedly sought medical treatment for the infectious stages of the disease and has consistently withdrawn from medical treatment once symptoms abate. She has also exhibited a pattern of behavior which is consistent with one who does not understand the full import of her condition nor the risks she poses to others, both the public and her family. On the contrary, she has repeatedly tried to hide the history of her condition from medical personnel. Although the court is sympathetic to the fact that she has recently undergone an epiphany of sorts, there is nothing in the record which would indicate that once she leaves the controlled setting of the hospital she would have the self-discipline to continue her cooperation. Moreover, her past behavior and lack of compliance with outpatient treatment when her listed residence was her mother's house, makes it all the more difficult to have confidence that her mother's good intentions will prevail over the respondent's inclinations to avoid treatments. In any event, the court will reevaluate the progress of the respondent's ability to cooperate in a less restrictive setting during its next review of the order in ninety days. ...

■ ■ Critical Thinking ■

Which kinds of procedural protections did the West Virginia court find to be insufficient? Why?

What were the procedural protections followed by the New York City Department of Health in dealing with resistant TB patients? How do these protections compare to what the West Virginia court ordered its state health department to do?

How might a government agency benefit from making the effort to insure that someone like Antoinette R. gets a full and fair process before she is confined?

Substantive Due Process

As we have seen, the procedural branch of due process doctrine requires the government to use a fair and impartial process before it takes actions that would deprive a person of life, liberty, or property. But are there some liberties that government cannot infringe without a compelling public need to, even if the individual receives all the *procedural* protections identified in *Greene*?

The answer is yes, which takes us into the substantive branch of due process. To quote the Supreme Court:

The Due Process Clause guarantees more than fair process, and the "liberty" it protects includes more than the absence of physical restraint. The Clause also provides heightened protection against government interference with certain fundamental rights and liberty interests.

Washington v. Glucksberg (1997)

The deprivation of physical liberty through confinement is one example of a fundamental right, and so it triggers both procedural due process and substantive due process considerations.

This is merely the first step:

> *Determining that a person has a "liberty interest" under the Due Process Clause does not end the inquiry; whether [an individual's] constitutional rights have been violated must be determined by balancing his liberty interests against the relevant state interests.*
>
> *Cruzan v. Missouri Dept. of Health* (1990)

How does a court balance an individual's liberty interest against the state's interest in taking some action that would diminish it? In almost every instance, the outcome of a case will turn on whether the liberty interest has been classified as a *fundamental* right. In other words, some liberty interests are more important than others, and, because of their importance, the government may not infringe them without showing that the infringement is *narrowly tailored* to achieving a *compelling* state interest.

Certain fundamental rights are set out in the text of the Constitution, such as the right of free expression or the right to non-establishment of religion. Others have been the product of judicial interpretation, such as the right to travel, the right to exercise parental authority as to one's children, and the right of privacy. Here's a list of rights found by the Supreme Court to be fundamental:

> *In a long line of cases, we have held that, in addition to the specific freedoms protected by the Bill of Rights, the "liberty" specially protected by the Due Process Clause includes the rights to marry; to have children; to direct the education and upbringing of one's children; to marital privacy; to use contraception; to bodily integrity ... to abortion ... [and] the traditional right to refuse unwanted lifesaving medical treatment.*
>
> *Washington v. Glucksberg* (1997)

In a famous dissenting opinion in a 1961 birth control case, later adopted as reasoning by a majority of the Court, Justice Harlan explained the logic behind identifying specially protected rights:

> *Were due process merely a procedural safeguard, it would fail to reach those situations where the deprivation of life, liberty or property was accomplished by legislation which ... could, given even the fairest possible procedure in application to*

individuals, nevertheless destroy the enjoyment of all three. Thus the guaranties of due process, though having their roots in Magna Carta's 'per legem terrae' and considered as procedural safeguards 'against executive usurpation and tyranny', have in this country 'become bulwarks also against arbitrary legislation'. …

Due process has not been reduced to any formula; its content cannot be determined by reference to any code. The best that can be said is that through the course of this Court's decisions it has represented the balance which our Nation, built upon postulates of respect for the liberty of the individual, has struck between that liberty and the demands of organized society. If the supplying of content to this Constitutional concept has of necessity been a rational process, it certainly has not been one where judges have felt free to roam where unguided speculation might take them. The balance of which I speak is the balance struck by this country, having regard to what history teaches are the traditions from which it developed as well as the traditions from which it broke. That tradition is a living thing. A decision of this Court which radically departs from it could not long survive, while a decision which builds on what has survived is likely to be sound. No formula could serve as a substitute, in this area, for judgment and restraint …

… [T]he full scope of the liberty guaranteed by the Due Process Clause cannot be found in or limited by the precise terms of the specific guarantees elsewhere provided in the Constitution. This 'liberty' is not a series of isolated points pricked out in terms of the taking of property; the freedom of speech, press, and religion; the right to keep and bear arms; the freedom from unreasonable searches and seizures; and so on. It is a rational continuum which, broadly speaking, includes a freedom from all substantial arbitrary impositions and purposeless restraints, and which also recognizes, what a reasonable and sensitive judgment must, that certain interests require particularly careful scrutiny of the state needs asserted to justify their abridgment. …

Poe v. Ullman (1961)

Not surprisingly, because the protection afforded to fundamental rights is so strong and so difficult for the government to curtail, substantive due process law has become quite politically controversial. In a 1997 case ruling that the liberty interest for a person desiring assisted suicide was not fundamental, then Chief Justice Rehnquist described how the Justices approached this area of law:

> [W]e ha[ve] always been reluctant to expand the concept of substantive due process, because guideposts for responsible decision-making in this unchartered area are scarce and open-ended. By extending constitutional protection to an asserted right or liberty interest, we, to a great extent, place the matter outside the arena of public debate and legislative action. We must therefore exercise the utmost care whenever we are asked to break new ground in this field, lest the liberty protected by the Due Process Clause be subtly transformed into the policy preferences of the Members of this Court.
>
> ... Our Nation's history, legal traditions, and practices provide the crucial guideposts for responsible decision-making ... [T]he development of this Court's substantive-due-process jurisprudence has been a process whereby the outlines of the "liberty" specially protected by the Fourteenth Amendment – never fully clarified, to be sure, and perhaps not capable of being fully clarified – have at least been carefully refined by concrete examples involving fundamental rights found to be deeply rooted in our legal tradition. This approach tends to rein in the subjective elements that are necessarily present in due-process judicial review.
>
> Washington v. Glucksberg (1997)

Comparing the Standards

The two indicia invoked most often as the basis for classifying a liberty interest as fundamental are that it is deeply rooted in the nation's history and traditions and that it is central to the concept of ordered liberty.

What analysis do the courts use if they find that a particular liberty interest is *not* fundamental? Let's imagine that someone asserts his freedom to decide where to park his car, and thereby challenges a parking ticket issued when the meter ran out because it penalizes his exercise of that freedom. A court would find that, although he does have a reasonable degree of freedom to decide where to park his car, that liberty interest does not rise to the level of a fundamental right. So, the court would ask simply whether the government's action was *rationally* related to a *legitimate* state interest. Managing parking patterns on city streets is a legitimate interest of government, and imposing reasonable time limits on parking is a rational way to further that interest.

In summation, compare the two standards:

- To justify a government action infringing a fundamental right, the infringement must be narrowly tailored to achieve a compelling state interest.
- To justify a government action infringing a lesser liberty interest, the infringement must be rationally related to a legitimate state interest.

It isn't impossible that a law curbing a fundamental interest will be upheld, despite the difficulty of meeting this standard. For example, the individual's right to travel guarantees freedom of movement. This guarantees that a government edict could not stop Americans from leaving their hometown and moving to a new location. In a hurricane, however, if a curfew order were to be issued, that would almost certainly be upheld because the order not to leave one's home after dark would be limited in time and place (narrowly tailored) and would be necessary to protecting the public's safety (a compelling interest).

On the other hand, some government actions might be so arbitrary, or undertaken for improper reasons, that they would fail to meet even a rational basis standard. A curfew issued at the whim of a mayor would surely be struck down, even on rational basis review.

Equal Protection of the Law

So far we have focused on the *kinds of procedures* government must follow and on the *kinds of actions* that individuals have a right to engage in. The Equal Protection Clause prohibits government from using certain *classifications as to groups of people*, when it passes or enforces laws. The paradigmatic example throughout American history has been race; racial classifications are so suspect, so imbued with a history of oppression, that they are virtually always prohibited.

In San Francisco in 1900, the Equal Protection Clause, race discrimination and public health collided when plague broke out in the city. The local board of health responded by imposing a quarantine around Chinatown, in effect imprisoning everyone within the boundaries of the quarantine whether they were infected or not. Members of the Chinese–American community challenged the quarantine in federal court, producing the following decision:

Jew Ho v. Williamson
U.S. Court of Appeals, 1900

> [W]hile the board of supervisors has quarantined a district bounded by streets, the operation of the quarantine is such as to run along in the rear of certain houses, and that certain houses are excluded, while others are included; that, for instance, upon Stockton street, in the block numbered from 900 to 1,000, there are two places belonging to persons of another race, and these persons and places are excluded from this quarantine, although the Chinese similarly situated are included, and although the quarantine, in terms, is imposed upon all the persons within the blocks bounded by such streets. The evidence here is clear that this is made to operate against the Chinese population only, and the reason given for it is that the Chinese may communicate the disease from one to the other. That explanation, in the judgment of the court, is not sufficient.
>
> [In] Yick Wo v. Hopkins, [which] arose in this state, out of the operation of an ordinance of this city respecting Chinese laundries, the Supreme Court [stated]:
>
> [T]he facts shown establish an administration [of the ordinance] directed so exclusively against a particular class of persons as to warrant and require the conclusion that, whatever may have been the intent of the ordinances as adopted, they are applied by the public authorities charged with their administration ... with a mind so unequal and oppressive as to amount to a practical denial by the state of that equal protection of the laws. ... Though the law itself be fair on its face and impartial in appearance, yet, if it is applied and administered by public authority with an evil eye and an unequal hand, so as practically to make unjust and illegal discriminations, between persons in similar circumstances, material to their rights, the denial of equal justice is still within the prohibition of the constitution. ...
>
> In the case at bar, assuming that the board of supervisors had just grounds for quarantining the district which has been

described, it seems that the board of health, in executing the ordinance, left out certain persons, members of races other than Chinese. This is precisely the point noticed by the Supreme Court [in Yick Wo, that the law was administered] 'with an evil eye and an unequal hand.' ... Therefore the court must hold that this ordinance is invalid and cannot be maintained, that it is contrary to the provisions of the Fourteenth Amendment of the Constitution of the United States, and that the board of health has no authority or right to enforce any ordinance in this city that shall discriminate against any class of persons in favor of another.

Equal protection law has grown enormously in importance in more than 100 years since *Jew Ho* was decided. The guiding principle is that all persons similarly situated should be treated alike. For example, in *Jew Ho*, Chinese and non-Chinese living on the same block and therefore subject to the same risk of plague were nevertheless treated differently. Today, the courts have developed a tiered analysis for equal protection claims that is similar to the two standards we saw for substantive due process claims. The three tiers of equal protection law are dependent on the nature of the characteristic upon which a law is classifying individuals.

1. Some classifications are characterized as *inherently suspect*. Government actions that classify persons based on those characteristics will be struck down unless the classification is narrowly tailored to achieve a compelling state interest. Race, alienage, and national origin fall into this category.

2. Others are subject to *heightened or intermediate scrutiny* because the Court has found that they are usually, but not always, irrational. Sex discrimination falls into this category. To be upheld, sex-based classification must bear a substantial relationship to an important governmental interest.

3. Finally, lawmakers must draw an almost endless number of classifications to govern. Most such classifications are benign; for example, a law that sets out different rules for landlords and tenants. For these, courts will use a *rational basis* test.

The Fourteenth Amendment's promise that no person shall be denied the equal protection of the laws must coexist with the practical necessity that most legislation classifies for one purpose or another, with resulting disadvantage to

various groups or persons. We have attempted to reconcile
the principle with the reality by stating that, if a law neither
burdens a fundamental right nor targets a suspect class, we
will uphold the legislative classification so long as it bears a
rational relation to some legitimate end.

Romer v. Evans (1995)

The Three Tests

When the law differentiates among Americans based on certain characteristics that have been associated with a history of discrimination, the
courts will apply one of the two higher tier tests. This is a way for the
courts to insure that legislators or other officials do not rely on unfair
criteria for administering public programs.

> *[W]hen a statute classifies by race, alienage, or national*
> *origin, [t]hese factors are so seldom relevant to the achieve-*
> *ment of any legitimate state interest that laws grounded*
> *in such considerations are deemed to reflect prejudice and*
> *antipathy – a view that those in the burdened class are not as*
> *worthy or deserving as others. For these reasons and because*
> *such discrimination is unlikely to be soon rectified by legis-*
> *lative means, these laws are subjected to strict scrutiny and*
> *will be sustained only if they are suitably tailored to serve a*
> *compelling state interest. ...*

> *Legislative classifications based on gender also call for a*
> *heightened standard of review. That factor generally provides*
> *no sensible ground for differential treatment. [W]hat differ-*
> *entiates sex from such non-suspect statutes as intelligence or*
> *physical disability ... is that the sex characteristic frequently*
> *bears no relation to ability to perform or contribute to*
> *society. Rather than resting on meaningful considerations,*
> *statutes distributing benefits and burdens between the sexes*
> *in different ways very likely reflect outmoded notions of the*
> *relative capabilities of men and women. A gender classifica-*
> *tion fails unless it is substantially related to a sufficiently*
> *important governmental interest. Because illegitimacy is*
> *beyond the individual's control and bears no relation to the*
> *individual's ability to participate in and contribute to society,*
> *official discriminations resting on that characteristic are also*
> *subject to somewhat heightened review. Those restrictions*

will survive equal protection scrutiny to the extent they are substantially related to a legitimate state interest.

We have declined, however, to extend heightened review to differential treatment based on age ... While the treatment of the aged in this Nation has not been wholly free of discrimination, such persons, unlike, say, those who have been discriminated against on the basis of race or national origin, have not experienced a history of purposeful unequal treatment or been subjected to unique disabilities on the basis of stereotyped characteristics not truly indicative of their abilities.

[W]here individuals in the group affected by a law have distinguishing characteristics relevant to interests the State has the authority to implement, the courts have been very reluctant ... to closely scrutinize legislative choices as to whether, how, and to what extent those interests should be pursued.

Cleburne v. Cleburne Living Center (1985)

In many ways, the cases that the Supreme Court has decided under the weakest – rational basis – test can be the most confusing because the Court will sometimes use a more searching version of this analysis when a classification appears to be based on other kinds of prejudice not covered in the first two tests. In a gay rights case, for example, the Court used the least powerful test but applied it with enough stringency to strike down the law.

[E]ven in the ordinary equal protection case calling for the most deferential of standards, we insist on knowing the relation between the classification adopted and the object to be attained. The search for the link between classification and objective gives substance to the Equal Protection Clause; it provides guidance and discipline for the legislature, which is entitled to know what sorts of laws it can pass; and it marks the limits of our own authority. In the ordinary case, a law will be sustained if it can be said to advance a legitimate government interest, even if the law seems unwise or works to the disadvantage of a particular group, or if the rationale for it seems tenuous. The laws [that we have upheld against equal protection challenges] were narrow enough in scope and grounded in a sufficient factual context for us to ascertain

some relation between the classification and the purpose it served. By requiring that the classification bear a rational relationship to an independent and legitimate legislative end, we ensure that classifications are not drawn [simply] for the purpose of disadvantaging the group burdened by the law.

Romer v. Evans (1995)

Justice O'Connor described when the Supreme Court will use what amounts to heightened rational basis as the standard of review in situations in which the law's end is itself illegitimate, regardless of the fit between end and means:

Laws such as economic or tax legislation that are scrutinized under rational basis review normally pass constitutional muster, since the Constitution presumes that even improvident decisions will eventually be rectified by the democratic processes. We have consistently held, however, that some objectives, such as a bare ... desire to harm a politically unpopular group, are not legitimate state interests. When a law exhibits such a desire to harm a politically unpopular group, we have applied a more searching form of rational basis review to strike down such laws under the Equal Protection Clause. ...

Moral disapproval of [a] group, like a bare desire to harm the group, is an interest that is insufficient to satisfy rational basis review under the Equal Protection Clause. Indeed, we have never held that moral disapproval, without any other asserted state interest, is a sufficient rationale under the Equal Protection Clause to justify a law that discriminates among groups of persons.

Lawrence v. Texas (2003)

Discrimination against Noncitizens: A Complex Area of Law

One of the questions arising under Equal Protection law that has given the courts the most difficulty has been determining when noncitizens, or aliens, can be subjected to differential treatment. Read the two cases below and see if you can identify all the factors that the Supreme Court has taken into account in determining which standard of review should be used when the federal government or a state government discriminates against aliens.

Mathews v. Diaz
U.S. Supreme Court, 1976

There are literally millions of aliens within the jurisdiction of the United States. The Fifth Amendment, as well as the Fourteenth Amendment, protects every one of these persons from deprivation of life, liberty, or property without due process of law. Even one whose presence in this country is unlawful, involuntary, or transitory is entitled to that constitutional protection.

The fact that all persons, aliens and citizens alike, are protected by the Due Process Clause does not lead to the further conclusion that all aliens are entitled to enjoy all the advantages of citizenship or, indeed, to the conclusion that all aliens must be placed in a single homogeneous legal classification. For a host of constitutional and statutory provisions rest on the premise that a legitimate distinction between citizens and aliens may justify attributes and benefits for one class not accorded to the other; and the class of aliens is itself a heterogeneous multitude of persons with a wide-ranging variety of ties to this country.

In the exercise of its broad power over naturalization and immigration, Congress regularly makes rules that would be unacceptable if applied to citizens. The exclusion of aliens and the reservation of the power to deport have no permissible counterpart in the Federal Government's power to regulate the conduct of its own citizenry. The fact that an Act of Congress treats aliens differently from citizens does not in itself imply that such disparate treatment is "invidious."

In particular, the fact that Congress has provided some welfare benefits for citizens does not require it to provide like benefits for all aliens. Neither the overnight visitor, the unfriendly agent of a hostile foreign power, the resident diplomat, nor the illegal entrant, can advance even a colorable constitutional claim to a share in the bounty that a conscientious sovereign makes available to its own citizens and some of its guests. The decision to share that bounty with our guests may take into account the character of the relationship between the alien and this country: Congress may decide that as the alien's tie grows stronger, so does the strength of his claim to an equal share of that munificence.

The real question presented by this case is not whether discrimination between citizens and aliens is permissible; rather, it is whether the statutory discrimination within the class of aliens allowing benefits to some aliens but not to others is permissible. [The benefit in question was enrollment in the Medicare program upon turning 65, a health insurance system that covers all Americans 65 and older.] We turn to that question.

For reasons long recognized as valid, the responsibility for regulating the relationship between the United States and our alien visitors has been committed to ... the Federal Government. Since decisions in these matters may implicate our relations with foreign powers, and since a wide variety of classifications must be defined in the light of changing political and economic circumstances, such decisions are frequently of a character more appropriate to either [Congress] or the [President]. This very case illustrates the need for flexibility in policy choices rather than the rigidity often characteristic of constitutional adjudication. Appellees Diaz and Clara are but two of over 440,000 Cuban refugees who arrived in the United States between 1961 and 1972. And the Cuban parolees are but one of several categories of aliens who have been admitted in order to make a humane response to a natural catastrophe or an international political situation. Any rule of constitutional law that would inhibit the flexibility of the political branches of government to respond to changing world conditions should be adopted only with the greatest caution. The[se] reasons ... also dictate a narrow standard of review of decisions made by the Congress or the President in the area of immigration and naturalization.

Since it is obvious that Congress has no constitutional duty to provide all aliens with the welfare benefits provided to citizens, the party challenging the constitutionality of the particular line Congress has drawn has the burden of advancing principled reasoning that will at once invalidate that line and yet tolerate a different line separating some aliens from others. In this case the appellees have challenged two requirements – first, that the alien be admitted as a permanent resident, and, second, that his residence be of a duration of at least five years. But if these requirements were eliminated, surely Congress would at least require that the alien's entry be lawful; even then, unless mere transients are to be held constitutionally entitled to benefits, some durational requirement would certainly be appropriate. In short, it is unquestionably reasonable for Congress to make an alien's eligibility depend on both the character and the duration of his residence. Since neither requirement is wholly irrational, this case essentially involves nothing more than a claim that it would have been more reasonable for Congress to select somewhat different requirements of the same kind.

We may assume that the five-year line drawn by Congress is longer than necessary to protect the fiscal integrity of the program. [Aliens must have resided in the U.S. for five years before becoming eligible for the benefits in question.] We may also assume that unnecessary hardship is incurred by persons just short of qualifying. But it remains true that some line is essential, that any line must produce some harsh and apparently arbitrary consequences, and, of greatest importance, that those who qualify under the test Congress has chosen may reasonably be presumed to have a greater affinity with the United States than those who do not. In short, citizens and those who are most like citizens qualify. Those who are less like citizens do not. ...

[Our earlier decision in] Graham v. Richardson provides the strongest support for appellees' position. That case holds that state statutes that deny welfare benefits to resident aliens, or to aliens not meeting a requirement of durational residence within the United States, violate the Equal Protection Clause of the Fourteenth Amendment and encroach upon the exclusive federal power over the entrance and residence of aliens. ... [But that latter ground of decision in Graham] actually supports our holding today that it is the business of the ... Federal Government, rather than that of ... the States ..., to regulate the conditions of entry and residence of aliens. The equal protection analysis also involves significantly different considerations because it concerns the relationship between aliens and the States rather than between aliens and the Federal Government.

[We further distinguish Graham by noting that] insofar as state welfare policy is concerned, there is little, if any, basis

*for treating persons who are citizens of another State differ-
ently from persons who are citizens of another country. Both
groups are noncitizens as far as the State's interests in administering its welfare programs are concerned. Thus, a division
by a State of the category of persons who are not citizens
of that State into subcategories of United States citizens
and aliens has no apparent justification, whereas, a comparable classification by the Federal Government is a routine
and normally legitimate part of its business. Furthermore,
whereas the Constitution inhibits every State's power to
restrict travel across its own borders, Congress is explicitly
empowered to exercise that type of control over travel across
the borders of the United States. ...*

Bernal v. Fainter
U.S. Supreme Court, 1984

*Petitioner, a native of Mexico, is a resident alien who has
lived in the United States since 1961. He works as a para-
legal for Texas Rural Legal Aid, Inc., helping migrant farm-
workers on employment and civil rights matters. In order to
administer oaths to these workers and to notarize their statements for use in civil litigation, petitioner applied in 1978
to become a notary public. Under Texas law, notaries public
authenticate written instruments, administer oaths, and take
out-of-court depositions. The Texas Secretary of State denied
petitioner's application because he failed to satisfy the statutory requirement that a notary public be a citizen of the
United States. ...*

*As a general matter, a state law that discriminates on the
basis of alienage can be sustained only if it can withstand
strict judicial scrutiny. In order to withstand strict scrutiny,
the law must advance a compelling state interest by the least
restrictive means available. Applying this principle, we have
invalidated an array of state statutes that denied aliens the
right to pursue various occupations [including state civil service jobs and licensure to practice law].*

*We have, however, developed a narrow exception to the rule
that discrimination based on alienage triggers strict scrutiny.
This exception has been labeled the "political function"*

exception and applies to laws that exclude aliens from positions intimately related to the process of democratic self-government. The contours of the "political function" exception are outlined by our prior decisions. ... [W]e held that a State may require police to be citizens because, in performing a fundamental obligation of government, police "are clothed with authority to exercise an almost infinite variety of discretionary powers" often involving the most sensitive areas of daily life. ... [W]e [also] held that a State may bar aliens who have not declared their intent to become citizens from teaching in the public schools because teachers, like police, possess a high degree of responsibility and discretion in the fulfillment of a basic governmental obligation. They have direct, day-to-day contact with students, exercise unsupervised discretion over them, act as role models, and influence their students about the government and the political process. [In a third case], we held that a State may bar aliens from positions as probation officers because they, like police and teachers, routinely exercise discretionary power, involving a basic governmental function, that places them in a position of direct authority over other individuals.

The rationale behind the political-function exception is that within broad boundaries a State may establish its own form of government and limit the right to govern to those who are full-fledged members of the political community. Some public positions are so closely bound up with the formulation and implementation of self-government that the State is permitted to exclude from those positions persons outside the political community, hence persons who have not become part of the process of democratic self-determination. ...

We have therefore lowered our standard of review when evaluating the validity of exclusions that entrust only to citizens important elective and non-elective positions whose operations 'go to the heart of representative government.' While not retreating from the position that restrictions on lawfully resident aliens that primarily affect economic interests are subject to heightened judicial scrutiny ... we have concluded that strict scrutiny is out of place when the restriction primarily serves a political function. ...

To determine whether a restriction based on alienage fits within the narrow political-function exception, we devised ... a two-part test.

First, the specificity of the classification will be examined: a classification that is substantially overinclusive or underinclusive tends to undercut the governmental claim that the classification serves legitimate political ends. ... Second, even if the classification is sufficiently tailored, it may be applied in the particular case only to persons holding state elective or important non-elective executive, legislative, and judicial positions, those officers who participate directly in the formulation, execution, or review of broad public policy and hence perform functions that go to the heart of representative government. ...

We recognize the critical need for a notary's duties to be carried out correctly and with integrity. But a notary's duties, important as they are, hardly implicate responsibilities that go to the heart of representative government. Rather, these duties are essentially clerical and ministerial. In contrast to state troopers, notaries do not routinely exercise the State's monopoly of legitimate coercive force. Nor do notaries routinely exercise the wide discretion typically enjoyed by public school teachers when they present materials that educate youth respecting the information and values necessary for the maintenance of a democratic political system. To be sure, considerable damage could result from the negligent or dishonest performance of a notary's duties. But the same could be said for the duties performed by cashiers, building inspectors, the janitors who clean up the offices of public officials, and numerous other categories of personnel upon whom we depend for careful, honest service. What distinguishes such personnel from those to whom the political-function exception is properly applied is that the latter are invested either with policymaking responsibility or broad discretion in the execution of public policy that requires the routine exercise of authority over individuals. Neither of these characteristics pertains to the functions performed by Texas notaries. ...

[Because the notary restriction does not meet the political-function exception, it will be subjected to strict scrutiny.] To satisfy strict scrutiny, the State must show that [the notary

public restriction] furthers a compelling state interest by the least restrictive means practically available. [Texas argues that the law] serves its 'legitimate concern that notaries be reasonably familiar with state law' and 'institutions and that notaries may be called upon years later to testify to acts they have performed'. However, both of these asserted justifications utterly fail to meet the stringent requirements of strict scrutiny. There is nothing in the record that indicates that resident aliens, as a class, are so incapable of familiarizing themselves with Texas law as to justify the State's absolute and classwide exclusion. The possibility that some resident aliens are unsuitable for the position cannot justify a wholesale ban against all resident aliens. Furthermore, if the State's concern with ensuring a notary's familiarity with state law were truly "compelling," one would expect the State to give some sort of test actually measuring a person's familiarity with the law. The State, however, administers no such test. To become a notary public in Texas, one is merely required to fill out an application that lists one's name and address and that answers four questions pertaining to one's age, citizenship, residency, and criminal record – nothing that reflects the State's asserted interest in insuring that notaries are familiar with Texas law. ... Without a factual underpinning, the State's asserted interest lacks the weight we have required of interests properly denominated as compelling. ...

■ ■ Critical Thinking ■

Why was the federal law with a discriminatory provision upheld and the state law struck down?

What standard of review did the Supreme Court apply to federal government policies? To state government policies?

What part of the standard does the "political exception" relate to?

These two cases illustrate the complexity of constitutional analysis. Not only are equal protection principles involved, but the Court also addresses federalism concerns about the differing roles of federal and state governments.

Measuring Risk and Protecting Liberty

The Constitution speaks in rather vague terms when it identifies rights to be protected, which leaves the heavy lifting of deciding exactly which criteria to use in any given case up to the courts. The most difficult situation is one that pits the most important government interests against the most important individual liberties. That is precisely the kind of problem that is likely to arise when government is responding to a genuine emergency, and takes actions that deprive people of liberty or property. What are the criteria for how those situations should be judged?

When Terrorism Threatens Health: How Far Are Limitations on Personal and Economic Liberties Justified?
Lawrence O. Gostin

> ... Disease-control measures invade ... the major spheres of personal liberty: vaccination, physical examination, and medical treatment interfere with bodily integrity; disease surveillance, reporting, and data collection interfere with informational privacy; and isolation, quarantine, and criminal sanctions for risk-taking behavior interfere with liberty. The effects of public health powers on economic interests are just as palpable. In many cases, personal control measures such as quarantine interfere with competitive markets. As the movement of people and goods are restricted, for example, businesses cannot freely sell their products and services; nor can they compete fairly with those who are not fettered by the exercise of control measures. Additionally, much public health regulation is directed squarely at business activities, thereby limiting freedom of enterprise: inspections and administrative searches; permits and licenses; occupational safety and health rules; nuisance abatements; and "takings," including regulatory takings. In each case, there is a constraint on economic liberty, albeit the freedom of contract, pursuit of a profession, or use of property.
>
> Homeland security is controversial because it places in conflict two sets of important values: the public's health and safety on the one hand and personal and economic liberties on the other. ... Although security and liberty sometimes are harmonious, more often than not they collide. Advancing the common good frequently requires limitations on individual interests. Society therefore faces hard trade-offs: individuals must forego some liberty to achieve a healthier and safer population; conversely, the government must permit some diminution of security to achieve a freer society. ...

The risk from bioterrorism can be stratified into three categories: significant risk, moderate risk, and negligible risk. The right question is, what powers should the state have to deal with each level of risk? Assuming the government's intervention is well targeted, the significant risk scenario unequivocally justifies the exercise of state power; arguably, a moderate level of risk could imbue the state with certain powers as well. Rather than inquiring whether liberty-limiting power is ever legitimate, commentators should ask what circumstances must exist to justify the exercise of authority. ...

If the state power to control health threats is legitimate, the central question then is, under what circumstances the power should be exercised. ... I would allow government to pursue public security through the full panoply of traditional powers, but require conformance with a structured set of standards and procedures set by elected officials in advance of a public health emergency. I [would] incorporate safeguards traditional to a liberal democracy, such as objective criteria for interventions (based upon scientific risk assessments), due process, and checks and balances. Yet, I would not make the state's burden so great as to chill effective disease surveillance and intervention. If the criteria and procedures required are excessively onerous, there remains too little space for the public interest. A framework can be structured into law that affords government the power to act, while deterring overreaching. ...

[An example of] negligible risk (arbitrarily exercised): An agency limits liberty capriciously without clear evidence of heightened risk or clear goals. In this category, the risk to the population is known to be low. Moreover, there is no reasonable suspicion based on an individualized assessment that the target of agency action poses a threat. Rather, the agency acts based on generalized or exaggerated fears.

Consider an agency decision to compulsorily vaccinate, treat, or isolate individuals without clear evidence of infection or exposure to infection. Alternatively, consider an agency decision to wiretap the telephone calls and monitor the e-mail communications of health care institutions and professionals without individualized evidence of risk. The agency action lacks justification because the population risk is low and the target of the intervention does not pose a known threat. ...

[The Importance of a] Well-Targeted Intervention: An agency action is most appropriate if it is well-targeted in the following ways. First, the agency acts with the [sole] intention of mitigating risk. Second, the action is actually likely to mitigate the risk. Third, the action is well-tailored so that it is not unreasonably over- or under-inclusive. Finally, the action is the least restrictive necessary to achieve the state's legitimate goals. Consider a government decision to require directly observed therapy for multi-drug resistant tuberculosis (M.TB). The agency appears to act with the intention of benefiting the person and preventing transmission of M.TB infection; the treatment is likely to achieve these goals; the treatment is well-tailored; and it is the least restrictive intervention under the circumstances.

... Government action is least appropriate if it restricts individual interests in a way that exceeds the scope of the threat or uses public health as a pretext for discrimination. The agency may overreach by interfering with liberty more than necessary to achieve legitimate goals, or by using a significant risk as a pretext for action that is not directed toward mitigating the risk. For example, the agency may conduct a fishing expedition of personal or business records, freely sharing data with law enforcement, immigration, and other government officials. Worse still, the agency may act based on stereotypes or animus of individuals or groups based on their race, religion, or ethnicity. Consider an agency decision to quarantine all members of a particular ethnic group, but not other similarly situated ethnic group members, in a given geographic area. This action would be arbitrary, perhaps based on exaggerated fear or even animus, and would not be necessary to detect or respond to a public health emergency. ...

A successful framework would allow the government to act quickly in response to an emergency, but not allow individual liberties to be reduced to an unacceptable level. The best way to work toward this balance is to make use of traditionally successful mechanisms, like the democratic process, checks and balances, clear criteria for decision-making, and judicial procedures designed to control the abuse of power by governmental agencies. In addition, the framework could [maximize the policy of] engag[ing] the community in voluntary measures of self-protection as a "less restrictive alternative" to compulsion. ...

Compare Professor Gostin's approach to the constitutional standards triggered under substantive due process or equal protection law. Is the Gostin approach more or less protective of individual liberty? Why?

The Writ of Habeas Corpus

Article I, Section 9 of the Constitution declares:

> The Privilege of the Writ of Habeas Corpus shall not be suspended, unless when in Cases of Rebellion or Invasion, the public Safety shall require it.

Habeas corpus is the mechanism, inherited from fourteenth century British law, which allows anyone confined by actions of government to challenge that confinement. It is not itself a ground for invalidating incarceration but rather a procedural mechanism that guarantees that anyone who is confined and seeking to be released can secure a court hearing to review the government's action. The phrase "habeas corpus" is Latin for "you [should] have the body."

> *As Blackstone phrased it, habeas corpus is the great and efficacious writ, in all manner of illegal confinement. As this Court [has] said, the office of the writ is to provide a prompt and efficacious remedy for ... intolerable restraints. ...*
>
> *There is no higher duty of a court, under our constitutional system, than the careful processing and adjudication of petitions for writs of habeas corpus, for it is in such proceedings that a person in custody charges that error, neglect, or evil purpose has resulted in his unlawful confinement and that he is deprived of his freedom contrary to law.*
>
> *Harris v. Nelson* (1969)

Look back at the *Greene* case in the beginning of this chapter – that lawsuit was brought as a habeas corpus action.

More recently, the scope of habeas corpus has come under question as part of the war on terror. In 2006, Congress passed the Military Commissions Act, which suspended habeas corpus for any alien determined to be an "unlawful enemy combatant engaged in hostilities or having supported hostilities against the United States." The primary effect of this law was to allow the government to detain persons indefinitely at Guantanamo and prevent them from challenging their incarceration as unlawful.

In *Boumediene v. Bush* (2008), the Supreme Court declared that the suspension of habeas corpus in the Military Commissions Act was unconstitutional. The Court's lengthy opinion concluded with these words: *"The laws and Constitution are designed to survive, and remain in force, in extraordinary times. Liberty and security can be reconciled; and in our system they are reconciled within the framework of the law. The Framers decided that habeas corpus, a right of first importance, must be a part of that framework, a part of that law."*

Important Terms

- "An evil eye and an unequal hand"
- Animus
- Compelling state interest
- Fundamental rights
- Less restrictive alternative
- Negative rights
- Positive rights
- Pretext
- Rational basis standard
- Similarly situated
- State action
- Strict scrutiny
- Suspect classification

Review Questions

1. Why did the framers limit the rights protected by the Constitution to defenses against actions by government?
2. Why is it important to have constitutional standards for the procedures used by government?
3. Are all liberty interests listed in the Constitution?
4. What are the criteria for fundamental rights?

5. Why aren't all classifications of groups of people unconstitutional?
6. In what situations are laws that discriminate against noncitizens most closely scrutinized? What is the reasoning behind that?
7. What markers does Professor Gostin use to distinguish between proper and improper exercises of government power in an emergency? Which do you agree with? Disagree with?

 **3**

Congress and the Agencies

What You Will Learn

- What are the most important federal emergency laws
- What is the process for declaring a national emergency
- How Congress can indirectly pressure states to take certain actions
- How Congress responded to September 11
- The process by which agencies issue regulations
- The standards by which courts review the agency regulatory process

Introduction

Throughout American history, the President has led the Executive Branch response to emergencies, often with no one questioning his inherent power to do so. Over time, however, and especially since the Supreme Court's decision in the *Youngstown* case that you read in Chapter 1, the role of the legislature has grown in importance. Today, the most significant federal emergency law is statutory.

This chapter describes three statutes related to emergencies and then examines the area of law – called administrative law – that governs the operation of agencies. Although federal agencies are part of the Executive Branch, they are created by statutes, which have been enacted by Congress. The traditional view has been that administrative agencies function as "transmission belts," entities that receive inputs from Congress in the form of statutes and then implement those legislative directives by promulgating rules that provide more detailed guidance. However, the reality of Washington lobbying – and the revolving door between government service and private lobbying – has vastly complicated that relatively simple understanding.

The first section on statutes describes the National Emergencies Act (NEA), the first comprehensive legislation to pull together the ground rules for exercising the power allotted to the President in various types of emergencies. The second addresses a group of statutes: those in which Congress uses its power to provide funds to state and local governments as a mechanism to influence them to adopt certain policies and practices. The third describes emergency laws enacted since September 11, an event that triggered a heightened level of attention to emergency preparedness.

One of the post–9/11 statutes – the Homeland Security Act – established the Department of Homeland Security. We will examine that particular department in some detail and use it as the springboard for exploring some of the most important principles of administrative law. The chapter closes with a more detailed examination of how administrative law is made and of the interests at stake when a big industry is involved.

The scope of this chapter is limited to *federal* law. Every state has its own set of laws that cover these emergencies and administrative procedure as well. There is a model state administrative procedure act that closely resembles the federal law. The emergency management laws at the state level are more variable; we will consider them separately in Chapter 10.

The National Emergencies Act

From the earliest days of the republic, through the Civil War, the world wars and to the present, the nation has had to grapple with how best to handle emergencies. During most of this history, Congress reacted separately and differently to each situation involving imminent or extraordinary threats. Most of the emergency laws enacted by Congress lasted only short periods, although one – the emergency declaration of the conflict in Korea – continued in effect for more than 40 years.

In the early 1970s, spurred in part by concerns over the war in Vietnam, Congress undertook the project of systematizing the laws of emergency. In 1973, Congress appointed a special committee on National Emergencies and Delegated Emergency Powers. It found that federal law contained 470 separate provisions that delegated extraordinary authority to the executive in a time of national emergency. The committee unanimously recommended new legislation to establish a clear, uniform procedure for presidential declaration and congressional regulation of emergencies.

In 1976, Congress enacted the NEA. The NEA provides the basic framework under which the President asserts his authority to deploy federal resources in a time of emergency. (See President Bush's declaration of emergency – Figure 3.1) Since it was enacted, the NEA has been invoked dozens of times, in situations ranging from prohibitions on engaging in financial transactions with terrorists or rogue governments, to a ban on imports from Burma, to the nation's response to September 11.

In 1977, Congress enacted the International Emergency Economic Powers Act (IEEPA), which authorizes the President to exercise controls over international economic transactions in which Americans were involved as one of the powers available to him during a declared national emergency. In addition to the IEEPA, certain other laws such as the Stafford Act, which deals with natural disasters, also apply to emergency situations (see Chapter 9).

We've included part of the text of the NEA in this section. Its essential functions include:

- Establishing the procedures for declaring a national emergency
- Requiring the President to specify which powers, under which statutes, he intends to invoke during the emergency
- Setting up reporting requirements while the declared emergency continues
- Establishing the methods for terminating a national emergency

National Emergencies Act
U.S. Code Title 50

§ 1621. [Declaration by President]

(a) With respect to Acts of Congress authorizing the exercise, during the period of a national emergency, of any special or extraordinary power, the President is authorized to declare such national emergency. Such proclamation shall immediately be transmitted to the Congress and published in the Federal Register.

(b) Any provisions of law conferring powers and authorities to be exercised during a national emergency shall be effective and remain in effect (1) only when the President specifically declares a national emergency, and (2) only in accordance with this chapter. ...

§ 1622. [Duration and termination]

(a) Any national emergency declared by the President in accordance with this subchapter shall terminate if –

(1) there is enacted into law a joint resolution terminating the emergency; or

(2) the President issues a proclamation terminating the emergency.

Any national emergency declared by the President shall be terminated on the date specified in any joint resolution referred to in clause (1) or on the date specified in a proclamation by the President terminating the emergency as provided in clause (2) of this subsection, whichever date is earlier, and any powers or authorities exercised by reason of said emergency shall cease to be exercised after such specified date ...

(b) Not later than six months after a national emergency is declared, and not later than the end of each six-month period thereafter that such emergency continues, each House of Congress shall meet to consider a vote on a joint resolution to determine whether that emergency shall be terminated.

(c) ... (5) [Sunset] ... Any national emergency declared by the President in accordance with this subchapter, and not otherwise previously terminated, shall terminate on the anniversary of the declaration of that emergency if, within the ninety-day period prior to each anniversary date, the President does not publish in the Federal Register and transmit to the Congress a notice stating that such emergency is to continue in effect after such anniversary.

§ 1631. [Which laws are triggered]
When the President declares a national emergency, no powers or authorities made available by statute for use in ... an emergency shall be exercised unless and until the President specifies the provisions of law under which he proposes that he, or other officers will act. Such specification may be made either in the declaration of a national emergency, or by ... Executive orders. ...

§ 1641. [Accountability and reporting]
(c) Expenditures ... When the President declares a national emergency or Congress declares war, the President shall transmit to Congress, within ninety days after the end of each six-month period after such declaration, a report on the total expenditures incurred by the United States Government during such six-month period which are directly attributable

to the exercise of powers and authorities conferred by such declaration. Not later than ninety days after the termination of each such emergency or war, the President shall transmit a final report on all such expenditures.

■ ■ ■ ▬▬▬▬▬▬▬▬▬▬▬▬▬▬▬▬▬▬▬▬▬▬▬

NEA Declaration Process Summary

1. President declares national emergency ("the proclamation")

2. Proclamation is published in the *Federal Register* and transmitted to Congress
   a. Congress can immediately terminate the emergency by joint resolution, or
   b. If it does not act immediately, Congress must meet every 6 months to consider whether to terminate the emergency

3. Proclamation starts the clock on the 1-year time limit on an emergency, unless its termination is otherwise specified in the proclamation or the President seeks extension (see #5 below)

4. During the emergency, the President can exercise "special powers" that are already designated as such in the United States Code (for example, to federalize large airports), *so long as* he identified the powers he wanted to invoke in
   a. The original proclamation, or
   b. Executive orders issued during the emergency

5. Emergency terminates
   a. On the date stated in the proclamation, or
   b. By a joint resolution of Congress, or
   c. On the anniversary of the proclamation, unless
      i. within 90 days prior to the anniversary date, the President issues a notice that the emergency must continue, publishes it in the Federal Register and transmits it to Congress
      ii. which starts the process over

▬▬▬▬▬▬▬▬▬▬▬▬▬▬▬▬▬▬▬▬▬▬ ■ ■ ■

On September 14, 2001, President Bush signed Proclamation 7463, which declared a national emergency in the aftermath of the terrorist attacks in the United States (see Figure 3.1).

48199

Federal Register	**Presidential Documents**
Vol. 66, No. 181	
Tuesday, September 18, 2001	

Title 3—

The President

Proclamation 7463 of September 14, 2001

Declaration of National Emergency by Reason of Certain Terrorist Attacks

By the President of the United States of America

A Proclamation

A national emergency exists by reason of the terrorist attacks at the World Trade Center, New York, New York, and the Pentagon, and the continuing and immediate threat of further attacks on the United States.

NOW, THEREFORE, I, GEORGE W. BUSH, President of the United States of America, by virtue of the authority vested in me as President by the Constitution and the laws of the United States, I hereby declare that the national emergency has existed since September 11, 2001, and, pursuant to the National Emergencies Act (50 U.S.C. 1601 *et seq.*), I intend to utilize the following statutes: sections 123, 123a, 527, 2201(c), 12006, and 12302 of title 10, United States Code, and sections 331, 359, and 367 of title 14, United States Code.

This proclamation immediately shall be published in the **Federal Register** or disseminated through the Emergency **Federal Register**, and transmitted to the Congress.

This proclamation is not intended to create any right or benefit, substantive or procedural, enforceable at law by a party against the United States, its agencies, its officers, or any person.

IN WITNESS WHEREOF, I have hereunto set my hand this fourteenth day of September, in the year of our Lord two thousand one, and of the Independence of the United States of America the two hundred and twenty-sixth.

[FR Doc. 01–23358
Filed 09–17–01; 8:45 am]
Billing code 3195–01–P

FIGURE 3.1 Proclamation 7463.

■ ■ Critical Thinking ■

Reread Professor Ackerman's proposal for "an emergency constitution" in Chapter 1. How do the provisions of the NEA differ from the Ackerman proposal? How are they similar?

Congressional Power under the Spending Clause

In practice, one of the most powerful tools that Congress has is its control of the federal government's purse strings. When Congress appropriates funds for various programs, it also establishes eligibility criteria for who can participate. In the area of education, for example, there is no clear authority in Article I for Congress to set achievement criteria for schools. Yet schools may have to demonstrate that their students meet certain achievement test levels to qualify for federal funding. This allows Congress to exercise a great deal of control indirectly that it could not exercise directly. The possibility of federal funds will provide enough incentive in most school systems for them to strive to meet the eligibility criteria.

Should it be constitutional for the Congress to exercise this kind of indirect power over states? The Supreme Court answered that question in the following case:

South Dakota v. Dole
U.S. Supreme Court, 1987

> *South Dakota permits persons 19 years of age or older to purchase beer containing up to 3.2% alcohol. In 1984 Congress enacted 23 U.S.C. § 158, which directs the Secretary of Transportation to withhold a percentage of federal highway funds otherwise allocable from States "in which the purchase or public possession ... of any alcoholic beverage by a person who is less than twenty-one years of age is lawful." The State sued in United States District Court seeking a declaratory judgment that § 158 violates the constitutional limitations on congressional exercise of the spending power. ...*
>
> *Here, Congress has acted indirectly under its spending power to encourage uniformity in the States' drinking ages. ... [W]e find this legislative effort within constitutional bounds even if Congress may not regulate drinking ages directly.*
>
> *The Constitution empowers Congress to "lay and collect Taxes, Duties, Imposts, and Excises, to pay the Debts and provide for the common Defence and general Welfare of the United States." Art. I, § 8, cl. 1. Incident to this power, Congress may attach conditions on the receipt of federal funds, and has repeatedly employed the power "to further broad policy objectives by conditioning receipt of federal moneys upon compliance by the recipient with federal statutory and administrative directives." [This Court has] determined that "the power of Congress to authorize expenditure of public moneys for public purposes is not limited by the direct grants of legislative power found in the Constitution." Thus, objectives not thought to be within Article I's "enumerated legislative fields" may nevertheless be attained through the use of the spending power and the conditional grant of federal funds.*
>
> *The spending power is of course not unlimited, but is instead subject to several general restrictions articulated in our cases.*

The first of these limitations is [that, in] considering whether a particular expenditure is intended to serve general public purposes, courts should defer substantially to the judgment of Congress. Second, we have required that if Congress desires to condition the States' receipt of federal funds, it "must do so unambiguously ..., enabl[ing] the States to exercise their choice knowingly, cognizant of the consequences of their participation." Third, our cases have suggested ... that conditions on federal grants might be illegitimate if they are unrelated "to the federal interest in particular national projects or programs. ..."

Our decisions have recognized that in some circumstances the financial inducement offered by Congress might be so coercive as to pass the point at which "pressure turns into compulsion." Here, however, Congress has directed only that a State desiring to establish a minimum drinking age lower than 21 lose a relatively small percentage of certain federal highway funds. Petitioner contends that the coercive nature of this program is evident from the degree of success it has achieved. We cannot conclude, however, that a conditional grant of federal money of this sort is unconstitutional simply by reason of its success in achieving the congressional objective.

When we consider, for a moment, that all South Dakota would lose if she adheres to her chosen course as to a suitable minimum drinking age is 5% of the funds otherwise obtainable under specified highway grant programs, the argument as to coercion is shown to be more rhetoric than fact. ...

Here Congress has offered relatively mild encouragement to the States to enact higher minimum drinking ages than they would otherwise choose. But the enactment of such laws remains the prerogative of the States not merely in theory but in fact. Even if Congress might lack the power to impose a national minimum drinking age directly, we conclude that encouragement to state action found in § 158 is a valid use of the spending power. ...

■ ■ Critical Thinking ■

As we saw in Chapter 1, it is a bedrock principle of American law that Congress can legislate only on those subjects (admittedly quite broad) as to which it has powers that are enumerated in Article I of the Constitution. The Supreme Court implicitly acknowledges in *Dole* that Congress has no Article I power to directly order the states to set certain speed limits on the highways within their jurisdiction. Is invocation of the Spending Clause power too easy a way around the doctrine of limited, enumerated powers? Or is it necessary for a twenty-first century national government to function? What are the deeper policy interests at stake in this case?

Although the Court in *Dole* accords broad deference to decisions by Congress on how to exercise its spending powers, it also identifies three criteria by which to judge whether Congress has crossed the line. What are they? Are they sufficient? Would the result have been different if the penalty under this program had been to lose all federal funds for highway construction?

Post-9/11 Emergency-Related Laws

Since the attacks of September 11, Congress has passed numerous laws dealing with the prevention of and preparedness for emergencies of various kinds.

The USA PATRIOT Act was enacted only 6 weeks after the attacks in New York and Washington and addressed criminal investigations and punishments. It provides federal law enforcement officials with greater leeway to track and intercept communications, to obtain documents and other information that was previously confidential, and to more closely regulate the dealings of American financial institutions. The PATRIOT Act also created several new crimes, including ones involving money laundering and solicitation for certain fraudulent charities, and expanded the definition of what actions could be considered crimes under the scope of providing "material support for terrorism."

Congress initially provided that the terms of the act would expire at the end of 2005, but most of its provisions have since been extended or made permanent. The PATRIOT Act has proven to be controversial, with civil liberties advocates challenging provisions related to surveillance, secrecy, and the grounds for deportation. One provision that has been altered since Congress first enacted the Act, as well as challenged in litigation, concerns the issuance of National Security Letters (NSLs), a device by which the FBI could obtain telephone or Internet records without court order and, at the same time, prohibit the telephone or Internet service provider from disclosing that the NSL had been issued. In 2005, Congress added more procedural protections for companies or individuals affected by NSLs. Lawsuits have been filed to challenge the constitutionality of NSLs, but there has been no ruling on that question from the Supreme Court.

EMERGENCY LAWS AROUND THE WORLD

Most nations have provided authority either in their constitutions or in laws for the government to exercise special powers during an emergency. Examples are shown in Table 3.1.

Table 3.1   Procedure for Declaring Emergencies in Various Countries

Country	Source of law	Levels of emergency	Who can declare	Termination
CANADA	Emergencies Act	War International threat Public order Public welfare	Prime Minister	After 90 days, unless extended by the PM or revoked by the PM or Parliament
FRANCE	Constitution Statute	Constitutional exception Siege Emergency	President Council of Ministers	After 12 days, unless extended by Parliament
GERMANY	Emergency Acts (constitutional and statutory components)	Defense-related emergencies International tension Domestic uprising Natural catastrophes	*Bundestag* [Parliament]; if nation attacked, defense emergency automatic	*Bundestag* or when emergency conditions cease
UNITED KINGDOM	Civil Contingencies Act	War Serious terrorist threat Event threatening serious damage to human welfare of the environment	Monarch Privy Council Prime Minister	After 7 days unless extended by Parliament

One of the much less controversial acts by Congress was its enactment of the Public Health Security and Bioterrorism Preparedness and Response Act in 2002. Just as the PATRIOT Act grew directly out of the reaction to September 11, this legislation was drafted in the wake of the anthrax attacks of October 2001. It authorized several billion dollars in public health spending to expand the national stockpile of emergency drugs, vaccines, and medical supplies and to provide grants to state and local governments for emergency preparedness planning.

The Bioterrorism Act also directed the Centers for Disease Control and Prevention (CDC), which is the federal government agency in charge of public health policy, to systematize the oversight of potentially dangerous biological agents. Any facility possessing one of these "select agents" (listed at www.selectagents.gov/agentToxinList.htm) must register with the government and follow detailed procedures to possess, use, or transfer the compound. The law also disqualifies individuals allowed to work with the chemicals if they have been convicted or indicted for a felony, if they have ever been committed to a mental institution, or if they were dishonorably discharged from military service.

The major impact of the third statute – the Homeland Security Act – was the establishment of a new Executive Branch agency, the Department of Homeland Security (DHS). The idea behind the DHS was to combine the federal government's apparatus for border security, protection of infrastructure, and response to emergencies into one department using an all-hazards approach. Agencies with many different missions and organizational cultures were moved into DHS, including the Federal Emergency Management Agency (FEMA), the Immigration and Naturalization Service, the Coast Guard, part of the Animal and Plant Health Inspection Service, Customs, and the Secret Service.

After the debacle of the Hurricane Katrina response in 2005, many critics urged that FEMA be re-instated as its own Cabinet-level agency. The experience of Katrina, together with the absence of other terrorist attacks in the United States from 2001 to date, also led to demands that DHS pay more attention to natural disaster preparedness than to the defense against security threats, which had dominated the Department's work. In response, Congress passed legislation restoring some of FEMA's previous operational structure, but it remains a component of DHS.

Administrative Agencies: DHS as Case Study

Like the other Cabinet-level departments of the federal government, DHS is organized into what are known as subcabinet components. The structural model parallels that of the President and the Cabinet. The top official is the Secretary of DHS; as of 2009, that official is Janet Napolitano, former Governor of Arizona. There is a Deputy Secretary, just as there is a Vice President. The department contains its own equivalent to the Cabinet, the subcabinet, which is composed of Under Secretaries and Assistant Secretaries. Just as the President has various high-level staff members, so does a Cabinet Secretary. The office of

U.S. DEPARTMENT OF HOMELAND SECURITY

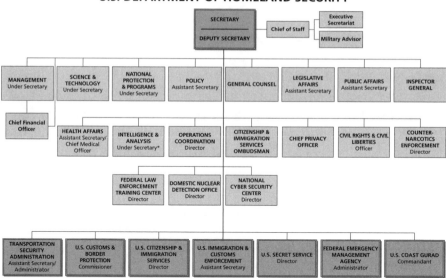

* Under Secretary for Intelligence & Analysis title created by Public Law 110–53, Aug. 3rd, 2007

FIGURE 3.2 The U.S. Department of Homeland Security Organizational Chart

the Secretary includes a chief of staff, a general counsel, and a chief financial officer, as well as speechwriters and various assistants.

DHS is organized as shown in Figure 3.2.

What Agencies Do

Agencies execute and enforce the laws that Congress passes. They act pursuant to the statutory mandates established for them by the legislature. Their functions may include promulgation of regulations that spell out more specifically the requirements for public or private entities that have been established by various laws; oversight of the provision of services; direct law enforcement; disbursement of funds; oversight of entities that receive funds; investigation of complaints; award of licenses; and many other activities that cannot easily be categorized.

For the purposes of this book, the most important function of agencies is rule-making, a term which refers to the adoption of regulations. Regulations are much like statutes in that they specify actions that private or public entities can, must, or cannot take. All regulations are developed pursuant to a statute enacted by Congress, which delegates authority to an agency to deal with the many particular issues and concerns that arise in any field, and that are too numerous for Congress to address in all their details. Moreover, administrative agencies employ experts within their respective fields. One of the chief rationales for delegating authority to agencies is that they can draw on this expertise more efficiently than Congress would be able to.

Coordination of Agencies

Within the Executive Branch, agency actions are coordinated and harmonized through the Office of Information and Regulatory Affairs (OIRA; pronounced oh-eye-ra), which is part of the Office of Management and Budget (OMB) and reports to the President. Using Executive Orders, presidents have established guidelines to be used by all agencies within the Executive Branch in weighing the benefits and disadvantages of possible regulations. President Clinton's Executive Order 12866, still in use, requires that an agency must submit for centralized review any proposed regulation that will have a major impact on the economy, environment, health, communities, or other government agencies or that raise novel legal or policy issues.

In addition, Executive Order 12866 requires each agency to submit an annual regulatory plan, which describes each major regulation under consideration or in the development process. OIRA circulates these plans among all federal agencies, to identify possible conflicts between agency positions. OIRA also convenes a regulatory working group that meets several times a year to discuss coordination and to hear input from state and local government officials and from the public.

The Process of Rule-Making

A statute called the Administrative Procedures Act (APA) established the ground rules for how agencies carry out their duties. The process by which government agencies develop, draft, and promulgate regulations is often called "APA rule-making."

Administrative regulations were of relatively little importance until the New Deal, when the rapid growth in the number of federal agencies and the expansion of their activities led to a massive increase in the decisions being made by agencies. This in turn led to concern about the lack of uniformity among the agencies in the processes they followed to issue regulations. In 1946, Congress passed the Administrative Procedure Act.

The APA defines "rule" as

> [T]he whole or a part of an agency statement of general or particular applicability and future effect, designed to implement, interpret, or prescribe law or policy ...

The Department of Justice expanded on this definition, and described rule-making as

> [A]gency action which regulates the future conduct of either groups of persons or a single person; it is essentially legislative in nature, not only because it operates in the future but because it is primarily concerned with policy considerations.
>
> U.S. Department of Justice, 1947

In other words, rules – a term used synonymously with regulations – are policy statements rather than determinations as to particular disputes. For example, a federal agency may issue a rule or a regulation as to how nuclear waste should be disposed of. If a company that produces nuclear waste was fined for failure to comply with the rule and then challenged the fine, there would be an adjudication by the agency of that dispute. The adjudication would produce a decision that would settle the question of whether that company was properly fined. The *adjudicatory* decision would not be a regulation.

The APA sets out the basic steps that all agencies must follow in adopting regulations. It requires that the agency provide public notice of the proposed regulation and allow for public comments before the regulation is finalized. The APA also provides that affected persons may challenge regulations in court if the agency failed to follow the required procedure.

The public notice requirement is satisfied when a document is published in the *Federal Register*, the official report of the U.S. Government. Published every weekday, the *Federal Register* includes official documents of the White House and federal agencies, such as proposed and final regulations and executive orders. It serves a function for the Executive Branch comparable to that served for Congress by the *Congressional Record*.

The Administrative Procedure Act
U.S. Code Title 5

§ 553. Rule making

… (b) General notice of proposed rule making shall be published in the Federal Register, unless persons subject thereto are named and either personally served or otherwise have actual notice thereof in accordance with law. The notice shall include –

(1) a statement of the time, place, and nature of public rule making proceedings;

(2) reference to the legal authority under which the rule is proposed; and

(3) either the terms or substance of the proposed rule or a description of the subjects and issues involved. …

(c) After notice required by this section, the agency shall give interested persons an opportunity to participate in the rule making through submission of written data, views, or arguments with or without opportunity for oral presentation. After consideration of the relevant matter presented, the agency shall incorporate in the rules adopted a concise general statement of their basis and purpose. …

(d) The required publication or service of a substantive rule shall be made not less than 30 days before its effective date …

(e) Each agency shall give an interested person the right to petition for the issuance, amendment, or repeal of a rule. …

§ 706. Scope of review

To the extent necessary to decision and when presented, the reviewing court shall decide all relevant questions of law, interpret constitutional and statutory provisions, and determine the meaning or applicability of the terms of an agency action. The reviewing court shall –

(1) compel agency action unlawfully withheld or unreasonably delayed; and

(2) hold unlawful and set aside agency action, findings, and conclusions found to be –

(A) arbitrary, capricious, an abuse of discretion, or otherwise not in accordance with law;

(B) contrary to constitutional right, power, privilege, or immunity;

(C) in excess of statutory jurisdiction, authority, or limitations, or short of statutory right;

(D) without observance of procedure required by law;

(E) unsupported by substantial evidence in a case subject to sections 556 and 557 of this title or otherwise reviewed on the record of an agency hearing provided by statute; or

(F) unwarranted by the facts to the extent that the facts are subject to trial de novo by the reviewing court.

In making the foregoing determinations, the court shall review the whole record or those parts of it cited by a party, and due account shall be taken of the rule of prejudicial error.

Law and government scholars Lisa Heinzerling and Mark Tushnet have described the functions served by this process as follows:

The notice-and-comment rule-making process is a hybrid of expertise and democratic accountability. The agency relies on its expertise to identify a problem to target and to develop a proposal. The public's comments largely reflect a concern for public accountability, but also reflect a concern for expertise – both the possibility that the agency's experts will have some sort of bias and the availability of different expertise outside the agency. And it can be argued that the reasoned elaboration with which the agency defends its rule following public comments itself serves as an accountability device.

Heinzerling and Tushnet (2006)

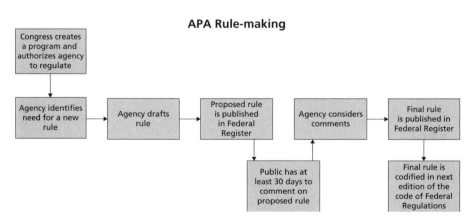

APA Rule-making

FIGURE 3.3

The APA in Action

The following case illustrates the complexity that can arise during efforts by a federal agency to regulate in an evolving environment, against the resistance of – or in collaboration with – powerful stakeholders. It involves the question of which kinds of seat belts and air bags should be required in automobiles. Its origins go back to the National Traffic and Motor Vehicle Safety Act of 1966, which directed the Secretary of Transportation to issue motor vehicle safety standards. Therein began the saga of regulatory action on passenger safety devices, which continued through the administrations of five presidents.

Motor Vehicle Manufacturers Ass'n v. State Farm Mutual Insur. Co.
U.S. Supreme Court, 1983

> *… The regulation whose rescission is at issue bears a complex and convoluted history. Over the course of approximately 60 rulemaking notices, the requirement has been imposed, amended, rescinded, reimposed, and now rescinded again.*

■ ■ ■ ▬▬▬▬▬▬▬▬▬▬▬▬▬▬▬▬▬▬▬▬▬▬▬▬▬

Johnson Administration

▬▬▬▬▬▬▬▬▬▬▬▬▬▬▬▬▬▬▬▬▬▬▬▬▬ ■ ■ ■

> *As originally issued by the Department of Transportation in 1967, Standard 208 simply required the installation of seatbelts in all automobiles. It soon became apparent that the level of seatbelt use was too low to reduce traffic injuries to an acceptable level. The Department therefore began consideration of "passive occupant restraint systems" – devices that do not depend for their effectiveness upon any action taken by the occupant except that necessary to operate the vehicle. Two types of automatic crash protection emerged: automatic seatbelts and airbags. The automatic seatbelt is a traditional safety belt, which when fastened to the interior of the door remains attached without impeding entry or exit from the vehicle, and deploys automatically without any action on the part of the passenger. The airbag is an inflatable device concealed in the dashboard and steering column. It automatically inflates when a sensor indicates that deceleration forces from an accident have exceeded a preset minimum, then rapidly deflates to dissipate those forces. The life-saving*

potential of these devices was immediately recognized, and in 1977, after substantial on-the-road experience with both devices, it was estimated by [the National Highway Traffic Safety Administration (NHTSA) – the component within the Department of Transportation responsible for this issue –] that passive restraints could prevent approximately 12,000 deaths and over 100,000 serious injuries annually.

■ ■ ■ ━━━━━━━━━━━━━━━━━━━━━━━━━━━━━━━━

Nixon Administration

━━━━━━━━━━━━━━━━━━━━━━━━━━━━━━━━ ■ ■ ■

In 1969, the Department formally proposed a standard requiring the installation of passive restraints, thereby commencing a lengthy series of proceedings. In 1970, the agency revised Standard 208 to include passive protection requirements, and in 1972, the agency amended the standard to require full passive protection for all front seat occupants of vehicles manufactured after August 15, 1975. In the interim, vehicles built between August 1973 and August 1975 were to carry either passive restraints or lap and shoulder belts coupled with an "ignition interlock" that would prevent starting the vehicle if the belts were not connected. ...

In preparing for the upcoming model year, most car makers chose the "ignition interlock" option, a decision which was highly unpopular, and led Congress to amend the Act to prohibit a motor vehicle safety standard from requiring or permitting compliance by means of an ignition interlock or a continuous buzzer designed to indicate that safety belts were not in use. The[se] 1974 Amendments also provided that any safety standard that could be satisfied by a system other than seatbelts would have to be submitted to Congress where it could be vetoed by concurrent resolution of both houses.

■ ■ ■ ━━━━━━━━━━━━━━━━━━━━━━━━━━━━━━━━

Ford Administration

━━━━━━━━━━━━━━━━━━━━━━━━━━━━━━━━ ■ ■ ■

The effective date for mandatory passive restraint systems was extended for a year until August 31, 1976. But in June 1976, Secretary of Transportation William Coleman initiated a new rulemaking on the issue. After hearing testimony and reviewing written comments, Coleman extended the optional alternatives indefinitely and suspended the passive restraint requirement. Although he found passive restraints technologically and economically feasible, the Secretary based his decision on the expectation that there would be widespread public resistance to the new systems. He instead proposed a demonstration project involving up to 500,000 cars installed with passive restraints, in order to smooth the way for public acceptance of mandatory passive restraints at a later date.

■ ■ ■ ━━━━━━━━━━━━━━━━━━━━━━━━━━━━━━

Carter Administration

━━━━━━━━━━━━━━━━━━━━━━━━━━━━━━ ■ ■ ■

Coleman's successor as Secretary of Transportation disagreed. Within months of assuming office, Secretary Brock Adams decided that the demonstration project was unnecessary. He issued a new mandatory passive restraint regulation, known as Modified Standard 208. The Modified Standard mandated the phasing in of passive restraints beginning with large cars in model year 1982 and extending to all cars by model year 1984. The two principal systems that would satisfy the Standard were airbags and passive belts; the choice of which system to install was left to the manufacturers. … Over the next several years, the automobile industry geared up to comply with Modified Standard 208.

■ ■ ■ ━━━━━━━━━━━━━━━━━━━━━━━━━━━━━━

Reagan Administration

━━━━━━━━━━━━━━━━━━━━━━━━━━━━━━ ■ ■ ■

In February 1981, however, Secretary of Transportation Andrew Lewis reopened the rulemaking due to changed economic circumstances and, in particular, the difficulties of the automobile industry. Two months later, the agency ordered a one-year delay in the application of the standard to large cars, extending the deadline to September 1982, and at the same time, proposed the possible rescission of the entire standard. After receiving written comments and holding public hearings, NHTSA issued a final rule that rescinded the passive restraint requirement contained in Modified Standard 208. ...

The Department of Transportation ... argues that under [the "arbitrary and capricious" standard], a reviewing court may not set aside an agency rule that is rational, based on consideration of the relevant factors and within the scope of the authority delegated to the agency by the statute. We do not disagree ... The scope of review under the "arbitrary and capricious" standard is narrow and a court is not to substitute its judgment for that of the agency. Nevertheless, the agency must examine the relevant data and articulate a satisfactory explanation for its action including a rational connection between the facts found and the choice made. In reviewing that explanation, we must consider whether the decision was based on a consideration of the relevant factors and whether there has been a clear error of judgment. Normally, an agency rule would be arbitrary and capricious if the agency has relied on factors which Congress has not intended it to consider, entirely failed to consider an important aspect of the problem, offered an explanation for its decision that runs counter to the evidence before the agency, or is so implausible that it could not be ascribed to a difference in view or the product of agency expertise. ...

The ultimate question before us is whether NHTSA's rescission of the passive restraint requirement of Standard 208 was arbitrary and capricious. We conclude ... that it was. We also conclude ... that further consideration of the issue by the agency is therefore required. We deal separately with the rescission as it applies to airbags and as it applies to seatbelts.

[Airbags]

The first and most obvious reason for finding the rescission arbitrary and capricious is that NHTSA apparently gave no consideration whatever to modifying the Standard to require that airbag technology be utilized. Standard 208 sought to achieve automatic crash protection by requiring automobile manufacturers to install either of two passive restraint devices:

airbags or automatic seatbelts. There was no suggestion in the long rulemaking process that led to Standard 208 that if only one of these options were feasible, no passive restraint standard should be promulgated. Indeed, the agency's original proposed standard contemplated the installation of inflatable restraints in all cars. Automatic belts were added [in 1971] as a means of complying with the standard because they were believed to be as effective as airbags in achieving the goal of occupant crash protection. At that time, the passive belt approved by the agency could not be detached. Only later [in 1974] at a manufacturer's behest, did the agency approve of the detachability feature – and only after assurances that the feature would not compromise the safety benefits of the restraint. Although it was then foreseen that 60% of the new cars would contain airbags and 40% would have automatic seatbelts, the ratio between the two was not significant as long as the passive belt would also assure greater passenger safety.

The agency has now determined that the detachable automatic belts will not attain anticipated safety benefits because so many individuals will detach the mechanism. Even if this conclusion were acceptable in its entirety, standing alone it would not justify any more than an amendment of Standard 208 to disallow compliance by means of the one technology which will not provide effective passenger protection. It does not cast doubt on the need for a passive restraint standard or upon the efficacy of airbag technology. ...

Given the effectiveness ascribed to airbag technology by the agency, the mandate of the Safety Act to achieve traffic safety would suggest that the logical response to the faults of detachable seatbelts would be to require the installation of airbags. At the very least this alternative way of achieving the objectives of the Act should have been addressed and adequate reasons given for its abandonment. But the agency not only did not require compliance through airbags, it did not even consider the possibility in its 1981 rulemaking. Not one sentence of its rulemaking statement discusses the airbags-only option. ...

The automobile industry has opted for the passive belt over the airbag, but surely it is not enough that the regulated industry has eschewed a given safety device. For nearly a decade, the automobile industry waged the regulatory equivalent of war against the airbag and lost – the inflatable restraint was proven sufficiently effective. Now the automobile industry has decided to employ a seatbelt system which will not meet the safety objectives of Standard 208. This hardly constitutes cause to revoke the standard itself. Indeed, the Motor Vehicle Safety Act was necessary because the industry was not sufficiently responsive to safety concerns. The Act intended that safety standards not depend on current technology and could be "technology-forcing" in the sense of inducing the development of superior safety design. If, under the statute, the agency should not defer to the industry's failure to develop safer cars, which it surely should not do, a fortiori it may not revoke a safety standard which can be satisfied by current technology simply because the industry has opted for an ineffective seatbelt design. ...

[Seatbelts]

Although the issue is closer, we also find that the agency was too quick to dismiss the safety benefits of automatic seatbelts. NHTSA's critical finding was that, in light of the industry's plans to install readily detachable passive belts, it could not reliably predict "even a 5 percentage point increase as the minimum level of expected usage increase." ...

Rescission of the passive restraint requirement would not be arbitrary and capricious simply because there was no evidence in direct support of the agency's conclusion. It is not infrequent that the available data does not settle a regulatory issue and the agency must then exercise its judgment in moving from the facts and probabilities on the record to a policy conclusion. Recognizing that policymaking in a complex society must account for uncertainty, however, does not imply that it is sufficient for an agency to merely recite the terms "substantial uncertainty" as a justification for its actions. The agency must explain the evidence which is available, and must offer a rational connection between the facts found and the choice made. ...

In this case, the agency's explanation for rescission of the passive restraint requirement is not sufficient to enable us to conclude that the rescission was the product of reasoned decision-making. ...We start with the accepted ground that if used, seatbelts unquestionably would save many thousands of lives and would prevent tens of thousands of crippling injuries. ... [T]he safety benefits of wearing seatbelts are not in doubt and it is not challenged that were those benefits to accrue, the monetary costs of implementing the standard would be easily justified. We move next to the fact that there is no direct evidence in support of the agency's finding that detachable automatic belts cannot be predicted to yield a substantial increase in usage. The empirical evidence on the record, consisting of surveys of drivers of automobiles equipped with passive belts, reveals more than a doubling of the usage rate experienced with manual belts. Much of the agency's rulemaking statement – and much of the controversy in this case – centers on the conclusions that should be drawn from these studies. The agency maintained that the doubling of seatbelt usage in these studies could not be extrapolated to an across-the-board mandatory standard because the passive seatbelts were guarded by ignition interlocks and purchasers of the tested cars are somewhat atypical. ...

... NHTSA opines that "it cannot reliably predict even a 5 percentage point increase as the minimum level of increased usage." But this and other statements that passive belts will not yield substantial increases in seatbelt usage apparently take no account of the critical difference between detachable automatic belts and current manual belts. A detached passive belt does require an affirmative act to reconnect it, but – unlike a manual seat belt – the passive belt, once reattached, will continue to function automatically unless again disconnected. Thus, inertia – a factor which the agency's own studies have found significant in explaining the current low usage rates for seatbelts – works in favor of, not against, use of the protective device. Since 20 to 50% of motorists currently wear seatbelts on some occasions, there would seem to be grounds to believe that seatbelt use by occasional users will be substantially increased by the detachable passive belts. Whether this is in fact the case is a matter for the agency to decide, but it must bring its expertise to bear on the question.

The agency is correct to look at the costs as well as the benefits of Standard 208. The agency's conclusion that the incremental costs of the requirements were no longer reasonable was predicated on its prediction that the safety benefits of the regulation might be minimal. Specifically, the agency's fears that the public may resent paying more for the automatic belt systems is expressly dependent on the assumption that detachable automatic belts will not produce more than "negligible safety benefits." When the agency reexamines its findings as to the likely increase in seatbelt usage, it must also reconsider its judgment of the reasonableness of the monetary and other costs associated with the Standard. In reaching its judgment, NHTSA should bear in mind that Congress intended safety to be the preeminent factor under the Motor Vehicle Safety Act ...

.... [W]e ... conclude that the agency has failed to supply the requisite "reasoned analysis" in this case.

■ ■ Critical Thinking ■

Administrative agencies are sometimes called the fourth branch of government. What are the checks and balances on their power?

What was the basis for the Supreme Court's finding that the agency's decisions were arbitrary? What else should the agency have done to engage in "reasoned decision-making"?

Important Terms

- Arbitrary and capricious standard
- Federal Register
- Homeland Security Act
- Notice-and-comment rule-making
- OIRA and OMB
- Proclamation of emergency
- Regulations
- Spending Clause
- USA PATRIOT Act

Review Questions

1. When courts are reviewing the process used by an agency to develop the content of regulations, what is the benchmark or standard for validity?
2. How are national emergencies declared? Terminated?
3. How does the Spending Clause enlarge the powers of Congress beyond Article I?
4. What does OMB do?
5. What broader purposes are served by the steps in the APA rule-making process?

4

The Domestic Use of Military Troops

What You Will Learn

- Which federal laws establish restrictions on the use of the military
- The public policy concerns behind such restrictions
- The history of how military troops have been used to quell unrest within the United States
- The difference between the Army, the Army Reserve, and the National Guard
- The distinctive conditions associated with martial law

Introduction

Since the founding of the Republic, the use of active duty military forces against Americans on American soil has been a contentious issue. There is a strong tradition in the United States of civilian control of the military and of concern about the presence of a large standing army. One can see the framers' response to these concerns in the architecture of the Constitution. The Constitution provides that the President and Congress share control over the uniformed armed services by virtue of the different responsibilities assigned to each. In addition, the federal government shares with the states control over the militia (now the National Guard).

Article I, Section 8 assigns to Congress the power to raise, support, organize, and regulate the armed forces; to provide for the "calling forth" of the militia to execute federal law and suppress insurrections; and to provide for organizing, arming, and disciplining the militia while they are deployed in federal service. Article II, Section 2 specifies that the President shall be commander in chief of the armed forces while Article II. Section 3 provides the President with the general power to "take Care that the Laws be faithfully executed." The Third Amendment specifically bars any branch of government from ordering that civilians allow soldiers to be quartered in their homes during peacetime.

What began as state militias are now state National Guard units. The National Guard is a uniformed service that governors can use to keep and restore order and protect lives and property. Although governors have the authority to call out the National Guard when needed, the Constitution forbids states from maintaining standing armies (Article I, Section 10). In turn, however, it makes the federal government responsible for protecting states against invasion and insurrection (Article IV, Section 4). Certainly, in the event of a foreign attack on American soil or a domestic rebellion, the President can deploy military units to respond. The President has the power to "call forth" National Guard units for assignment either in the United States or elsewhere, if needed.

History

During the nation's first century, the federal government's use of military forces within the United States was episodic. In 1794, President Washington mobilized the militia (there were too few regular army troops available) to suppress the Whiskey Rebellion in Pennsylvania. Washington's authority to send troops was the Calling Forth Act, which was written to expire after three years. In 1807, Congress passed the Insurrection Act, which delineated the situations in which the President could send federal troops to quell domestic disorders.

In the years just before and after the Civil War, troops were sometimes deployed as part of civilian posses – to enforce the Fugitive Slave Law before the war and to enforce Reconstruction laws afterward. The source of this power was the Judiciary Act of 1789, under which U.S. marshals could call up members of the state militia to serve in a posse. The U.S. Marshals Service is a unit within the Justice Department that is responsible for providing security in the federal courts and for serving papers and enforcing court orders, including making arrests. The word "posse" is a shortened version of the Latin phrase "posse comitātūs," (pronounced com-ee-tay'-tus), which Black's Law Dictionary defines as

> *n.* [Latin "power of the county"] A group of citizens who are called together to help the sheriff keep the peace or conduct rescue operations.
>
> Black's Law Dictionary (2004)

One example of the use of the militia for law enforcement purposes was to assist marshals at the polls in the 1876 presidential election. After the election, disputes arose over votes in South Carolina, Louisiana, and Florida, where it was alleged that the military presence intimidated voters into supporting Republican candidates, including Rutherford B. Hayes. When the final count showed that Democrat Samuel Tilden had won the popular vote, a deal was struck in which Southern Democrats agreed to deliver enough electoral votes to give the Presidency to Hayes in return for a promise that federal troops would leave the southern states. Reconstruction ended, and less than two years later, Congress enacted the Posse Comitātūs Act.

The Posse Comitātūs Act

The Posse Comitātūs Act (PCA) has been amended slightly since its original enactment, and now provides as follows:

The Posse Comitātūs Act
U.S. Code, Title 18 Section 1385

> Whoever, except in cases and under circumstances expressly authorized by the Constitution or Act of Congress, willfully uses any part of the Army or the Air Force as a posse comitātūs or otherwise to execute the laws shall be fined under this title or imprisoned not more than 2 years, or both.

Acting pursuant to the "expressly authorized" language, Congress has passed several laws that create exceptions to the PCA. The two most significant are the Insurrection Act, discussed below, and the Stafford Act, which deals with responses to natural disasters and is the subject of Chapter 9. Congress has also enacted authorization for the armed forces to share equipment with civilian law enforcement agencies. In addition to these specific exceptions, government officials and legal scholars have debated the extent to which the President may have "inherent authority" to use troops to enforce the law within the United States when emergency conditions seem to require an immediate response. (Recall President Truman's unsuccessful invocation of "inherent powers" to seize the steel mills in the *Youngstown* case in 1952. We discuss this case in Chapter 1.)

Congress reaffirmed the PCA, although in hedged language, when it enacted the Homeland Security Act in 2002. A section of that law is titled "Sense of Congress reaffirming the continued importance and applicability of the [PCA]." It provides as follows:

Homeland Security Act
U.S. Code, Title 6 Section 466

> (a) FINDINGS – Congress finds the following: …

> (3) The Posse Comitātūs Act has served the Nation well in limiting the use of the Armed Forces to enforce the law.

(4) Nevertheless, by its express terms, the Posse Comitātūs Act is not a complete barrier to the use of the Armed Forces for a range of domestic purposes, including law enforcement functions, when the use of the Armed Forces is authorized by Act of Congress or the President determines that the use of the Armed Forces is required to fulfill the President's obligations under the Constitution to respond promptly in time of war, insurrection, or other serious emergency. ...

(b) SENSE OF CONGRESS – Congress reaffirms the continued importance of [the PCA], and it is the sense of Congress that nothing in this Act should be construed to alter the applicability of such section to any use of the Armed Forces as a posse comitātūs to execute the laws.

■ ■ Critical Thinking ■

Consider the language in Section (a)(4) above, beginning "or the President determines." Is this a proper codification of the concept that the President has indeterminate "inherent powers"? What are the checks and balances on this kind of authority?

The Scope of the PCA

What does the PCA mean when it prohibits "us[ing] any part of the Army or Air Force"? For starters, why only those two services? As a practical matter, the Navy may be less likely to be engaged in domestic law enforcement. For the sake of consistency, though, Defense Department regulations extend the prohibitions of the PCA to the Navy (of which the Marine Corps is a part). The Coast Guard is different, however. From its inception, the Coast Guard has been a uniformed service dedicated to domestic use; it has never been part of the Defense Department. It was originally part of the Treasury Department and is now part of the Department of Homeland Security (see Chapter 3). Thus, there is no barrier to using the Coast Guard for law enforcement purposes. Whether the PCA applies to the National Guard depends on whether the Guard units in question have been federalized (see the box at the end of this chapter titled "The Dual Role of the National Guard").

The Wounded Knee Standoff

One of the most controversial modern uses of military troops for law enforcement purposes occurred in 1973, when President Nixon ordered Army and National Guard troops to end the occupation by Lakota Sioux Indians of a building on their reservation. In the three-month confrontation that followed, two people were killed and one paralyzed by gunfire. The bitterness aroused by this action was deepened by the fact that it occurred at Wounded Knee, S.D., where Army troops in 1890 massacred more than 200 Sioux, including dozens of women, children, and elders.

The litigation that followed the 1973 Wounded Knee standoff included criminal prosecutions of those thought to have led the group seizing federal property. The defendants countered that government officials themselves had violated the law by violating the PCA. A series of court decisions distilled the following three tests for whether the PCA had been violated:

- Whether civil law enforcement agents made direct active use of military personnel to execute the laws;
- Whether the use of military personnel pervaded the activities of civilian law enforcement actions; and
- Whether military personnel subjected civilians to exercises of military power that were regulatory, prescriptive, or compulsory in nature.

A second category of cases arising from the 1973 Wounded Knee incident were civil suits brought by Native Americans for violation of their constitutional rights. The following case was one in which residents of the reservation sued federal officials. The appeals court reversed the trial court's dismissal of their complaint.

Bissonette v. Haig
U.S. Court of Appeals, 1985

> *This is an action for damages caused by defendants' alleged violations of the Constitution of the United States. The complaint alleges, among other things, that the defendants seized and confined plaintiffs within an "armed perimeter" by the unlawful use of military force, and that this conduct violated not only a federal statute but also the Fourth Amendment. The use of federal military force, plaintiffs argue, without lawful authority and in violation of the Posse Comitātūs*

Act, was an "unreasonable" seizure of their persons within the meaning of the Fourth Amendment. [The Fourth Amendment prohibits unreasonable searches and seizures.] We hold that the complaint states a claim upon which relief may be granted. The judgment of the District Court, dismissing the complaint with prejudice for failure to state a claim, will therefore be reversed, and the cause remanded for further proceedings consistent with this opinion.

I. This case arises out of the occupation of the village of Wounded Knee, South Dakota, on the Pine Ridge Reservation by an armed group of Indians on February 27, 1973. On the evening when the occupation began, members of the Federal Bureau of Investigation, the United States Marshals Service, and the Bureau of Indian Affairs Police sealed off the village by establishing roadblocks at all major entry and exit roads. The standoff between the Indians and the law-enforcement authorities ended about ten weeks later with the surrender of the Indians occupying the village.

In February 1975, the plaintiffs, most of whom at the time of the occupation were residents of the Pine Ridge Indian Reservation, brought this action in the District Court for the District of Columbia alleging that the defendants, who were military personnel or federal officials, conspired to seize and assault them and destroy their property in violation of several constitutional and statutory provisions. ...

II. In their amended complaint, plaintiffs ... claim that they were unreasonably seized and confined in the village of Wounded Knee contrary to the Fourth Amendment and their rights to free movement and travel. ... This case comes to us on appeal from a dismissal for failure to state a claim, and we therefore accept for present purposes the factual allegations of the complaint. ...

... We believe that the Constitution, certain acts of Congress, and the decisions of the Supreme Court embody certain limitations on the use of military personnel in enforcing the civil law, and that searches and seizures in circumstances which exceed those limits are unreasonable under the Fourth Amendment.

*... Reasonableness is determined by balancing the inter-
ests for and against the seizure. Usually, the interests
arrayed against a seizure are those of the individual in
privacy, freedom of movement, or, in the case of a seizure by deadly force, life. Here, however, the opposing
interests are more societal and governmental than strictly
individual in character. They concern the special threats
to constitutional government inherent in military enforcement of civilian law. ...*

*Civilian rule is basic to our system of government. The use
of military forces to seize civilians can expose civilian government to the threat of military rule and the suspension of
constitutional liberties. On a lesser scale, military enforcement of the civil law leaves the protection of vital Fourth and
Fifth Amendment rights in the hands of persons who are not
trained to uphold these rights. It may also chill the exercise
of fundamental rights, such as the rights to speak freely and
to vote, and create the atmosphere of fear and hostility which
exists in territories occupied by enemy forces.*

*The interest in limiting military involvement in civilian
affairs has a long tradition beginning with the Declaration
of Independence and continued in the Constitution, certain acts of Congress, and decisions of the Supreme Court.
The Declaration of Independence states among the grounds
for severing ties with Great Britain that the King "has kept
among us, in times of peace, Standing Armies without
Consent of our Legislature ... [and] has affected to render
the Military independent of and superior to the Civil power."
These concerns were later raised at the Constitutional
Convention. Luther Martin of Maryland said, "when a
government wishes to deprive its citizens of freedom, and
reduce them to slavery, it generally makes use of a standing
army." ...*

... [I]n Laird v. Tatum, *statements the [Supreme] Court
made ... reaffirm ... limitations [found in the Constitution and
in statutes]:*

*"The concerns of the Executive and Legislative Branches ...
reflect a traditional and strong resistance of Americans to any*

military intrusion into civilian affairs. That tradition has deep roots in our history and found early expression, for example, in the Third Amendment's explicit prohibition against quartering soldiers in private homes without consent and in the constitutional provisions for civilian control of the military. Those prohibitions are not directly presented by this case, but their philosophical underpinnings explain our traditional insistence on limitations on military operations in peacetime. Indeed, when presented with claims of judicially cognizable injury resulting from military intrusion into the civilian sector, federal courts are fully empowered to consider claims of those asserting such injury; there is nothing in our Nation's history or in this Court's decided cases, including our holding today, that can properly be seen as giving any indication that actual or threatened injury by reason of unlawful activities of the military would go unnoticed or unremedied."

The governmental interests favoring military assistance to civilian law enforcement are primarily twofold: first, to maintain order in times of domestic violence or rebellion; and second, to improve the efficiency of civilian law enforcement by giving it the benefit of military technologies, equipment, information, and training personnel. These interests can and have been accommodated by acts of Congress to the overriding interest of preserving civilian government and law enforcement. ... [Under the Insurrection Act] the President may call upon the military only after having determined that domestic unrest makes it "impracticable to enforce the laws of the United States by the ordinary course of judicial proceedings," and he may do so only after having issued a proclamation ordering the insurgents to disperse. Those steps were not taken here.

We believe that the limits established by Congress on the use of the military for civilian law enforcement provide a reliable guidepost by which to evaluate the reasonableness for Fourth Amendment purposes of the seizures and searches in question here. Congress has acted to establish reasonable limits on the President's use of military forces in emergency situations, and in doing so has circumscribed whatever, if any, inherent power the President may have had absent such legislation. This is the teaching of Youngstown Sheet & Tube Co. v. Sawyer. *There the President attempted to justify his seizure of the steel mills on grounds of inherent executive power to protect national security. Justice Black, writing for the Court, rejected this assertion of executive authority, and in addition four of the five judges concurring in the Court's opinion or judgment wrote separate opinions expressing the view that Congress had precluded the exercise of inherent executive authority by specifically refusing to give the President the power of seizure.*

… The legal traditions which we have briefly summarized establish that the use of military force for domestic law-enforcement purposes is in a special category, and that both the courts and Congress have been alert to keep it there. In short, if the use of military personnel is both unauthorized by any statute, and contrary to a specific criminal prohibition, and if citizens are seized or searched by military means in such a case, we have no hesitation in declaring that such searches and seizures are constitutionally "unreasonable." We do not mean to say that every search or seizure that violates a statute of any kind is necessarily a violation of the Fourth Amendment. But the statute prohibiting (if the allegations in the complaint can be proved) the conduct engaged in by defendants here is, as we have attempted to explain, not just any act of Congress. It is the embodiment of a long tradition of suspicion and hostility towards the use of military force for domestic purposes.

Plaintiffs' Fourth Amendment case, therefore, must stand or fall on the proposition that military activity in connection with the occupation of Wounded Knee violated the Posse Comitātūs Act. …

… [M]ilitary involvement, even when not expressly authorized by the Constitution or a statute, does not violate the Posse Comitātūs Act unless it actually regulates, forbids, or compels some conduct on the part of those claiming relief. A mere threat of some future injury would be insufficient. In addition, … the mere furnishing of materials and supplies cannot violate the statute. … [T]he use of military personnel, planes, and cameras to fly surveillance and the advice of military officers in dealing with the disorder – advice, that is, as distinguished from active participation or direction – [these are also permitted].

The question becomes, then, whether the present complaint alleges more than these kinds of activities. ... We of course have no way of knowing what plaintiffs would be able to prove if this case goes to trial, but the complaint, considered simply as a pleading, goes well beyond an allegation that defendants simply furnished supplies, aerial surveillance, and advice. It specifically charges that "the several Defendants maintained or caused to be maintained roadblocks and armed patrols constituting an armed perimeter around the village of Wounded Knee. ..." Defendants' actions, it is charged, "seized, confined, and made prisoners [of plaintiffs] against their will... ." These allegations amount to a claim that defendants' activities, allegedly in violation of the Posse Comitātūs Act, were "regulatory, proscriptive, or compulsory," in the sense that these activities directly restrained plaintiffs' freedom of movement. No more is required to survive a motion to dismiss. We hold, therefore, that plaintiffs' first set of claims, alleging an unreasonable seizure in violation of the Fourth Amendment because of defendants' confinement of plaintiffs within an armed perimeter, does state a cause of action. ...

■ ■ Critical Thinking ■

What are the principles behind the longstanding American aversion to sending federal troops to maintain order? Are they still important?

Weapons of Mass Destruction

More recently, public fear about an attack using chemical, biological or nuclear weapons has increased. In response, Congress enacted the following statute, geared to a scenario involving military assistance to federal law enforcement authorities, especially the Federal Bureau of Investigation:

Emergency situations involving chemical or biological weapons of mass destruction
U.S. Code, Title 10 Section 382

(a) In general – The Secretary of Defense, upon the request of the Attorney General, may provide assistance in support of Department of Justice activities relating to the enforcement of [criminal laws] during an emergency situation involving a biological or chemical weapon of mass destruction. Department of Defense resources, including personnel of the Department of Defense, may be used to provide such assistance if –

(1) the Secretary of Defense and the Attorney General jointly determine that an emergency situation exists; and

(2) the Secretary of Defense determines that the provision of such assistance will not adversely affect the military preparedness of the United States.

(b) Emergency situations covered – In this section, the term "emergency situation involving a biological or chemical weapon of mass destruction" means a circumstance involving a biological or chemical weapon of mass destruction –

(1) that poses a serious threat to the interests of the United States; and

(2) in which –

(A) civilian expertise and capabilities are not readily available to provide the required assistance to counter the threat immediately posed by the weapon involved;

(B) special capabilities and expertise of the Department of Defense are necessary and critical to counter the threat posed by the weapon involved; and

(C) enforcement of [criminal laws] would be seriously impaired if the Department of Defense assistance were not provided. …

(d)(2)(A) Except as provided in subparagraph (B), the regulations may not authorize the following actions:

(i) Arrest.

(ii) Any direct participation in conducting a search for or seizure of evidence related to a violation of [criminal law].

(iii) Any direct participation in the collection of intelligence for law enforcement purposes.

(B) The regulations may authorize an action described in subparagraph (A) to be taken under the following conditions:

(i) The action is considered necessary for the immediate protection of human life, and civilian law enforcement officials are not capable of taking the action. …

■ ■ Critical Thinking ■

Compare the language of the act you have just read to the language of the Insurrection Act below. How does this law arguably alter the Insurrection Act's requirements?

The Insurrection Act

As noted above, the Insurrection Act predates the PCA, and thus was at least part of what Congress intended by its reference in the PCA to statutes that explicitly authorize deployment of federal troops for law enforcement purposes within the United States. The Insurrection Act has been invoked a number of times, including to enforce court orders desegregating schools and in response to widespread looting and violence.

The most recent controversy over the Insurrection Act grew out of the failure of relief efforts immediately after Hurricane Katrina in 2005. Congressional hearings and agency reports sought to identify where and when the mistakes had been made, and some suggested that the President hesitated to send federal troops because he lacked clear authority under the PCA. During the same time period, in fall 2005, there was also widespread concern about and planning for a possible influenza pandemic reaching the United States. The *Washington Post* reported that Bush administration officials wanted to insure that military units would be available for enforcement of quarantine orders, should that become necessary.

In that context, Congress adopted an amendment to the Insurrection Act that diminished the control of governors over National Guard units and expanded the number of situations in which the President could deploy military forces to include natural disasters and health emergencies. The amendment was a small part of a much larger authorization bill and passed without debate. When they realized what had occurred, all 50 governors urged Congress to repeal the new language. A year later, Congress did precisely that. The Insurrection Act now provides as follows:

The Insurrection Act
U.S. Code, Title 10

§ 331. Aid to State governments

Whenever there is an insurrection in any State against its government, the President may, upon the request of its legislature or of its governor if the legislature cannot be convened, call into Federal service such of the militia of the other States, in the number requested by that State, and use such of the armed forces, as he considers necessary to suppress the insurrection.

§ 332. Use of militia and armed forces to enforce Federal authority

Whenever the President considers that unlawful obstructions, combinations, or assemblages, or rebellion against the authority of the United States, make it impracticable to enforce the laws of the United States in any State by the ordinary course of judicial proceedings, he may call into Federal service such of the militia of any State, and use such of the armed forces, as he considers necessary to enforce those laws or to suppress the rebellion.

§ 333. Interference with State and Federal law

The President, by using the militia or the armed forces, or both, or by any other means, shall take such measures as he considers necessary to suppress, in a State, any insurrection, domestic violence, unlawful combination, or conspiracy, if it –

(1) so hinders the execution of the laws of that State, and of the United States within the State, that any part or class of its people is deprived of a right, privilege, immunity, or protection named in the Constitution and secured by law, and the constituted authorities of that State are unable, fail, or refuse to protect that right, privilege, or immunity, or to give that protection; or

(2) opposes or obstructs the execution of the laws of the United States or impedes the course of justice under those laws.

In any situation covered by clause (1), the State shall be considered to have denied the equal protection of the laws secured by the Constitution.

§ 334. Proclamation to disperse

Whenever the President considers it necessary to use the militia or the armed forces under this chapter, he shall, by proclamation, immediately order the insurgents to disperse and retire peaceably to their abodes within a limited time.

■ ■ Critical Thinking ■

Diagram the different preconditions for troop deployment and the different functions that troops are authorized to serve. Under the current language of the Insurrection Act, could federal troops be sent to enforce a quarantine order?

Martial Law

In the midst of the post-Katrina rescue efforts, White House Press Secretary Scott McClellan announced that "martial law has been declared." He was incorrect, but not alone in his confusion. Many people conflate martial law with any deployment of troops to quell disturbances. As the Supreme Court noted, "the term 'martial law' carries no precise meaning. The Constitution does not refer to 'martial law' at all, and no Act of Congress has defined the term." *Duncan v. Kahanamoku* (1946). Martial law has a particular meaning, though – it signifies that military authority has *replaced* civilian authority and that civilian courts have been supplanted by military tribunals. When Hawaii was placed under martial law for almost three years after the attack on Pearl Harbor, for example, local police forces were under the command of the military, as were the local courts.

Although there is a consensus that a President could declare martial law in the event of an extreme emergency, it has happened only rarely in American history. Given their powers under the Insurrection Act (above) and the National Emergencies Act (see Chapter 3), presidents have not sought the extraordinary powers associated with martial law except during the Civil War and World War II. In every national emergency since World War II, including September 11, civil authority has continued to function and there has been no serious suggestion that the President should impose martial law.

At the state level, the issue of martial law has received more attention. Governors have imposed martial law – which can then be enforced by the National Guard – with much greater frequency than have presidents. The following provides a summary description:

Martial law authority in the states is delegated by statute to the state executive. In total, eighteen states statutorily provide for the governor to declare martial law. While the statutes contain much boilerplate, there are enough differences among them to provide a spectrum of martial law authority in the states.

At one end of the spectrum, Washington empowers its governor to proclaim "complete martial law," defined as the "subordination of all civil authority to the military." The governor must be of the opinion that the "re-establishment or maintenance of law and order may be promoted." The only condition is the presence of troops in the specific localities under martial law. The statute even permits "military tribunals" to try persons apprehended in such a locality, and for the limited suspension of habeas corpus.

At the other end of the spectrum, Iowa allows its governor to "establish a military district under martial law" only when the general assembly is convened, which provides a certain oversight function. When the general assembly is not in session, the governor can establish martial law "only after the governor has issued a proclamation convening an extraordinary session of the general assembly." Iowa also provides by statute that any justice of the Iowa Supreme Court may transfer a pending civil or criminal case from the district under martial law to any other jurisdiction for adjudication.

The majority of states fall somewhere in between these two extremes.

Weida (2004)

Figure 4.1 is an example of a proclamation of martial law. In this example, martial law was declared in 1913 in the aftermath of a flood.

■ ■ Critical Thinking ■

Watch a film that depicts the imposition of martial law, such as "The Seige." How realistic do you think it is? How are the burdens and advantages of martial law depicted?

FIGURE 4.1 Ohio Governor James M. Cox's Proclamation of Martial Law in 1913.

Important Terms

- Federalizing the National Guard
- Martial law
- Militia
- Posse comitātūs
- Regulatory, prescriptive, or compulsory
- U.S. marshals

THE DUAL ROLE OF THE NATIONAL GUARD

The National Guard has a unique dual mission that consists of both federal and state roles. The President can activate the National Guard for participation in federal missions, either domestically or abroad. When federalized, the Guard units are commanded by the commander of the theater in which they are operating and, ultimately, by the President as commander in chief. When not federalized, the only federal mission of the National Guard is to maintain properly trained and equipped units that are available for prompt mobilization.

For state missions, the governor, through the state adjutant general, commands Guard forces. Each state and territory has its own National Guard. The governor can call the National Guard into action during local or statewide emergencies, such as storms, fires, earthquakes, civil disturbances, or to support law enforcement. When National Guard units are under state command, they are not subject to the PCA and therefore can be used in law enforcement activities.

The Militia Act of 1903 reorganized and renamed the various state militias into what is today the National Guard. The Army National Guard is part of the U.S. Army and comprises almost half of the Army's available combat forces and approximately one-third of its support organization. The Air National Guard is part of the U.S. Air Force. The Army and Air Force National Guards are trained and equipped as part of their respective services and use the same ranks and insignia.

The Army and Air National Guards are very similar to the Army Reserve and Air Force Reserve, respectively. The primary difference lies in the level of government to which they are subordinated. The Army Reserve and Air Force Reserve are subordinated to the federal government while the National Guards are subordinated to the various state governments, except when called into federal service.

Review Questions

1. What is the relationship between the Posse Comitātūs Act and the Insurrection Act? Between the Insurrection Act and martial law?
2. How is the National Guard different from other services? How is the Coast Guard different from other services?
3. When can National Guard troops lawfully be used for law enforcement?
4. What kinds of activities must military commanders avoid to insure that they do not violate the Posse Comitātūs Act?

PART

II

The Law of Health Emergencies

 **5**

Federal Public Health Law

What You Will Learn

- The kinds of constitutional questions that arise when public health officials exercise the power of quarantine
- How federalism shapes the system of American public health laws
- The history of the shift from exclusive state control over quarantine to shared federal-state control
- How legal powers are divided today between state and federal public health officers

Introduction

Together, this chapter and the next one will explain the origins and current operations of public health emergency law, at both the federal and state levels. Consider as you read a hypothetical proposed by David Fidler, a law professor at Indiana University. Professor Fidler imagined a scene in which Dr. Evil, who is considering possible targets for a bioterrorist attack, seeks legal advice. Rumpole the Malevolent, his lawyer, advises Dr. Evil that "[y]our ideal legal target for a bioweapon attack is a country that, first of all, has a fragmented legal system, in that relevant legal powers to respond to a public health emergency are divided among actors at the national and local levels. Federalism is, for instance, a fragmented legal system" (Fidler, 2001). Should the United States change its system? Is it feasible to do so?

History

When the colonies first formed the United States, there was no national public health law. In a time when traveling any significant distance was rare, infectious disease outbreaks and epidemics were often localized, to an extent that is difficult to imagine today. Recall from Chapter 1 that the Supreme Court stated in *Jacobson v. Massachusetts* that enactment of quarantine and other health laws fell within the "police power" of each state. Before 1796, quarantines were solely the responsibility of state and local governments. Early federal involvement was minor. When Congress first passed a law to address quarantine, in 1796, it simply allowed the national government to assist state governments in the event of disease outbreaks. That general policy preference has endured. The structure of public health law today continues to be based on the premise that state and local health officials will, at least initially, take lead responsibility for most public health emergencies. But the federal role has grown dramatically.

The origin of independent federal public health authority derives from laws designed to provide medical care for eighteenth-century merchant seamen, a group who traveled constantly and often had little access to care when they became ill in unfamiliar cities. Moreover, their illnesses threatened the mercantile trade that was essential to the economy of the fledging nation. The origins of what is now the U.S. Public Health Service (PHS) began in 1798, when Congress established a fund to provide treatment for sick and injured merchant seamen.

The marine hospital fund, as it was known, was financed by deductions from the sailors' wages used to build hospitals in port cities. By the end of the Civil War, many of these hospitals had been occupied by either the Union or Confederate armies, and only a handful were still operational. The trend toward federal control began after the Civil War. In 1870, the Secretary of the Treasury, in whose department the marine hospital fund was administered, initiated a major organizational reform of the system.

In the following decade, two critical events happened. The Treasury Department realigned the loose network of remaining hospitals into a Marine Hospital Service (MHS), administered centrally. A new position of supervising surgeon (later, the Surgeon General) was created to oversee the MHS. The second major event resulted from an 1877 yellow fever epidemic that spread rapidly from New Orleans up the Mississippi River, a signal to the nation that increased mobility made localized control of infectious disease inadequate. Congress reacted by passing the National Quarantine Act of 1878, which conferred quarantine authority for the first time on a federal government agency, the MHS, and authorized the construction of federal quarantine facilities.

The first supervising surgeon, John Maynard Woodworth, continued the era of change by adopting a military model for the physicians in the MHS. They began wearing uniforms and served in the MHS as troops did in the military, subject to deployment to sites where they were needed. This development was formalized in 1889, with the renaming of the MHS physician group as the Commissioned Corps. In 1902, Congress changed the organizational name again, to the Public Health and Marine Hospital Service. Today, there remains a Commissioned Corps of health care professionals (including dentists, nurses, and pharmacists as well as doctors) in the PHS.

In the first half of the twentieth century, the Corps was increasingly used for military purposes. It had served an important role in the Spanish–American War in 1898, when PHS doctors cared for wounded service members and operated quarantine stations to prevent troops infected with yellow fever from returning to the states from Cuba or Puerto Rico. The 1902 legislation authorized the President to use PHS officers in times of threatened or actual war. President Wilson signed an Executive Order in 1917 that provided for the PHS to be deployed in World War I. A 1943 law went further and authorized the President to convert the PHS into a military service during times of war.

The early twentieth century also saw the states that had their own quarantine facilities begin to turn them over voluntarily to the national government. This development came because the governments of states where major ports were located wanted to shift the cost of immigration-related health examinations and monitoring to Washington, where there was more expertise and a larger budget. In addition, local politics fostered graft. Politicians often rewarded supporters by appointing them as health officers to oversee incoming ships, a situation ripe for corruption. By 1921, all of the states had relinquished their role in policing persons and goods coming to the United States from abroad.

COMMITTEE OF DOCTORS URGES NEW YORK STATE TO TURN OVER MARITIME QUARANTINE TO FEDERAL GOVERNMENT

Quarantine work is essentially scientific in its nature, and our committee is a unit in feeling that such work cannot be carried on efficiently unless the tenure of office be independent of changes in administration and politics. The United States Public Health Service, by its organization, the character, training, and experience of its personnel and its opportunities for constant communication with all foreign ports, is admirably equipped to administer quarantine in a most efficient manner ... One of the most important reasons for a national control is the absolutely imperative need that the office of Health Officer of a

> *port be taken out of politics. ... Under Federal control, there is continuity of service, uniformity of procedure and policy [and] constant supervision over the acts of the health officers ...*
>
> Dr. Charles L. Dana
> New York Times, January 2, 1916

In 1946, what had been a malaria control project centered in southern states became the Communicable Disease Center, with its headquarters in Atlanta. After several changes to the name, it became the Centers for Disease Control and Prevention (CDC). Operating as a branch of the PHS, CDC has the most advanced disease surveillance system in the world.

Federal Public Health Law Today

The PHS is now a component of the U.S. Department of Health and Human Services (DHHS). The core of federal public health law is found in the statutes that grant authority for various actions to DHHS, PHS, and CDC. The bedrock question in this field is still how legal authority should be divided between federal and state governments. In reading the statutory sections that follow, ask yourself how Congress has delineated the different roles for federal and state officials in a time of public health crisis.

The Public Health Service Act
U.S. Code, Title 42

§ 243 General grant of author for cooperation

(a) Enforcement of quarantine regulations; prevention of communicable diseases

The Secretary [of the Department of Health and Human Services] is authorized to accept from State and local authorities any assistance in the enforcement of quarantine regulations made pursuant to this chapter which such authorities may be able and willing to provide. The Secretary shall also assist States and their political subdivisions in the prevention and suppression of communicable diseases and with respect to other public health matters ...

(c) Development of plan …

(1) The Secretary is authorized to develop [and implement] a plan under which … resources of the Service … may be effectively used to control epidemics of any disease or condition and to meet other health emergencies or problems. …

(2) The Secretary may, at the request of the appropriate State or local authority, extend temporary (not in excess of six months) assistance to States or localities in meeting health emergencies of such a nature as to warrant Federal assistance. …

§ 247d. Public health emergencies

(a) Emergencies

If the Secretary determines, after consultation with such public health officials as may be necessary, that –

(1) a disease or disorder presents a public health emergency; or

(2) a public health emergency, including significant outbreaks of infectious diseases or bioterrorist attacks, otherwise exists,

the Secretary may take such action as may be appropriate to respond to the public health emergency … Any such determination of a public health emergency terminates upon the Secretary declaring that the emergency no longer exists, or upon the expiration of the 90-day period beginning on the date on which the determination is made by the Secretary, whichever occurs first. Determinations that terminate under the preceding sentence may be renewed by the Secretary … Not later than 48 hours after making a determination under this subsection of a public health emergency (including a renewal), the Secretary shall submit to the Congress written notification of the determination. …

§ 264. Regulations to control communicable diseases

(a) Promulgation and enforcement by Surgeon General

The Surgeon General, with the approval of the Secretary, is authorized to make and enforce such regulations as in his judgment are necessary to prevent the introduction, transmission, or spread of communicable diseases from foreign countries into the States or possessions, or from one State or possession into any other State or possession. ...

(b) Apprehension, detention, or conditional release of individuals

Regulations prescribed under this section shall not provide for the apprehension, detention, or conditional release of individuals except for the purpose of preventing the introduction, transmission, or spread of such communicable diseases as may be specified from time to time in Executive orders of the President ...

(c) Application of regulations to persons entering from foreign countries

Except as provided in subsection (d) of this section, regulations prescribed under this section, insofar as they provide for the apprehension, detention, examination, or conditional release of individuals, shall be applicable only to individuals coming into a State or possession from a foreign country or a possession.

(d)(1) Apprehension and examination of persons reasonably believed to be infected

Regulations prescribed under this section may provide for the apprehension and examination of any individual reasonably believed to be infected with a communicable disease in a qualifying stage and (A) to be moving or about to move from a State to another State; or (B) to be a probable source of infection to individuals who, while infected with such disease in a qualifying stage, will be moving from a State to another State. Such regulations may provide that if upon examination any such individual is found to be infected, he may be detained for such time and in such manner as may be reasonably necessary. For purposes of this subsection, the term "State" includes, in addition to the several States, only the District of Columbia.

(2) For purposes of this subsection, the term "qualifying stage" with respect to a communicable disease, means that such disease

(A) is in a communicable stage; or

(B) is in a pre-communicable stage, if the disease would be likely to cause a public health emergency if transmitted to other individuals. ...

§ 266. Special quarantine powers in time of war

To protect the military and naval forces and war workers of the United States, in time of war, against any communicable disease specified in Executive orders ..., the Secretary, in consultation with the Surgeon General, is authorized to provide by regulations for the apprehension and examination, in time of war, of any individual reasonably believed (1) to be infected with such disease and (2) to be a probable source of infection to members of the armed forces of the United States or to individuals engaged in the production or transportation of arms, munitions, ships, food, clothing, or other supplies for the armed forces. Such regulations may provide that if upon examination any such individual is found to be so infected, he may be detained for such time and in such manner as may be reasonably necessary.

§ 270. Quarantine regulations governing ... civil aircraft

The Surgeon General is authorized to provide by regulations for the application to air navigation and aircraft of any of the provisions of sections 267 to 269 of this title and regulations prescribed thereunder, ... to such extent and upon such conditions as he deems necessary for the safeguarding of the public health.

§ 271. Penalties for violation of quarantine laws

Any person who violates any regulation prescribed under sections 264 to 266 of this title, ... or who enters or departs from the limits of any quarantine station ... in disregard of quarantine rules and regulations or without permission of the quarantine officer in charge, shall be punished by a fine of not more than $1,000 or by imprisonment for not more than one year, or both.

■ ■ Critical Thinking ■

What are the most significant limitations on when the federal health officials can act to stop an infectious disease from spreading? Why doesn't the statute simply grant all authority to deal with infectious diseases to federal officials?

What conditions are necessary for a situation to qualify as a "public health emergency" under the Act? How do the federal public health powers differ once an emergency is declared? Is there any effective limitation on these powers? What about the constitutional rights of persons who might be quarantined?

What factors must be present for DHHS to have authority to quarantine individuals?

One of these factors relates to diseases specified in Executive Orders. Following is the current Executive Order identifying diseases as to which DHHS has that power.

EXECUTIVE ORDER 13295
REVISED LIST OF QUARANTINABLE
COMMUNICABLE DISEASES

By the authority vested in me as President by the Constitution and the laws of the United States of America, including section 361(b) of the Public Health Service Act (42 U.S.C. 264(b)), it is hereby ordered as follows:

Section 1. Based upon the recommendation of the Secretary of Health and Human Services (the 'Secretary'), in consultation with the Surgeon General, and for the purpose of specifying certain communicable diseases for regulations providing for the apprehension, detention, or conditional release of individuals to prevent the introduction, transmission, or spread of suspected communicable diseases, the following communicable diseases are hereby specified pursuant to section 361(b) of the Public Health Service Act:

(a) Cholera; Diphtheria; infectious Tuberculosis; Plague; Smallpox; Yellow Fever; and Viral Hemorrhagic Fevers (Lassa, Marburg, Ebola, Crimean-Congo, South American, and others not yet isolated or named).

(b) Severe Acute Respiratory Syndrome (SARS), which is a disease associated with fever and signs and symptoms of pneumonia or other respiratory illness, is transmitted from person to person predominantly by the aerosolized or droplet route, and, if spread in the population, would have severe public health consequences.

Section 2. The Secretary, in the Secretary's discretion, shall determine whether a particular condition constitutes a communicable disease of the type specified in section 1 of this order.

Section 3. The functions of the President under sections 362 and 364(a) of the Public Health Service Act (42 U.S.C. 265 and 267(a)) are assigned to the Secretary.

Section 4. This order is not intended to, and does not, create any right or benefit enforceable at law or equity by any party against the United States, its departments, agencies, entities, officers, employees or agents, or any other person. …

> George W. Bush
> The White House
> April 04, 2003

In 2005, President Bush amended this order by Executive Order 13375, which added the following to Section 1 of the 2003 Order:

(c) Influenza caused by novel or re-emergent influenza viruses that are causing, or have the potential to cause, a pandemic.

If the CDC learned that several individuals with severe infectious bronchitis were about to enter the United States, what could CDC officials do?

Regulations for Domestic Diseases

Recall that in Chapter 4 we learned that agencies often promulgate regulations to fill in the details that are not specified in statutes. Note that in several sections of the PHS Act above, Congress specifically called on DHHS to develop regulations. Do the following regulations help you identify where the line has been drawn between federal and state public health power?

■ ■ ■ ▬▬▬▬▬▬▬▬▬▬▬▬▬▬▬▬▬▬▬▬▬▬▬▬▬▬

As used in the federal regulations:

- *Communicable diseases* means illnesses due to infectious agents or their toxic products, which may be transmitted from a reservoir to a susceptible host either directly as from an infected person or animal or indirectly through the agency of an intermediate plant or animal host, vector, or the inanimate environment.
- *Communicable period* means the period or periods during which the etiologic agent may be transferred directly or indirectly from the body of the infected person or animal to the body of another.
- *Incubation period* means the period between the implanting of disease organisms in a susceptible person and the appearance of clinical manifestation of the disease.

▬▬▬▬▬▬▬▬▬▬▬▬▬▬▬▬▬▬▬▬▬▬▬▬▬ ■ ■ ■

Interstate Quarantine
Code of Federal Regulations, Title 42, Part 70

§ 70.2 Measures in the event of inadequate local control

Whenever the Director of the Centers for Disease Control and Prevention determines that the measures taken by health authorities of any State or possession (including political subdivisions thereof) are insufficient to prevent the spread of any of the communicable diseases from such State or possession to any other State or possession, he/she may take such measures to prevent such spread of the diseases as he/she deems reasonably necessary ...

§ 70.4 Report of disease

The master of any vessel or person in charge of any conveyance engaged in interstate traffic, on which a case or suspected case of a communicable disease develops shall, as soon as practicable, notify the local health authority at the next port of call, station, or stop, and shall take such measures to prevent the spread of the disease as the local health authority directs.

§ 70.5 Certain communicable diseases; special requirements

The following provisions are applicable with respect to any person who is in the communicable period of cholera, plague, smallpox, typhus or yellow fever, or who, having been exposed to any such disease, is in the incubation period thereof:

(a) Requirements relating to travelers.

(1) No such person shall travel from one State or possession to another, or on a conveyance engaged in interstate traffic, without a written permit of the Surgeon General or his/her authorized representative.

(2) Application for a permit may be made directly to the Surgeon General or to his/her representative authorized to issue permits. ...

§ 70.6 Apprehension and detention of persons with specific diseases

Regulations prescribed in this part authorize the detention, isolation, quarantine, or conditional release of individuals, for the purpose of preventing the introduction, transmission, and spread of the communicable diseases listed in [the applicable] Executive Order.

■ ■ Critical Thinking ■

Are there portions of the regulations that seem outdated? Which ones and why? The diseases for which travel permits are required have been largely eradicated in the United States. If one of those diseases were to reappear, what do you think the public reaction would be to a travel permit requirement?

The regulations provide no guidelines for determining whether state or local measures are "insufficient to prevent the spread of ... communicable diseases." How much discretion do you think the federal officials should have in making that decision? What would the practical restraints be on initiating a federal takeover?

The regulations authorize the "apprehension and detention" of persons with certain diseases; which ones? They do not, however, provide for any due process protections for persons who are detained. Imagine that a person has been placed in quarantine and seeks a court order to secure certain rights. How should a judge respond? Recall the *Greene* case in Chapter 2.

Regulations for International Travelers Arriving in the United States

The CDC has a separate set of regulations for persons entering any state from a foreign country (whether they are returning citizens or foreign nationals). The power that the CDC can exercise over international travelers stems from the following regulation:

Foreign Quarantine
Code of Federal Regulations, Title 42, Part 71

> § 71.32 (a) Whenever the Director [of the CDC] has reason to believe that any arriving person is infected with or has been exposed to any of the communicable diseases listed in the [current] Executive Order, he/she may isolate, quarantine or place the person under surveillance and may order disinfection or disinfestation, fumigation, as he/she considers necessary to prevent the introduction, transmission or spread of the listed communicable diseases. ...

As with the regulations for domestic interstate travelers, this regulation makes no explicit provision for procedural protections for a person who is detained.

Changes to the CDC's Quarantine Regulations

In the fall of 2005, the CDC published a notice of proposed rulemaking (see Chapter 4) in which significant changes were proposed to the above regulations. As this book goes to press in 2009, the agency has taken no action either to finalize or withdraw them. The most controversial aspects of the proposed regulations concern (1) the nature of the new due process protections that would be afforded to those who are isolated or quarantined and (2) the obligations placed on airlines and their passengers. We will examine each in turn.

■ ■ ■ ▬▬▬▬▬▬▬▬▬▬▬▬▬▬▬▬▬▬▬▬

Many people confuse two commonly used terms: isolation and quarantine.

- *Isolation* means the separation and restriction of movement of persons who are *known* to have a specific infectious illness, during the period when the disease is communicable.
- *Quarantine* means the separation and restriction of movement of persons who are not ill but who have been *exposed or are believed to have been exposed* to an infectious disease, during the period when it would be communicable.

▬▬▬▬▬▬▬▬▬▬▬▬▬▬▬▬▬▬▬▬ ■ ■ ■

Due Process Changes – for Better or Worse?

As is true of the current regulations, the proposed regulations would be triggered by a link to a risk of interstate transmission and the inclusion of the disease in question in the list in the current Executive Order. In an effort to modernize their procedures, the CDC also set forth a procedure for how the due process rights of detained individuals would be protected. Here is how the CDC describes its plan:

> The proposed regulation establishes administrative procedures that afford individuals with due process commensurate with the degree of deprivation and the circumstances of controlling the spread of communicable disease. CDC quarantine officers are typically the first line of defense in preventing the importation of communicable diseases into the United States. Quarantine officers routinely conduct rapid assessments of ill passengers at airports and other ports of entry to assess the presence of communicable disease. Such assessments generally occur on a voluntary basis with the consent of the ill passenger. Where the quarantine officer reasonably believes that an ill passenger has a quarantinable disease, and the passenger is otherwise non-compliant, the quarantine officer may order the provisional quarantine of the passenger by serving the passenger with a written order, verbally ordering that the passenger be provisionally quarantined, or by ordering that actual restrictions be placed

on a non-compliant passenger. The quarantine officer's reasonable belief would be informed by objective scientific evidence such as clinical criteria indicative of one of the specified quarantinable diseases, e.g., high fever, respiratory distress, and/or chills, accompanied by epidemiologic criteria such as travel to or from an affected area and/or contact with known cases.

Provisionally quarantined individuals are provided with a written order in support of the agency's determination at the time that provisional quarantine commences or as soon thereafter as the circumstances reasonably permit. The written provisional quarantine order provides the individual with notice regarding the legal and scientific basis for their provisional quarantine, the location of detention, and the suspected quarantinable disease. Under the proposed regulations, CDC may provisionally quarantine an individual for up to three business days unless the Director determines that the individual should be released or served with a quarantine order.

CDC does not intend to provide individuals with administrative hearings during this initial three-day period of provisional quarantine, but rather will afford an opportunity for a full administrative hearing in the event that the individual or group of individuals is served with a quarantine order, which potentially would involve a longer period of detention. ...

CDC believes that the provisional quarantine of individuals for up to three business days without an administrative hearing is reasonable because such a time frame is necessary to determine whether the individual has one of the specified quarantinable diseases. A provisional quarantine order is likely to be premised on the need to investigate based on reasonable suspicion of exposure or infection, whereas a quarantine order is more likely to be premised on a medical determination that the individual actually has one of the quarantinable diseases. Thus, during this initial three business day period, there may be very little for a hearing officer to review in terms of factual and scientific evidence of exposure or infection. Three business days may be necessary to collect medical samples, transport such samples to laboratories, and conduct diagnostic testing, all of which would help inform the Director's determination that the individual is infected with a quarantinable disease and that further quarantine is necessary.

In addition, because provisional quarantine may last no more than three business days, allowing for a full hearing, with witnesses, almost guarantees that no decision on the provisional quarantine will actually be reached until after the provisional period has ended, thus making such a hearing virtually meaningless in terms of granting release from the provisional quarantine.

In the event that further quarantine or isolation is necessary, the Director would issue an additional order based on scientific principles such as clinical manifestations, diagnostic or other medical tests, epidemiologic information, laboratory tests, physical examination, or other available evidence of exposure or infection. The length of quarantine or isolation would not exceed the period of incubation and communicability for the communicable disease as determined by the Director.

… [A]n opportunity for judicial review of the agency's decision exists via the filing of a petition for a writ of habeas corpus. This judicial review mechanism affords individuals under quarantine with the full panoply of due process rights typical of a court hearing. A petition for a writ of habeas corpus is the traditional mechanism by which individuals may contest their detention by the federal government.

In addition to this judicial review mechanism, as previously mentioned, the proposed regulations establish a procedure for individuals under quarantine to request an administrative hearing. The purpose of the administrative hearing is not to review any legal or constitutional issues that may exist, but rather only to review the factual and scientific evidence concerning the agency's decision, e.g., whether the individual has been exposed to or infected with a quarantinable disease. Such an administrative hearing would comport with the basic elements of due process. Under the proposed regulations, the Director would notice the hearing and designate a hearing officer to review the available evidence of exposure or infection and make findings as to whether the individual should be released or remain in quarantine.

Federal Register (2005)

Essentially the same set of procedures – providing for provisional quarantine as well as quarantine, with limited review rights – would apply to international as well as interstate travelers under the proposed regulations.

■ ■ Critical Thinking ■

Persons could be informed that they were being taken into provisional quarantine by a written order, but also by verbal notice or even simply by being told that they must step into the custody of federal public health officers. Why might this be problematic from a due process perspective? Why might the CDC believe that such methods were necessary? What is your view?

The CDC states that it is sufficient and "traditional" for the only method of challenging such detention to be for the individual to file a lawsuit seeking a writ of habeas corpus. (Recall what we learned about habeas corpus in Chapter 2.) Should other protections be in place as well? If so, what?

The Role of Airlines

Where once the federal quarantine authority applied primarily to shipping, today the most common situation in which questions about quarantine of international travelers are likely to arise would involve the arrival of an international flight. The quarantine regulations proposed by CDC in 2005 would establish new rules for airlines and passengers, including:

- Any airline operating an international flight bound for a U.S. airport must report to CDC before it landed whether any death or illness (as defined by CDC) had occurred on board.
- On each flight, the following information "shall be solicited" from each passenger and made available to the CDC upon request: full name, emergency contact, e-mail address, home address, passport number, name of traveling companions, a personal phone number (preferably cell or home number rather than work number), and ports of call visited.

In addition, the CDC could order medical examination and monitoring for arriving passengers. The new rules would require that persons who receive an examination order "shall provide the Director with such information as the Director may order, including, but not limited to, familial and social contacts, travel itinerary, medical history, place of work, and vaccination status." If a person refused to be examined, he or she would be subject to quarantine until the incubation period for the disease ended.

■ ■ Critical Thinking ■

From the perspective of the airline industry, do you think the proposed new rules are workable and fair? How would you argue for or against their adoption if you were an airline lobbyist

From the perspective of the individual traveler, do you have any objections to the proposed rules? What do you think public reaction would be if they were instituted? Are there alternative methods that you could suggest?

Important Terms

- Centers for Disease Control and Prevention
- Isolation
- Public health emergency
- Quarantinable communicable disease
- Quarantine
- Surgeon General of the United States

Review Questions

1. We began the chapter by posing the question of whether the divided nature of public health legal authorities might prove problematic in an emergency. What is your view as we finish the chapter?
2. Describe in your own words the historical evolution and growth of federal government power in this field. Consider the impact of other events at various points, such as wars, economic depressions, urbanization, and immigration.
3. To make sure that you have it clearly in mind, diagram the steps in imposing first provisional quarantine and then quarantine.
4. Imagine that you have just arrived at a large metropolitan airport. Friends and family are expecting you. Instead of disembarking in the normal way, however, you and the other passengers are taken to a special area marked "U.S. Government." You are told that officials have just learned

that someone on the flight has a highly contagious form of tuberculosis. As a result, everyone is being taken to a nearby military base where you will live in the barracks for at least the next 3 days. While there, you will be provided with food, toiletries and housed in a small private room with a TV set and telephone. How would you respond?

6

State Public Health Law

What You Will Learn

- The origins and development of state and local public health laws
- The history of public health abuses of the quarantine power
- How and why a new genre of public health law was created to provide even broader powers to cope with emergency situations

Introduction

Public health laws were among the earliest topics for legislation in the American colonies and the primacy of state authority in this area has continued into the present. One major change has been that, with the increasing attention to individual rights and liberties since the 1950s, public health law has been modernized to incorporate essential protections. This improvement was all the more necessary in light of a series of abuses of the quarantine power by public health officials, mostly in the late nineteenth and early twentieth centuries. In addition, the heightened focus on events like the 2001 anthrax attacks has led to a new genre of public health statute: emergency health powers acts.

History

Historian Elizabeth Tandy summarized the experiences of America's first European settlers in this way: "The colonization of America was a bitter fight with disease and death from the very moment the resolute emigrants set foot on the little vessels which were to carry them on their long voyage" (Tandy, 1923). Although we may tend to think of violence and the risk of starvation as being the most daunting obstacles for John Winthrop, William Penn, and others, infectious diseases were an equally fearsome and constant threat. Winthrop, writing to his wife in 1630, described the high death toll during the first winter in the Plymouth settlement from a disease that "grew out of an ill diet at sea and proved infectious" (Tandy, 1923).

■ ■ ■ ▬▬▬▬▬▬▬▬▬▬▬▬▬▬▬▬▬▬▬▬▬▬▬▬▬

Where does the word "quarantine" come from and what does it mean?

The practice of quarantine began in 1374 in Venice as a way to protect its residents from the plague that was brought to the city by persons and goods disembarking from commercial ships. Ships arriving at the port from locations known to have suffered outbreaks of the plague were required to sit at anchor for 40 days before landing. The word "quarantine" comes from the Italian phrase "quaranta gironi," which means 40 days.

▬▬▬▬▬▬▬▬▬▬▬▬▬▬▬▬▬▬▬▬▬▬▬▬▬ ■ ■ ■

As waves of smallpox and yellow fever swept through the settlements, many of the earliest laws enacted by American colonists concerned public health and protection from disease. Boston enacted a municipal ordinance providing legal authority for disease control in 1647; New York City followed suit in 1663 (Gostin, 2008). Citizens frequently acted after experiencing a disease outbreak: Philadelphia created the first municipal board of health in the new world after a yellow fever epidemic devastated the city in 1793, killing or causing the dispersal of almost 40 percent of the city's population (Novak, 1996). This historical background helps to explain the primacy of state and local authority in the field of public health (see Chapter 5) and provides the context for the Supreme Court's reasoning in *Jacobson v. Massachusetts* in Chapter 1.

Jacobson Revisited

Return to Chapter 1 and read the *Jacobson* decision again. In Chapter 1, we analyzed *Jacobson* for how it illustrated federalism – the dynamic between state and federal authority in American government. We also noted that the Court both upheld governmental authority over public health policy and outlined situations in which such authority would be too arbitrary to be upheld – for example, when there was proof that an individual would be medically harmed by a particular vaccination.

In rereading the opinion, note how the concept of "police power" is interwoven with the theme of localization. The Court ruled that the inherent police power of state governments – a power that the states "did not surrender when becoming [members] of the union" – provided authority for the commonwealth of Massachusetts and the Cambridge Board of Health to require smallpox vaccinations. At least in part, that conceptualization of a state-based plenary [or absolute] power to define the government actions necessary to achieve the common good was founded on the premise that public health was an example of "matters completely within [a state's] territory and which do not by their necessary operation affect the people of other states." Today, that degree of localization seems archaic. We discussed in Chapter 5 some of the costs of vesting state and local governments with primary responsibility for public health. Yet we will see from the historical evolution of public health authority in the colonies how the localized focus originated.

■ ■ ■ ▬▬▬▬▬▬▬▬▬▬▬▬▬▬▬▬▬▬▬▬▬▬▬

Case Study – Philadelphia's Lazaretto Quarantine Station

In 1793, the nation's capital was still located in Philadelphia. As a result, when a yellow fever epidemic virtually closed the city down that year, killing 10 percent of the city's population and sickening thousands more, it was a major threat to the young nation and its leaders, as well as a local public health crisis. Six years later, the city's new board of health had a facility built outside the city, which they named the Lazaretto Quarantine Station. The origin of the word "lazaretto," like that of "quarantine," lay in fourteenth-century Italy. "Lazaretto" derives from the story of Lazarus, a leper; the word means pest house, or house of quarantine. The function of this lazaretto was the same as those established three centuries earlier: to examine all arriving ships, passengers, and cargo and to house the ill and those exposed to illness who were on board, as well as to disinfect the ship and its cargo.

The Lazaretto was positioned downstream of Philadelphia on the Delaware River. From there, a lookout was on watch to spot incoming vessels, which were stopped and inspected by Lazaretto staff, who included a quarantine master and a resident physician. They boarded each ship and conducted an inspection. If there were no signs of infection, the required certifications were completed and the ship could proceed to Philadelphia the next day.

If any crew or passengers showed signs of illness, however, a much longer process ensued. All those aboard were housed in the Lazaretto hospital until those who had become sick during the voyage either recovered or died. The ship itself was fumigated, scoured, and whitewashed. It took from a week to a month before the ship and its crew and passengers were released to continue their voyage to Philadelphia.

In the latter half of the nineteenth century, the nature of the work at the Lazaretto changed in several ways, which were typical of the changes occurring at all American port cities. Steamboats had replaced sailing vessels as transatlantic transportation, and the faster times of ocean crossings meant that there was often less risk of disease occurring at sea. Steamships also brought much higher levels of passenger traffic and a major surge in immigration to the United States. The number of passengers going through the Lazaretto inspection process jumped from 500 to 4,000 in the year after steamship service began in Philadelphia. By 1879, nearly 30,000 people a year were emigrating to Philadelphia.

The swelling number of immigrants vastly increased the burden and cost of operating the Lazaretto, and the following year – 1880 – the state of Pennsylvania turned the Lazaretto over to federal authorities. (As we saw in the last chapter, the same set of issues contributed to demands in New York City to relinquish local operation of quarantine facilities.) The Lazaretto closed in 1895, replaced with a new quarantine facility located farther from Philadelphia, which operated until 1919. Ironically, after federal officials closed the Lazaretto, private investors drawn by its waterfront location transformed the Lazaretto into a resort known as the Orchard Club.

Source: www.ushistory.org/laz/history

The history of public health law in the states is far from entirely laudable, however. Local citizens were often unnerved by the proximity of quarantine facilities like the Lazaretto (see box) or terrified that they were at risk of contracting a dread disease that officials could not prevent or effectively control – especially before the advent of antibiotics. In reaction, the public sometimes lashed out.

In 1858, the residents of Staten Island, New York (one of the five boroughs of New York City), destroyed a local quarantine facility. The magazine *Harper's Weekly* reported that the presence of the hospital had been a growing source of anger to residents who thought that the hospital was "breeding pestilence ... and occasioning every year yellow fever panics." When a state commission failed to order its closure, "the Staten Islanders took matters into their own hands. On Sept 1 ... a large party, 'disguised and armed,' attacked the hospital from two sides, removed the patients, and set the buildings on fire."

Even uglier were the condemnations of groups of people believed to be of particular danger, but whose only real fault lay in being outsiders in a time of panic, and thus perfect scapegoats. Racist and anti-immigrant attitudes combined with the enormous discretionary power accorded to public health officials and produced a series of shameful results. And unlike the outburst by the Staten Island mob, these actions were formal and considered, taken by government officials who utilized the power and legitimacy of the state.

In 1892, four cases of typhoid fever were discovered in a tenement house in New York City among passengers who had recently arrived on the ship Massila, which carried a large number of eastern European immigrants. In response, city health officials ordered the quarantine of "every single Russian Jewish passenger" who had been on the ship, as well as the smaller number of Italian immigrants that the ship had carried. In addition, the persons who had been exposed to the Massila passengers after they arrived, mostly their neighbors in crowded ethnic ghettos, were also put under quarantine. They were taken to North Brother Island, in the East River, and kept in the cottages used there for others who were quarantined during this period, including Mary Mallon, known in the press as "Typhoid Mary." Of the approximately 1,200 persons who were detained, approximately 1,100 were healthy, newcomers to New York who happened to live close to the former Massila passengers who had become ill (Markel, 1999).

As legal historian Felice Batlan described the effects of the Massila quarantine:

> These men, women, and children were detained for twenty-one days after the last case of typhus developed among any of those quarantined. As thousands of immigrants and city residents were detained in quarantine, the death rate among residents began to rise dramatically. Although the Health Department found it perplexing that the death rate from typhus was small for passengers and high among residents, the conditions of quarantine itself may have produced these deaths. The quarantine represented a tremendous mobilization of essentially unchecked municipal power with serious life and death consequences.
>
> Batlan (2007)

A few years later, on the west coast, a similar event occurred when cases of bubonic plague appeared in San Francisco among Chinese immigrants. The official reaction was aimed more at the vulnerable

Chinese community than at the disease itself. The result was the filing of two lawsuits that established key principles to help curb similar abuses in later public health reactions.

In their first response to the disease, federal and local public health authorities collaborated to use an experimental vaccine for the required inoculation of all Chinese residents in San Francisco. In addition, the Chinese – and no one else – were prohibited from leaving the city without showing proof that they had been vaccinated. Law enforcement officers were stationed at major transportation points to enforce the order, and railroads were forbidden from selling tickets to "Asiatics or other races particularly liable" to bubonic plague unless they had a vaccination certificate (Batlan, 2007).

The Chinese Consolidated Benevolent Association filed suit and won a decision in federal court invalidating the orders. The court found that there was no rational basis for requiring only Chinese residents to be inoculated before leaving the city and that the health officials had violated the Equal Protection Clause because the plaintiffs were singled out on account of their race (*Wong Wai v. Williamson,* 1900). However, the panic continued and local officials again acted in an irrational manner.

Faced with a court order prohibiting their first effort, the Board of Health recommended and the Board of Supervisors enacted a quarantine, which the police department enforced, that applied solely to Chinese residents. The city directed that no one could enter or leave Chinatown and specified the geographic boundary lines of the neighborhood. Only Chinese residents, and no white residents, were affected. Cordoned off with barbed wire as food shortages mounted, residents again brought suit to challenge the city's policy.

The result was the *Jew Ho v. Williamson* decision in Chapter 2. Reread that opinion now. Again the court found that the public health officials had enforced a policy that was both discriminatory and irrational. In fact, the court noted the quarantine of an entire community was likely to *increase* transmission of the disease, because healthy Chinatown residents now lacked a way to distance themselves from neighbors who were ill, since they were all trapped together in one small geographic area.

The New York and San Francisco quarantines directed against immigrants were perhaps the most famous examples of disease control efforts that public health officials later came to regret. In part because of this history, in part simply because of the enormous discretionary power that public health agencies have traditionally wielded, today's health departments have become much more sensitive to the rights of the individuals whose liberty interests are at stake when public panic threatens to subvert policies based on scientific knowledge. Yet abuses are still possible. In 1998 in Fresno County, California, an elderly non-English-speaking woman with tuberculosis, who apparently did not understand the medical directions she was given, was jailed for 10 months when local officials ignored a law requiring that persons detained for treatment of tuberculosis must be housed in a medical facility rather than in a prison (*Souvannarath v. Hadden*, 2002).

Emergency Health Powers Laws

As is evident from this history, state and local health departments have long had the legal authority to declare quarantines or to take other measures, such as requiring vaccination, to respond to outbreaks of disease. But in the wake of the 2001 anthrax attack and the generally heightened fear of terrorist activity after September 11, the U.S. Centers for Disease Control and Prevention (CDC) asked the Center for Law and the Public's Health based at Georgetown and Johns Hopkins universities to develop a new legal framework to address such situations. The Center developed a Model State Emergency Health Powers Act (MSEHPA) that has been adopted in whole or in part by more than 30 states.

The philosophy behind the MSEHPA is that existing public health laws would be inadequate if there were a widespread emergency today. According to one of the authors of MSEHPA, the massive efforts needed to respond to a public health emergency "are possible only through enhanced, expedited powers and access to vast resources. Emergency statutes and regulations are designed to provide such power and resources" (Hodge and Anderson, 2008). Because state and local agencies have long had the primary responsibility for public health policy, the model law was intentionally designed as one for state legislatures, rather than Congress, to adopt.

The MSEHPA contains some of the same structural components as the National Emergencies Act that we analyzed in Chapter 3 (and the Stafford Act that we will address in Chapter 9). It establishes the criteria for a formal declaration of emergency, which then triggers an authorization for greater powers in the chief executive (here, the governor) than she or he otherwise has. It spells out what those powers are. And it provides a process for termination or continuation of the state of emergency.

The goal behind MSEHPA is to increase flexibility and adaptability so that health officials can respond to unexpected crises without unnecessary delay. According to Professor James Hodge –

> [E]mergency managers, public health practitioners, health-care workers, volunteers, and others may not be able to fully determine the legality of their actions during emergencies. Some responders may act without significant regard for any legal ramifications; others may choose not to act at all because of this legal uncertainty. Neither of these consequences is acceptable because each has the potential to stymie important public health interventions.
>
> Hodge and Anderson (2008)

An obvious concern when the government is given greater power is whether there are adequate checks and balances placed on that authority. Another of the MSEHPA's authors has identified four principles for limiting the powers of the state even in an emergency:

> Agency actions should be (1) necessary to avert a significant risk, in the first instance in the judgment of health officials and ultimately, with reasonable deference [to the decisions of the health agency], to the satisfaction of a judge [who would review the agency's decisions]; (2) reasonably well-tailored to address the risk, in the sense [that] officials do not over-reach or go beyond a necessary and appropriate response; (3) authorized in a manner allowing public scrutiny and oversight; and (4) correctable in the event of an unreasonable mistake.
>
> Gostin et al. (2002)

Keep those four principles in mind and ask yourself whether you think they have been adequately addressed as you read the following portions of the New Jersey statute based on MSEHPA.

■ ■ Critical Thinking ■

What kinds of specific legal mechanisms might be used to implement Gostin's four principles? Are those mechanisms present in the New Jersey statute (see page 137)?

Puppy Love: Bioterrorism, Civil Rights and Public Health
George J. Annas, 2003

... [T]he first false premise underlying emergency public health legislation is that the facts warrant categorizing bioterrorism as ... more risky than nuclear or conventional bombs ... Exaggerated risks, of course, produce extreme responses. Public health planning should be based on science, especially the science of epidemiology, and accurate risk assessment and facts, not the free-floating anxiety and fear that the government uses to justify more control over individual citizens.

[The] second false premise is that health and human rights cease to complement each other in emergencies, so that the most effective way to respond to a bioterrorist attack, should one occur, is to immediately trade off human rights for public health and safety. [I do not] think that the government can never interfere with the civil rights of an individual. But, ... I [do] believe such situations will be extremely rare (e.g., a person with active, contagious tuberculosis who refuses to take medication while insisting on congregating with others), and ... I believe bioterrorist attacks do not justify arbitrary governmental action ..., at least if there are (and there almost always will be) other less restrictive alternatives.

... I believe that a government response that is seen by its citizens as arbitrary and compulsory will backfire, and actually be counterproductive ... Infected individuals, for example, will avoid hospitals and public health officials, rather than voluntarily seek out care, as thousands did during the anthrax attacks. They will thus be much more likely to spread the disease when they flee ... Some may actually take up arms and actively resist the government should it try to impose martial law. ...

... As Senator Sam Nunn, who played the part of the president in the tabletop exercise Dark Winter [which simulated a smallpox attack], concluded after it ended: "There is no force on earth strong enough to get 250 million Americans to do something that they do not believe is in their own best interests or that of their families."...

... Abuse of power will predictably instill panic in the public, as it did in China and Taiwan during the SARS epidemic. Even totalitarian dictatorships cannot control their populations by fear alone in the twenty-first century. ... Justice Brandeis was right when he wrote:

Experience will teach us to be most on our guard to protect liberty when the Government's purposes are beneficent. Men born to freedom are naturally alert to repel invasion of their liberty by evil-minded rulers. The greatest dangers to liberty lurk in insidious encroachment by men of zeal, well-meaning but without understanding.

... In the current environment of instant communication ..., it is much more important for public health officials to manage information than it is to manage people. The only effective way to govern Americans is to provide them with complete and factual information about what is and is not known about an attack or epidemic, and what steps they can take to protect themselves and their families from harm. ...

Declaring a Public Health Emergency

The threshold and trigger for everything that follows in MSEHPA is the governor's decision to declare a public health emergency. For that reason, the grounds and process by which the declaration occurs are critically important to the legitimacy and perceived legitimacy of later actions.

As an initial matter, one needs to ask, what *is* a public health emergency such that the state should have additional powers beyond those in the regular public health laws. And when and how should a state of emergency be terminated?

For the sake of convenience, we are going to examine one state's public health emergency law in some detail, because no two states have exactly the same laws. New Jersey adopted an Emergency Health Powers Act (EHPA) in 2005 that is based largely on the MSEHPA. Thus, we are going to focus on New Jersey statutory law.

The New Jersey EHPA defines "public health emergency" as follows:

[A]n occurrence or imminent threat of an occurrence that:

a. is caused or is reasonably believed to be caused by any of the following:

(1) bioterrorism or an accidental release of one or more biological agents;

(2) the appearance of a novel or previously controlled or eradicated biological agent;

(3) a natural disaster;

(4) a chemical attack or accidental release of toxic chemicals; or

(5) a nuclear attack or nuclear accident; and

b. poses a high probability of any of the following harms:

(1) a large number of deaths, illness or injury in the affected population;

(2) a large number of serious or long-term impairments in the affected population; or

(3) exposure to a biological agent or chemical that poses a significant risk of substantial future harm to a large number of people in the affected population.

N.J. Stat. 26:13-2

Pause and consider: does this definition sweep too broadly? Would AIDS, for example, be included? Compare these criteria to the federal government's list of quarantinable communicable diseases in Chapter 5. Do both provisions cover the same diseases? Does it matter if there are differences?

The New Jersey statute says this about the initiation and termination of a declared public health emergency:

a. The Governor, in consultation with the commissioner and the Director of the State Office of Emergency Management, may declare a public health emergency. In declaring a public health emergency, the Governor shall issue an order that specifies:

(1) the nature of the public health emergency;

(2) the geographic area subject to the declaration;

(3) the conditions that have brought about the public health emergency to the extent known; and

(4) the expected duration of the state of public health emergency, if less than 30 days. Such order may also prescribe necessary actions or countermeasures to protect the public's health.

b. Any public health emergency declared pursuant to this act shall be terminated automatically after 30 days unless renewed by the Governor under the same standards and procedures set forth [above].

N.J. Stat. 26:13-3

■ ■ Critical Thinking ■

Which branches of government appear to play no role in the declaration or termination of a public health emergency? What are the arguments for and against a specified role for them? Are there checks and balances against a governor's abuse of power to declare public health emergencies? Can you envision how such a declaration could be challenged?

The Powers of Government during an Emergency

The New Jersey law, like the MSEHPA, outlines a number of additional powers that the state government will have during an emergency in a wide variety of areas: mandatory testing and treatment, confidentiality of medical information, the disposal of human remains, seizure of property, and the rationing of medications or vaccines. Some of those topics will come up in later chapters, but for now we are going to concentrate on isolation and quarantine – the two actions that illustrate the most extreme of government's powers: the power to deprive the individual of liberty.

Following are the sections of the New Jersey EHPA that set forth the procedures for isolation and quarantine:

The following isolation and quarantine procedures shall be in effect during a state of public health emergency:

a. The commissioner may exercise, for such period as the state of public health emergency exists, the following emergency powers over persons:

(1) to designate, including an individual's home when appropriate, and establish and maintain suitable places of isolation and quarantine;

(2) to issue and enforce orders for the isolation or quarantine of individuals subject to the procedures specified in this section; and

(3) to require isolation or quarantine of any person by the least restrictive means necessary to protect the public health, subject to the other provisions of this section. All reasonable means shall be taken to prevent the transmission of infection among the isolated or quarantined individuals, as well as among the personnel maintaining and caring for individuals in isolation or quarantine.

b. The following standards shall apply for quarantine or isolation.

(1) Persons shall be isolated or quarantined if it is determined by a preponderance of the evidence that the person to be isolated or quarantined poses a risk of transmitting an infectious disease to others. A person's refusal to accept medical examination, vaccination, or treatment … shall constitute prima facie evidence that the person should be quarantined or isolated.

(2) Isolation or quarantine of any person shall be terminated by the commissioner when the person no longer poses a risk of transmitting an infectious disease to others.

c. (1) To the extent possible, the premises in which persons are isolated or quarantined shall be maintained in a safe and hygienic manner, designed to minimize the likelihood of further transmission of infection or other harm to persons subject to isolation or quarantine. Adequate food, clothing, medication, means of communication, other necessities and competent medical care shall be provided.

(2) An isolated person shall be confined separately from a quarantined person, unless otherwise determined by the commissioner.

■ ■ ■

Remember: what is the difference between isolation and quarantine?

(3) The health status of isolated and quarantined persons shall be monitored regularly to determine if their status should change. If a quarantined person subsequently becomes infected or is reasonably believed to have become infected with a contagious or possibly contagious disease, the person shall promptly be moved to isolation.

d. (1) A person subject to isolation or quarantine shall obey the commissioner's orders, shall not go beyond the isolation or quarantine premises, and shall not put himself in contact with any person not subject to isolation or quarantine other than a physician or other health care provider, or person authorized to enter the isolation or quarantine premises by the commissioner.

(2) No person, other than a person authorized by the commissioner, may enter the isolation or quarantine premises. Any person entering an isolation or quarantine premises may be isolated or quarantined.

e. (1) Except as provided in paragraph (4) of this subsection, the commissioner shall petition the Superior Court for an order authorizing the isolation or quarantine of a person or groups of persons.

(2) A petition pursuant to paragraph (1) of this subsection shall specify the following:

(a) the identity of the person or group of persons, by name or shared characteristics, subject to isolation or quarantine;

(b) the premises designated for isolation or quarantine;

(c) the date and time at which the commissioner requests isolation or quarantine to commence;

(d) the suspected contagious disease, if known;

(e) a statement of the terms and conditions of isolation and quarantine;

(f) a statement of the basis upon which isolation or quarantine is justified; and

(g) a statement of what effort, if any, has been made to give notice of the hearing to the person or group of persons to be isolated or quarantined, or the reason supporting the claim that notice should not be required.

(3) Except as provided in paragraph (4) of this subsection, before isolating or quarantining a person, the commissioner shall obtain a written order, which may be an ex parte order [an order issued without the other party being present], from the Superior Court authorizing such action. The order shall be requested as part of a petition filed in compliance with paragraphs (1) and (2) of this subsection. The court shall grant an order upon finding by a preponderance of the evidence that isolation or quarantine is warranted pursuant to the provisions of this section. A copy of the authorizing order shall be provided to the person ordered to be isolated or quarantined, along with notification that the person has a right to a hearing pursuant to paragraph (5) of this subsection.

■ ■ ■ ━━━━━━━━━━━━━━━━━━━━━━━━━━━━

Are the procedures set forth in the following section an adequate substitute for the requirement of a court order?

━━━━━━━━━━━━━━━━━━━━━━━━━━━━ ■ ■ ■

(4) Notwithstanding the provisions of paragraphs (1) through (3) of this subsection to the contrary, the commissioner may issue a verbal order, to be followed by a written order requiring the immediate, temporary isolation or quarantine of a person or group of persons, including those persons who have entered an isolation or quarantine premises, without first obtaining an order from the court if the commissioner determines that any delay in the isolation or quarantine of the person would significantly jeopardize the ability to prevent or limit the transmission of infectious or possibly infectious disease to others. The commissioner's written order shall specify:

(a) the identity of the person or group of persons, by name or shared characteristics, subject to isolation or quarantine;

(b) the premises designated for isolation or quarantine;

(c) the date and time at which the isolation or quarantine commences;

(d) the suspected contagious disease, if known;

(e) a statement of the terms and conditions of isolation and quarantine;

(f) a statement of the basis upon which isolation or quarantine is justified; and

(g) the availability of a hearing to contest the order.

The commissioner shall provide notice of the order for isolation or quarantine upon the person or group of persons specified in the order. If the commissioner determines that service of the notice required is impractical because of the number of persons or geographical areas affected, or other good cause, the commissioner shall ensure that the affected persons are fully informed of the order using the best possible means available. A copy of the order shall also be posted in a conspicuous place in the isolation or quarantine premises.

Following the issuance of the commissioner's order directing isolation or quarantine, the commissioner shall file a petition pursuant to paragraphs (1) through (3) of this subsection as soon as possible, but not later than 72 hours thereafter.

(5) The court shall grant a hearing within 72 hours of the filing of a petition when a person has been isolated or quarantined pursuant to paragraph (3) or (4) of this subsection. In any proceedings brought for relief under this subsection, the court may extend the time for a hearing upon a showing by the commissioner that extraordinary circumstances exist that justify the extension. ...

■ ■ ■ ━━━━━━━━━━━━━━━━━━━━━━━━━━━━━━━

The following section concerns contesting the *continuance* of isolation or quarantine.

━━━━━━━━━━━━━━━━━━━━━━━━━━━━━━━ ■ ■ ■

f. (1) Following a hearing as provided for in paragraph (5) of subsection e of this section, on or after a period of time of no less than 10 days but not more than 21 days, as determined by the commissioner based on the generally recognized incubation period of the infectious disease warranting the isolation or quarantine, a person isolated or quarantined pursuant to the provisions of this section may request a court hearing to contest his continued isolation or quarantine. The court may proceed in a summary manner.

The hearing shall be held within 72 hours of receipt of the request, excluding Saturdays, Sundays and legal holidays. A request for a hearing shall not act to stay the order of isolation or quarantine. At the hearing, the commissioner must show by a preponderance of the evidence that continuation of the isolation or quarantine is warranted because the person poses a significant risk of transmitting a disease to others with serious consequences.

■ ■ ■ ━━━━━━━━━━━━━━━━━━━━━━━━━━━

The following section concerns contesting the *conditions* under which one is held in isolation or quarantine.

━━━━━━━━━━━━━━━━━━━━━━━━━━━ ■ ■ ■

(2) A person isolated or quarantined pursuant to the provisions of this section may request at any time a hearing in the Superior Court for injunctive relief regarding his treatment and the terms and conditions of the quarantine or isolation. Upon receiving a request for either type of hearing described in this paragraph, the court shall fix a date for a hearing. The court may proceed in a summary manner. The hearing shall be held no later than 10 days after the receipt of the request by the court. A request for a hearing shall not act to stay the order of isolation or quarantine.

(3) If, upon a hearing, the court finds that the isolation or quarantine of the individual is not warranted under the provisions of this section, then the person shall be immediately released from isolation or quarantine. If the court finds that the isolation or quarantine of the person is not in compliance

with the provisions of subsection c. of this section, the court may fashion remedies appropriate to the circumstances of the state of public health emergency and in keeping with the provisions of this section.

g. ... The petitioner shall have the right to be represented by counsel.

N.J. Stat. 26:13-15

■ ■ Critical Thinking ■

What are the checks and balances in this section of the statute that will protect individual liberties? How do the types of court hearings authorized in the New Jersey law differ from each other? How long could a person be held with no hearing?

As an exercise, diagram the procedures that the Commissioner must follow.

Important Terms

- Checks and balances
- Emergency Health Powers Act
- Least restrictive means necessary
- Police powers

Review Questions

1. What are the conceptual links between anti-immigrant prejudice and fear of communicable diseases?
2. What pragmatic reasons might a public health official have for wanting to build protections of individual liberty into the law?
3. Given that "regular" public health powers include isolation and quarantine, do you think that a formal emergency powers law is necessary? Why or why not? Whom do you think benefits most from the presence of such a law – public health and other state officials or the public at large?
4. The New Jersey statute provides that if a court finds that a quarantine or isolation order was improper, it can grant "appropriate" remedies. What kinds of remedies do you think would be appropriate?

7

Contemporary Issues in Public Health Emergency Law

What You Will Learn

- Today's most urgent public health issues
- How health agencies define bioterrorism and "new" diseases, and what forms they are likely to take
- How health agencies responded to the anthrax attack and SARS
- The legal and ethical questions that will shape the response to future emergencies

Introduction

In this chapter, we explore the two threats that dominate contemporary discussion in public health emergency law: bioterrorism and the emergence of new infectious diseases for which there may be no effective treatment. We will examine them through the lens of the legal issues they raise. In particular, we focus on three topics: the legal and ethical principles for approaching the problem of how to ration and distribute medications when there is not enough to treat everyone in the population; how a mass quarantine in today's society could be effective and what its cost would be; and the questions raised by the possibility of imposing domestic and international travel restrictions. We will begin by describing the most important underlying facts related to bioterrorism and emerging infectious diseases.

Definitions of Bioterrorism

There are multiple definitions of bioterrorism, whether generated by government agencies such as the CDC or found in federal and state law. They generally include some or all the following factors:

- The intentional use or threat of use of any biological agent to cause harm in a human, animal, plant, or other living organism

- The same use or threat of use to degrade the quality of food, air, or the water supply
- With the goal of influencing government conduct or policy
- With the goal of intimidating or coercing a civilian population

■ ▨ ■ ▬▬▬▬▬▬▬▬▬▬▬▬▬▬▬▬▬▬▬▬▬▬

The Most Feared Pathogens

The CDC has identified the six most dangerous pathogens that could be used in a bioterrorist attack (see Table 7.1).

Table 7.1   The Six Most Dangerous Pathogens

Name	Description	Symptoms	Treatment
Anthrax (excluding cutaneous)	Transmission by inhaling; kills 85% of those infected often within 1 to 3 days	Fever and fatigue; Progresses to chest pain, cough, rapid decline	Antibiotics (cipro) before symptoms appear; vaccine not widely available
Smallpox	Physical contact with infected fluids or objects or inhalation of droplets; fatal in 30% of unvaccinated patients	Fever, aches, vomiting; Rash develops into pustules	No treatment, but vaccine within 4 days after exposure may mitigate
Pneumonic plague	Airborne; almost 100% fatality rate if untreated	Fever, headache, bloody cough; Progresses to respiratory failure and death	Antibiotics within 48 hours of exposure
Viral hemor-rhagic fevers	Viruses spread by mosquitoes, rodents and ticks; Ebola death rate up to 90%, Dengue rate 1%	Some variance; include fever, aches, exhaustion, internal bleeding	Antiviral treatments vary for the specific form
Botulism	Transmission by inhaling, could be aerosolized; too few cases to know fatality rate	Toxin blocks nerve signals and muscle movement; paralysis; inability to swallow	Ventilator; antitoxin given quickly may stop progression
Tularemia	Inhaling or contact with contaminated substances; could be aerosolized; overall mortality low but untreated severe cases from 30 to 60% fatalities	Fever, headaches, chills, infection of eyes, skin, mucosal tissue	Antibiotics usually successful in naturally occurring cases

Source: CDC, Gostin 2003.

Table 7.2 lists events throughout history that involved biological weaponry and bioterrorism.

Table 7.2   Select Historical Events Involving Biological Weapons and Bioterrorism

<1000 B.C.E	Scythian archers tipped arrows with blood, manure, and tissue from dead bodies.
Fifth century	Assyrians poisoned enemy wells with rye ergot (*Claviceps purpurea*), a fungus containing mycotoxins.
590 B.C.E	Athenians poisoned enemy water supplies with helebore, an herb purgative, during the Siege of Krissa.
Third century B.C.E	Persian, Greek, and Roman Literature describe the use of dead animals being used to contaminate enemy water supplies.
184 B.C.E	Carthaginian General Hannibal ordered his sailors to hurl clay pots filled with poisonous snakes onto the decks of enemy ships during a naval battle. Hannibal won the battle.
1155	Holy Roman Emperor Barbarossa poisons wells with decomposing human bodies.
1346	Tartur army catapulted deceased bodies of plague victims over city walls during the siege of Caffa.
1495	Spanish sell wine mixed with the blood of lepers to their enemies.
1763	British distribute variola virus contaminated blankets to Native Americans resulting in a smallpox outbreak.
1797	Napoleon floods fields around Mantua to promote malaria.
1915 to 1918	Germans attempt to infect Allied horses with anthrax and glanders.
1932 to 1945	Japanese operate Unit 731 in Manchuria conducting experiments that included infecting prisoners with a variety of lethal pathogens.
1942	British test anthrax bombs on Gruinard Island off the coast of Scotland.
1950 to 1969	U.S. and U.S.S.R. grow offensive biological weapons programs.
1969	U.S. President Nixon ends the U.S. offensive biological weapons program.
1972	U.S. and U.S.S.R. sign the Biological Weapons Convention agreeing an end to offensive programs.
1978	Assassination of Bulgarian exile Georgi Markov in London with an injected ricin pellet.
1979	Accidental anthrax release from a secret Soviet facility in Sverdlovsk kills 66.
1984	In Dalles, Oregon, the Rajneeshee cult contaminated local salad bars with salmonella sickening more than 750 people.

(Continued)

Table 7.2 Select Historical Events Involving Biological Weapons and Bioterrorism (*Continued*)

1990	Japanese Aum Shinrikyo cult unsuccessfully attempts botulinum toxin releases in Tokyo.
1991	U.S. troops receive anthrax vaccinations.
1991	After the first Gulf War, U.N. inspectors begin inspections of biological weapons capability in Iraq. Iraqi government officials confirm that they had researched the use of anthrax and botulism.
1993	Aum Shinrikyo cult unsuccessfully attempts a second botulinum toxin attack on the wedding of the Crown Prince. Later the same month, they unsuccessfully attempted to release anthrax from a Tokyo high rise.
2001	Anthrax contaminated letters mailed to U.S. Senate offices and media outlets, sickening 22 and killing five.
2004	Ricin sent to U.S. Senate Majority Leader Bill Frist's office.

■ ■ ■

The Anthrax Attacks of 2001

... [O]n 4 October 2001, health officials in Florida announced that Robert Stevens, a tabloid photo editor at American Media, Inc (AMI), had been diagnosed with pulmonary anthrax – the first such case in the United States in almost 25 years. Initially, the patient's condition was attributed to a natural source. However, after two of the victim's co-workers fell ill and anthrax spores were discovered throughout the building in which they worked, these initial assessments soon gave way to apprehension. Other cases began to appear at media outlets in New York City. These new cases revealed the possible source of the exposure: almost all of those infected in New York had come into direct contact with letters containing a mysterious powder.

In mid-October, the crisis reached Washington, D.C., when an anthrax-laden letter was opened in the office of Senator Tom Daschle. Several workers at the postal facility that processed the letter fell ill with pulmonary anthrax. Congressional office buildings were evacuated and virtually all federal government mail delivery in the nation's capital was halted as a result. An additional letter, addressed to Senator Patrick Leahy, was found during a search of quarantined mail, bringing the total number of anthrax-laden letters sent to at least four. With the realization that these infections stemmed from a deliberate act, what originally started out as public health response increasingly became a law enforcement investigation.

By the end of November 2001, ... the outbreak had run its course, and no additional letters were discovered. The results were sobering: a total of 22 people had been infected with either cutaneous or pulmonary anthrax, and five of those infected with the pulmonary form died. ...

The first bioterrorist attack on the United States in the 21st century is revealing in many respects. The government's response to the attacks proved to a difficult undertaking characterized by a significant amount of on-the-job learning ... From the unconventional delivery mode and conflicting estimates of exposure to questions over the appropriate timing and nature of treatment, government agencies frequently provided substantially different, sometimes contradictory, information and advice to those potentially exposed, to the media, and to the public as a whole. ...

[T]here were only 18 reported cases [of pulmonary anthrax] in the United States between 1900 and 1978, and none through the turn of the century. As a result, very few physicians had any direct experience with anthrax, its identification, and its symptomology. ... [T]he initial cases in Florida were initially diagnosed with pneumonia. ...

[A] large number of hoaxes and false alarms ... followed the actual attacks. Laboratories across the continent were deluged with requests to conduct tests on everything from suspicious-looking white powder to plant seeds to stuffed animals. According to statistics from the CDC, its laboratories and other [labs] tested over 125,000 samples during the period following the first reports of the outbreak. In several cases, some state and local laboratories were so overloaded with testing requests that they contemplated setting up triage procedures to prioritize tests. ...

A key feature of the public health response to the anthrax letters was the widespread use of antibiotic prophylaxis. Shortly after the contamination at AMI was confirmed, the CDC airlifted enough antibiotics for 1,000 people to Florida ... With Congress, major television networks and newspapers targets of the attacks, this aspect of the response received considerable attention. The brand name "Cipro" became a household word almost overnight ... In prescribing antibiotics, the CDC identified approximately 10,000 people ... as at risk due to potential exposure. However, the number of people on antibiotics extended far beyond the population immediately at risk. At the peak of the outbreak, more than 30,000 people were taking various types of antibiotics. This figure does not include the "worried well" who obtained prescriptions from their private physicians or over the Internet. While specific data are unavailable, some sources of antibiotics reported increases as high as 300 to 600 per cent compared to previous sales. ... [P]harmacies in Florida and later in New York reported skyrocketing demands ...

Center for Counterproliferation Research, National Defense University (2002)

Figure 7.1 shows one of the anthrax-tainted letters that was mailed in the fall of 2001.

Figure 7.2 shows an example of a cutaneous anthrax lesion.

Emerging Infectious Diseases

The University of Iowa's Center for Emerging Infectious Diseases defines this term as "infectious diseases whose incidence in humans has increased in the past two decades or threatens to increase in the near future." The National Institute of Allergies and Infectious Diseases of the National Institutes of Health offers this explanation of the threat they pose to public health:

Despite remarkable advances in medical research and treatments during the 20th century, infectious diseases remain among the leading causes of death worldwide for three reasons: (1) emergence of new infectious diseases; (2) re-emergence of old infectious diseases; and (3) persistence of intractable infectious diseases. Emerging diseases include outbreaks of previously unknown diseases or known diseases whose incidence

FIGURE 7.1 An Anthrax-Tainted Letter Addressed to Senator Patrick Leahy
Source: Federal Bureau of Investigation. http://www.fbi.gov/page2/august08/anthrax_gallery1.html

in humans has significantly increased in the past two decades. Re-emerging diseases are known diseases that have reappeared after a significant decline in incidence. Within the past two decades, innovative research and improved diagnostic and detection methods have revealed a number of previously unknown human pathogens. For example, within the last decade, chronic gastric ulcers, which were formerly thought to be caused by stress or diet, were found to be the result of infection by the bacterium *Helicobacter pylori*.

New infectious diseases continue to evolve and "emerge." Changes in human demographics, behavior, land use, etc. are contributing to new disease emergence by changing

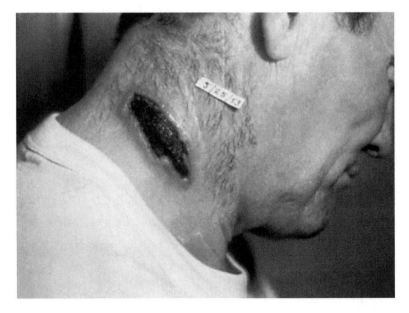

FIGURE 7.2 A Cutaneous Anthrax Lesion on the Neck
Photo courtesy of CDC/Public Health Image Library PHIL ID# 1934.

transmission dynamics to bring people into closer and more frequent contact with pathogens. This may involve exposure to animal or arthropod carriers of disease. Increasing trade in exotic animals for pets and as food sources has contributed to the rise in opportunity for pathogens to jump from animal reservoirs to humans. For example, close contact with exotic rodents imported to the United States as pets was found to be the origin of the recent U.S. outbreak of monkeypox, and use of exotic civet cats for meat in China was found to be the route by which the SARS coronavirus made the transition from animal to human hosts.

In addition to the continual discovery of new human pathogens, old infectious disease enemies are "re-emerging." Natural genetic variations, recombinations, and adaptations allow new strains of known pathogens to appear to which the immune system has not been previously exposed and is therefore not primed to recognize (e.g., influenza). Furthermore, human behavior plays an important role in re-emergence. Increased and sometimes imprudent use of antimicrobial drugs and pesticides has led to the development of resistant pathogens, allowing many diseases that were formerly treatable with drugs to make a comeback (e.g., tuberculosis, malaria, nosocomial [resulting from hospital care], and food-borne infections). Recently, decreased compliance with vaccination policy has also led to re-emergence of diseases such as measles and pertussis, which were previously under control.

National Institutes of Health, National Institute of Allergy and Infectious Diseases, "Emerging and Re-Emerging Infectious Diseases," available at http://www3.niaid.nih.gov/topics/emerging/introduction.htm

Does the discovery of a new virus always signal the threat of a pandemic? No – three characteristics must be met before the situation becomes a public health emergency:

- The virus infects humans
- There is human-to-human transmission
- The virus causes serious disease in humans

The First Post-9/11 EID: SARS

The CDC describes SARS as follows:

Severe acute respiratory syndrome (SARS) is a viral respiratory illness caused by a coronavirus, called SARS-associated coronavirus (SARS-CoV). SARS was first reported in Asia in February 2003. Over the next few months, the illness spread to more than two dozen countries in North America, South America, Europe, and Asia before the SARS global outbreak of 2003 was contained. ...

According to the World Health Organization (WHO), a total of 8,098 people worldwide became sick with SARS during the 2003 outbreak. Of these, 774 died. In the United States, only eight people had laboratory evidence of SARS-CoV infection. All of these people had traveled to other parts of the world with SARS. SARS did not spread more widely in the community in the United States.

In general, SARS begins with a high fever (temperature greater than 100.4°F [>38.0°C]). Other symptoms may include headache, an overall feeling of discomfort, and body aches. Some people also have mild respiratory symptoms at the outset. About 10 percent to 20 percent of patients have diarrhea. After 2 to 7 days, SARS patients may develop a dry cough. Most patients develop pneumonia.

The main way that SARS seems to spread is by close person-to-person contact. The virus that causes SARS is thought to be transmitted most readily by respiratory droplets (droplet spread) produced when an infected person coughs or sneezes. Droplet spread can happen when droplets from the cough or sneeze of an infected person are propelled a short distance (generally up to 3 feet) through the air and deposited on the mucous membranes of the mouth, nose, or eyes of persons who are nearby. The virus also can spread when a person touches a surface or object contaminated with infectious droplets and then touches his or her mouth, nose, or eye(s). In addition, it is possible that the SARS virus might spread more broadly through the air (airborne spread) or by other ways that are not now known.

In the context of SARS, close contact means having cared for or lived with someone with SARS or having direct contact with respiratory secretions or body fluids of a patient with SARS. Examples of close contact include kissing or hugging, sharing eating or drinking utensils, talking to someone within 3 feet, and touching someone directly. Close contact does not include activities like walking by a person or briefly sitting across a waiting room or office.

The SARS Outbreak of 2003: Timeline

2002 – November 16: First known case of SARS is discovered in Guangdong province, China.

2003 – February 11: The Chinese Ministry of Health reports that there have been 300 cases including five deaths in Guangdong province from an "acute respiratory syndrome" that is consistent with atypical pneumonia.

March 11: Hong Kong health officials report an outbreak of an "acute respiratory syndrome" among hospital workers. There are also reports of a severe form of pneumonia among staff at a hospital in Hanoi.

March 15: The World Health Organization (WHO) confirms that there is a new "worldwide health threat" and that possible cases have been identified in Canada, Indonesia, Philippines, Singapore, Thailand, and Vietnam. The WHO issues guidelines warning travelers to Southeast Asia about the dangers of SARS.

March 19: The United Kingdom, Spain, Germany, and Slovenia report cases.

March 27: WHO recommends screening departing travelers from the worst affected areas.

March 30: Based on a sharp increase in cases in an apartment complex, the Hong Kong Department of Health issues an isolation order requiring residents of one 35-story building in the complex to remain in their apartments for 10 days. These persons are subsequently moved to rural isolation camps.

April 2: WHO recommends postponement of all nonessential travel to Hong Kong and the Guangdong province of China.

April 5: China issues an apology for its slow response to the SARS outbreak. The press reports allegations that Chinese officials covered up the true extent of the disease.

April 9: First SARS case reported in Africa.

April 14: Canadian scientists announce that they have sequenced the genome of the SARS virus.

April 16: The WHO announces that a new pathogen, a member of the coronavirus family never before seen in humans, is the cause of SARS.

April 17: First SARS case confirmed in India.

April 23: WHO recommends postponement of nonessential travel to Toronto. Beijing closes all schools for 2 weeks.

April 26: Health ministers from 13 Asian countries call for all international travelers to be screened for SARS.

April 27: Beijing closes all entertainment venues, including movie theaters, cafes, and clubs.

May 5: Chinese authorities quarantine 10,000 people in Nanjing.

May 15: China threatens to impose the death penalty or life imprisonment on anyone who breaks quarantine orders.

May 22: Taiwan reports 65 new cases in 1 day. More than 150 doctors and nurses have left hospital jobs because of fear of contracting SARS, shutting down or cutting services at nine hospitals.

June 13: The WHO withdraws travel warnings for four Chinese provinces but maintains the warning for Beijing.

June 17: WHO lifts its travel warning for Taiwan. Singapore and Vietnam have also been declared SARS-free, after 20 consecutive days without new cases.

June 24: Hong Kong and Beijing are removed from the WHO's list of infected areas.

July 2: WHO declares that Toronto is SARS-free.

July 5: Taiwan is the last country to be removed from the WHO's list of infected areas.

September 2003 – May 2004: New cases of SARS are reported in Singapore, Taiwan, and China, but there is little spread of the disease.

July 2004: The director of China's main disease control agency and the Hong Kong Health Secretary resign after criticism that they failed to adequately report and contain the initial outbreak.

Sources: BBC News, CDC, and WHO.

■ ■ Critical Thinking ■

How did anthrax and SARS present different legal and management problems for public health officers? Evaluate the official responses described above. What were the best and worst actions taken in each case? What are the bases for your characterizations?

Rationing Medications

Should an outbreak occur of a highly infectious pathogen – whether it is intentionally caused as part of a bioterrorist attack or a naturally occurring phenomenon such as SARS – there will be great urgency surrounding the issue of distribution of medications or vaccines. Scientists anticipate that if a new strain of influenza takes hold in humans, it will take several months to develop and produce a drug that can counteract it. For anthrax or smallpox, there are pharmaceutical countermeasures available, but the initially available quantities may be inadequate.

States have developed plans to coordinate with federal public health authorities to disseminate "push packs" of existing drugs from the Strategic National Stockpile (SNS) managed by the CDC. The SNS is a national repository of antibiotics, chemical antidotes, antitoxins, life-support medications, IV administration, airway maintenance supplies, and medical/surgical items. Push packs contain pharmaceuticals, antidotes, and medical supplies designed to provide rapid delivery of medical resources in the early hours of a public health emergency. Push packs are stored in strategically located, secure warehouses, and can be delivered within 12 hours after a state's request. It is then up to state and local health officials to distribute them in the affected areas. If the cause of the disease is quickly identified and there are known medications, the SNS program will arrange shipping of pharmaceutical products specific to that disease.

If there are not enough medications or vaccines available to protect an entire population, enormous ethical and legal questions arise. University of Virginia bioethicist John Arras has summarized the problem as follows:

> [T]he ethical challenges posed by a possible pandemic ... are nearly as formidable as the scientific and public health challenges. Assuming a high degree of mortality associated with the viral strain, a genuine pandemic would claim millions of lives worldwide and threaten the integrity of key medical, public health, social and political infrastructures. ... In the absence of social consensus on priorities, adhering to fair processes becomes critical for the public legitimation of rationing scarce life-saving resources ... [T]he rational principles we develop must remain vigilant against the ever-present temptation to discriminate against the poor and dispossessed, whether here at home or in the far reaches of the developing world.
>
> Arras (2006)

The Ethics Subcommittee of the Advisory Committee to the Director of the CDC prepared a set of ethical guidelines geared to a likely shortage of medications in the event of pandemic influenza. For the allocation of resources, they recommended the following analysis to the CDC:

> We have concluded that a classic utilitarian approach to defining priorities, "the greatest good for the greatest number," is not a morally adequate platform for pandemic influenza planning. We recommend an approach to ethical justification, that, like utilitarianism, evaluates the rightness or wrongness of actions or policies primarily by their consequences, but, we further recommend that planning should take into account other checks ... grounded in the ethical principles of respect for persons, non-maleficence and justice. For example, a classic utilitarian approach, which might accept imposing suffering on the few for the greater benefit of all, would be tempered by such principles as:
>
> • Refrain from harming or injuring individuals or communities.
> • Equal opportunity to access resources should be assured to those within agreed upon priority groups.

- Respect for individual autonomy by, for example, employment of the least restrictive interventions that are likely to be effective.

Distribution plans should also specify:

- What scarce goods are involved in the distribution plan? ...
- Who (or what agency) will decide about prioritization and distribution? A mechanism for authoritative interpretations of the rules in the case of a dispute or an appeal is needed.
- Who is eligible to be a recipient (for example, visitors to the local community or only residents)? ...
- What morally relevant criteria will be employed to assign higher or lower priorities to groups of individuals or individuals within the determined goal (preserving the functioning of society)? For example, are certain key services more essential than others? Within the organization or group of individuals who provide an essential service, are there justified criteria for determining further order of priority (e.g., those with more years of experience or those who have dealt with crises in the past)? ...

... [I]n planning for a pandemic where the primary objective is to preserve the function of society, it is necessary to identify certain individuals and groups of persons as "key" to the preservation of society and to accord to them a high priority for the distribution of certain goods such as vaccines and antiviral drugs. ... Care must be taken to avoid extension of the evaluation of social worth to other attributes that are not morally relevant. ...

Kinlaw and Levine (2007)

■ ■ Critical Thinking ■

Would a first-come, first-served approach be consistent with these ethical guidelines?

The CDC prepared a guide to rationing vaccines during a pandemic influenza outbreak (see Table 7.3). What do you think are the risks of breaching or omitting the ethical principles set out above if this order is followed? Would you change any of the CDC's priority rankings? If so, on what ethical or legal basis?

Table 7.3   The CDC's Guide to Rationing Vaccines During a Pandemic

Priority rank	Group to receive vaccine	Approximate number in group
1-A	Persons involved in manufacturing and distributing vaccines and antiviral medications; health care workers	9 million
1-B	Persons with multiple influenza high-risk conditions or history of hospitalization for pneumonia or influenza	26 million
1-C	Pregnant women and household contacts of infants and of persons who cannot be vaccinated for medical reasons	10.7 million
1-D	Essential public health emergency response workers and key government leaders	200,000
2-A	Infants to age 2, adults up to 65 with a single high-risk condition, healthy adults 65 and older	59 million
2-B	Remainder of public health emergency responders and essential workers in public safety, utilities, transportation and telecommunications	8.5 million
3	Other key government health officials and funeral home workers	200,000
4	Remainder of population	179 million

Source: www.hhs.gov.

Contemporary Mass Quarantine

Traditionally, isolation and quarantine orders have been issued to individuals or, in some cases, to relatively small groups of people (for example, passengers on a particular ship or flight). Should a pandemic level of transmission be reached, however, public health officials would not be able to catch up by identifying and trying to trace transmission on a case-by-case basis. On the other hand, complete enforcement of a mass quarantine order would probably overtax the capacity of local law enforcement.

One lesson that public health agencies learned during the 2003 SARS outbreak was that a menu of large-scale quarantine strategies could be effective. Governments were able to implement a number of social distancing mechanisms, such as cancellation of public events, closure of shopping malls and some public transportation, and other "snow day" measures. Persons who had been exposed to SARS but were not ill were asked to adhere to "home quarantine." Officials also developed the concept of "working quarantine," in which providers of essential services are permitted to work but must observe activity restrictions while off-duty. When schools, workplaces, and transportation facilities were not closed, infection control measures included fever screening before entry or the requirement of wearing face masks.

One result of these measures was the realization that quarantine did not have to be mandatory to be effective. Voluntary compliance with social distancing measures was greater than 90 percent in most settings (HHS Pandemic Influenza Plan 2005). However, the financial, social, and psychological impact of such policies was substantial. Moreover, their success required a high degree of cooperation involving not only government officials but also employers, media, and various service providers (see Chapter 8 for more discussion of the role of the private sector).

Figure 7.3 defines the principles of modern quarantine.

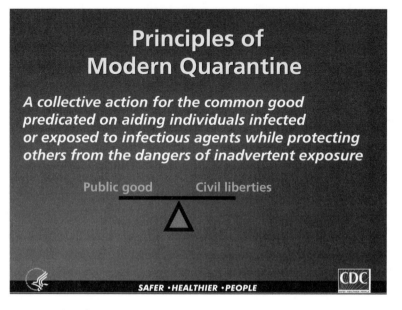

FIGURE 7.3 Principles of Modern Quarantine

■ ■ Critical Thinking ■

When a person is incarcerated, including being placed in a quarantine facility, the government assumes responsibility for providing food, medication, and other necessaries for so long as the incarceration lasts. Would that apply to persons in "home quarantine"? What would the criteria be? If the government does have that duty, how would it be fulfilled?

Travel Restrictions

The rapid transcontinental spread of SARS in 2003 eliminated any doubt that international travel would likely be a major vector of transmission for infectious disease in the future. Some have even speculated that bioterrorists might release a lethal pathogen in airports around the world, making the points of origin extremely difficult to trace and enhancing the odds for rapid dissemination of disease. If one of the characteristics of the disease is that persons who are infected but asymptomatic can transmit the infection, health officials will face major challenges in curbing its spread.

> During the 2003 global response to SARS, the control strategy for the United States included issuing travel notifications, distributing ... Alert Notices to travelers arriving from areas with SARS, and conducting visual inspections of arriving travelers ... CDC staff met more than 11,000 direct and indirect flights from SARS-affected areas and distributed more than 2.7 million Travel Health Alert Notices to arriving passengers as well as to persons arriving at 13 U.S. land border crossings near Toronto and departing passengers bound for the United States from the Toronto airport. ...
>
> ... CDC quarantine staff [also] met planes reporting an ill passenger ... If the ill passenger was determined to be a possible SARS case, the locating information was forward to state and local health departments for contact tracing.
>
> Border and travel-related activities implemented in countries more seriously affected by SARS included pre-departure temperature and symptom screening, arrival screening, "stop lists" ... of persons who were possible SARS cases or contacts ..., quarantine of travelers returning from other SARS-affected areas.
>
> HHS Pandemic Influenza Plan (2005)

Based on its experiences with SARS, CDC developed a new set of four levels of advisories to issue to travelers:

> *In the news* – notification of an occurrence of a disease of public health significance affecting a geographic area, but no increased risk of disease exposure if standard guidelines are followed
>
> *Outbreak notice* – notification that a disease outbreak is occurring in a limited geographic area or setting, creating an increased risk for disease exposure but one that is limited to specific settings
>
> *Travel health precaution* – notification that a disease outbreak of significant scope is occurring in a large geographic area and identifying specific precautions that travelers should take
>
> *Travel health warning* – notification that a widespread outbreak is expanding outside the area or populations that were initially affected, including the recommendation that nonessential travel be canceled.

Source: HHS Pandemic Flu Plan, 2005

■ ■ Critical Thinking ■

Note that none of the CDC alert levels forbid people from travelling. How effective do you think this advisory approach will be in curbing travel? Can you think of other legal measures that might be used as well?

Review the proposed federal quarantine regulations from Chapter 5. They were not in effect during the SARS outbreak. How would they have been helpful? Can you think of any disadvantages to having them in force for a new disease like SARS?

Important Terms

- Anthrax
- Bioterrorism
- Emerging infectious disease
- Push packs
- Re-emerging infectious disease
- SARS
- Social distancing
- Strategic National Stockpile
- Utilitarianism

Review Questions

1. What is the difference between bioterrorism and emerging infectious diseases?
2. What lessons did public health officials learn from the anthrax attacks? From SARS?
3. What factors are necessary for a new virus to be classified as a public health emergency?.

8

The Role of the Private Sector

What You Will Learn

- The ways in which public health emergencies could disrupt businesses, hospitals, and other segments of the economy
- The particular challenges that hospitals will face in responding to mass emergency conditions
- How the law has created a duty for employers to provide a safe workplace
- How multiple aspects of employment benefits law could become an essential factor if a long-term quarantine is in effect

Introduction

When we think of public health emergency law, we tend to concentrate on the legal authority given to government agencies to take steps to curb disease transmission. Indeed, that has been our focus in Chapters 5 to 7. In this chapter, we examine some of the ways in which a public health emergency could impact the private sector and the ways in which actions within the private sector could make the difference between success and failure for health interventions.

The Economic Dimensions of Emergencies

Although concern over loss of life and illness naturally takes precedence in an emergency, the economic consequences can also be severe. During the SARS outbreak, for example, which was relatively short and limited in scope, economists estimated that Hong Kong's gross domestic product dropped by more than 1.5 percent. In Singapore, SARS led to a 75 percent decline in visitors, a 50 percent fall in hotel occupancy, and a severe drop in the stock market (Williams, 2007). The economic cost of the September 11 attacks was estimated at more than $80 billion (Segal and Hearne, 2005); likewise, the overall economic impact of Hurricane Katrina topped $80 billion (Feinberg, 2006).

At the level of the individual company or enterprise, the numbers are smaller but the dislocation can be just as devastating. SARS caused one manager to acknowledge that while the company had continuity of operations plans for natural disasters and terrorist attacks, "we have never faced, or even seriously contemplated, the challenge of our own business being affected by an infectious disease" (Maiello, 2003). The impact on the private sector of public health emergencies such as we discussed in Chapter 7 could be extraordinary:

> Halting commercial transactions and the movement of goods to and from quarantined areas will have significant economic effects that may be profound and long term and reach well beyond the quarantine area. Much modern business practice relies on just-in-time supply chains. Shortages of food, fuel, medicines and medical supplies, essential personnel, and social services (sanitation) should be anticipated, and provisions must be in place to deal with such issues. Post quarantine stigmatization of the geographic location and of the population quarantined should be anticipated.
>
> Barbera (2001)

Some entire workplaces – especially schools, theaters, and public facilities – will be closed to interrupt transmission of a communicable disease. Thousands of people would be abruptly unable to work. In addition, the closure of schools would force many parents to stay home to care for children. Even institutions such as hospitals, whose mission is to provide services in a time of emergency, will face new and unfamiliar legal issues and demands.

SARS IN TORONTO

By far, the part of Toronto most severely compromised by SARS was its health care system. Because the first reported SARS patient in the area presented no history of contact with pneumonia (his mother, just back from Hong Kong, had died from undiagnosed pneumonia the week before), hospitals did not recognize right away that this was SARS. Thus, they placed infected individuals in double rooms, exposing other patients, their families, care providers, and other frontline workers to the virus. By the end of the epidemic, nearly half of the reported cases were among the health care workers;

three of them died. Even though all hospital procedures were reengineered within 72 hours once it became clear we were dealing with SARS, surveillance and infection control were still inadequate.

Beyond shortcomings in treating SARS itself, the burden on the health care system caused delays in testing for and treating other illnesses. Patients had to postpone or skip essential treatments such as chemotherapy and radiation. Family doctors and specialists were overwhelmed. I visited a physician who had a sign on his door telling patients to go to the nearest emergency room if they had a dry cough or fever. To avoid risk of infection, many people refused dental work, and many dentists refused patients.

Cooper (2006)

Emergency Rooms in an Emergency

Virtually every hospital in the United States derives part of its income from two federal programs: Medicare, which insures every American 65 or older, and Medicaid, which insures Americans who are indigent. As a condition of receiving those funds, hospitals with emergency rooms incur certain obligations. A federal law known as EMTALA (the Emergency Medical Treatment and Active Labor Act) requires them to provide two basic services. First, they must screen every patient who comes to the ER to determine whether they are experiencing a medical emergency. Second, if the patient has an emergency condition, the ER must either admit them to that hospital or stabilize their medical condition before transferring them to another hospital (42 U.S. Code § 1395dd).

If a hospital emergency room is filled to capacity, the hospital can go on "diversion status," which means that ambulances are directed to transport patients to the next nearest hospital. However, until the anthrax attacks during the fall of 2001, the U.S. Department of Health and Human Services (HHS), which enforces EMTALA, had never contemplated the possible impact of a community-wide public health emergency on the normal obligations of hospital ERs. After 2001, a series of statutory and regulatory changes altered EMTALA to establish new protocols that will apply if there is a formal declaration of emergency. As a result, both the screening and the stabilization duties have been somewhat altered.

As to screening, the Secretary of HHS may waive the normal EMTALA screening requirement and allow for "the direction or relocation of an individual to receive medical screening in an alternate location pursuant to an appropriate State emergency preparedness plan" (Project Bioshield Act of 2004). The Department also issued guidelines stating that, in the event of a declared emergency, if state or local governments have implemented community response plans designating certain facilities to handle particular categories of patients, then other hospitals in the area may transfer patients in those categories to a designated facility without risking a violation of EMTALA (DHHS 2004).

In addition to the standard screening and stabilization requirements, medical privacy rules also have been altered for times when a declared emergency is in effect. For example, HHS issued guidelines during the aftermath of Hurricane Katrina that made it easier for hospitals to share otherwise nondisclosable patient information when disclosure was necessary to identify, locate, and notify family members or otherwise assist in searches for persons who had been displaced by the storm. The changes to normal practices included the following:

- The requirement to obtain the patient's permission to speak with family members or friends was waived; and
- The requirement to allow patients to opt out of the hospital's publicly available informations listing of the names of patients and their general condition was waived.

Another important qualification to the general rules protecting the privacy of medical records is that disaster relief organizations, such as the American Red Cross, are not bound by the privacy requirements because they are not themselves medical care providers. Thus, hospitals are free to share patient information with the Red Cross without obtaining the patient's consent if complying with the consent process would interfere with the organization's ability to respond to the emergency.

■ ■ Critical Thinking ■

Many of these special rules allowing hospitals to operate differently during a declared emergency reflect a judgment that the ideal procedures may have to be compromised in a time of confusion. But the trade-offs generally come at the expense of protections for patients. Should standards for medical care vary by circumstance?

Workplace Safety

One legal issue that would affect some employers during an emergency concerns the safety of the workplace itself. From the perspective of the hospital staff, for example, a critical question would be whether they could be required to continue to work under unsafe conditions. The same issue could arise for workers in any critical infrastructure industry – such as communications or policing – in which continued functioning would be essential to the emergency response effort, but where the workplace itself had been contaminated or otherwise rendered unsafe.

Several laws apply to this question. The broadest one is a provision of the Occupational Safety and Health Act (OSHA) that applies to all employers. The so-called "general duty clause" states that "[e]ach employer ... shall furnish ... a place of employment which [is] free from recognized hazards that are causing or are likely to cause death or serious physical harm." (29 U.S. Code § 654(a)(1)). In interpreting this standard, courts ask whether a "reasonably prudent employer" through the exercise of due diligence would have realized what was necessary to avert a hazard (*Fairfield v. Occupational Safety & Health Review Commission*, 2002). An employer who was aware of the danger can be found liable based on the current state of knowledge in the field and what the employer should have known (*New York State Elec. & Gas Corp. v. Secretary of Labor*, 1996). Courts have also assessed whether measures existed that the employer could have taken which were feasible and likely to have been effective in preventing the danger (*Safeway Inc. v. Occupational Safety & Health Review Commission*, 2004).

OSHA also requires that all employers with more than 10 workers adopt written emergency action plans that include procedures for evacuation or sheltering in place and the identification of which employees would be responsible for critical tasks during an emergency (29 C.F.R. § 1910.38). The plans must address all "emergencies that the employer may reasonably expect in the workplace."

In addition to the OSHA requirements, the Federal Labor-Management Relations Act (LMRA) protects unionized employees from having to work in "abnormally dangerous conditions" and provides that a good faith refusal to work in such conditions shall not constitute an illegal strike (29 U.S. Code § 143). Courts have developed several formulations of the criteria that must be met for a workplace to be considered abnormally dangerous. Most focus on whether there is objective evidence that an employee's working conditions "might reasonably be considered 'abnormally dangerous'" in the particular circumstance (Leroy, 2004).

Postal Workers and the Anthrax Attacks

In fall 2001, there was a great deal of confusion as public health and law enforcement officials responded to the packets of anthrax sent through the mail. Because mail was the delivery method used by the perpetrator, postal workers were put at significant risk, and two died. Both of the following cases concern the safety of Postal Service employees. In the first, the court is faced with the question of assessing whether there is a continuing health or safety risk; and in the second, the issue is whether the actions by workplace managers were so unconscionable that damages are owed to the affected workers.

Miami Area Local, American Postal Workers Union v. U.S. Postal Service
U.S. District Court for the Southern District of Florida, 2001

> ... *In October of 2001, the United States struggled through the first widely-known bio-terrorist attack of the twenty-first century as law enforcement officers, scientists, postal workers, and ordinary citizens confronted a scourge of anthrax spores traced to letters apparently sent through the mail. On October 5, 2001, medical authorities confirmed that Bob Stevens, an employee of American Media, Inc. ["AMI"], in Boca Raton, Florida, died after inhaling anthrax spores. Medical authorities later confirmed a second case of inhalation anthrax at AMI in Boca Raton, which was successfully treated. Throughout the month, law enforcement officers found anthrax-tainted correspondence on Capitol Hill and at numerous media outlets, and discovered anthrax linked to confirmed anthrax cases at the West Trenton post office and Hamilton Township mail center in New Jersey, the Brentwood mail center in the District of Columbia, and the mail center at the State Department headquarters. The Centers for Disease Control and Prevention ["CDC"] in Atlanta, Georgia, confirmed that there were sixteen cases of anthrax (and four anthrax-attributed deaths) in October. Anthrax felled two postal workers. To date, investigators have found traces of anthrax spores at six postal facilities in the Postal Service's Central District of Florida. All of these facilities have been decontaminated. No facilities in the Postal Service's Southern District have tested positive for anthrax, and no Florida postal workers have tested positive*

for exposure to anthrax. Although limited in scope, these unpredictable and grave attacks set the nation on edge.

[The Miami Local filed a grievance pursuant to the union's contract with the USPS seeking protective equipment, testing and other measures. A number of issues were resolved.] [T] he only issues remaining before this Court are: (1) whether Miami Local is entitled to an Order, contrary to national policy, permitting window clerks to wear face masks when serving customers at the window pending arbitration; and (2) whether the Court may order arbitration on an expedited basis.

Based upon the testimony and exhibits the parties presented, the Court finds that ... [t]he Postal Service has followed the CDC's advice on the proper medical and preventative response to the anthrax threat. Moreover, the national APWU and USPS have agreed to close and decontaminate postal facilities where anthrax is found. In facilities where no trace of anthrax is found, the Postal Service has begun to issue protective equipment, including respirators and gloves; and environmental testing is being pursued aggressively.

Although the CDC has made certain interim recommendations for protecting postal workers from exposure to anthrax, the CDC has not recommended that window clerks wear masks while serving customers at the window. It is reasonable for the USPS to rely on the recommendations of the CDC regarding the appropriate response to the anthrax threat because it is the accepted medical authority.

Pursuant to existing national policy, window clerks may not wear masks while working at the window. If a window clerk is uncomfortable working at the window without a mask, the Postal Service will accommodate that person, and ensure that the employee is provided with work elsewhere in the facility where masks are permitted. Although the evidence is unclear, it appears that twenty percent of the 300 postal window clerks remain concerned about their health because they are not permitted to wear protective face masks while serving customers at the window. ...

[The Miami Local is seeking an injunction, which is a court order that would immediately compel the Postal Service to allow window clerks to wear facemasks until the issue can be arbitrated through the normal channels for union grievances. The union also wants the court to order that the arbitration be scheduled immediately. The law sets a high standard for obtaining an immediate injunction. The party seeking it must establish that there is a real threat of irreparable injury if the injunction is not granted.]

Miami Local's claim of irreparable injury is two-fold. First, it claims that the postal workers will suffer irreparable injury from the fear and stress that flows from not being permitted to wear masks at the window. Second, it claims that without arbitration on an expedited basis, the arbitration process will be a nullity.

As to its first claim, while it is true that there are window clerks who suffer from heightened levels of fear and stress because they are not permitted to wear masks while working at the window, the record is devoid of any evidence that their fear is based on an actual threat, or that any postal worker in Florida has suffered actual and imminent harm as a result of anthrax exposure. The CDC, the accepted medical authority, has indicated that there is no evidence at present that postal window clerks face an actual and imminent, or even an appreciable risk of contracting anthrax while servicing customers at the window. Therefore, the Court finds that this first claim of injury alleged by Miami Local is both remote and speculative.

As to its second claim, given the speed at which all of the other issues raised in Miami Local's grievance have been resolved at the national level, the Court must conclude that it is more likely than not that the Postal Service and the national APWU will address the remaining face mask issue in the same expeditious manner. Therefore, the Court finds that Miami Local has failed to establish irreparable injury as to both of its claims. ...

The public has a substantial interest in having matters of national scope and importance dealt with on a national level.

It is precisely in times such as these, that the Postal Service must utilize its limited resources in an efficient and effective manner. To force the Postal Service to address issues of national scope on a piecemeal and ad-hoc basis would hamper the unitary leadership and efficient use of resources that is required. Therefore, the Court finds that Miami Local has failed to establish that the threatened injury outweighs the threatened harm an injunction may impose on the defendants ...

Briscoe v. Potter
U.S. District Court for the District of Columbia, 2004

... On Tuesday, October 9, 2001, an unknown person(s) mailed from Trenton, New Jersey, an anthrax-laden letter addressed to United States Senator Tom Daschle at his office in Washington, D.C. That letter arrived in a mail bag at Brentwood [Postal Service facility] on or about Thursday, October 11, 2001. The mail bag was opened and its contents were separated into the Delivery Bar Code Sorter ("DBCS") machine # 17; the Daschle letter was fed manually into DBCS # 17 at approximately 7:10 a.m. The letter was then moved to the Government Mail section for delivery to the Hart Senate Office Building, where Senator Daschle's office is located. Between approximately 8:00 a.m. and 9:40 a.m., DBCS # 17 was opened in the normal course of operations and a large blower using compressed air was used to blow debris and dust from the conveyor belts and optical reading heads of the machine.

Source: http://www.fbi.gov/pressrel/pressrel01/102301.htm

The Daschle letter was delivered to the Hart Senate Office Building at approximately noon on Friday, October 12, 2001. It was opened in the Senator's personal office the following Monday, October 15, 2001. The envelope contained a fine white powder, which aroused suspicion. The Capitol Police were called and they performed a field test on the letter, which was ultimately found to contain anthrax spores. Subsequently, the ventilation system in the Hart Senate Office Building was shut down and the building was closed; bundles of letters and packages were quarantined and all mail delivery was suspended; staffers in Senator Daschle's office were tested and given antibiotics; and tours of the Capitol were canceled.

In contrast, the Brentwood facility continued to operate as usual. During a regularly-scheduled "floor" meeting on Monday, October 15, 2001, Larry Littlejohn, a Brentwood maintenance technician, asked his supervisor for a briefing on anthrax and proper safety procedures. The supervisor refused to provide the requested briefing, threatened Mr. Littlejohn with a seven-day suspension, and had him forcibly expelled from the building. ...

On Tuesday, October 16, 2001, all Senate employees were tested for anthrax exposure and given antibiotics as a countermeasure. The tests apparently "showed that at least twenty (20) Senate staffers had been exposed to anthrax, including staffers on a floor below Senator Daschle's office and at least one staffer who had not been at work when the letter was opened the previous day. On that same day, [an Army general] stated that the anthrax spores in the Daschle letter constituted "a very potent form of anthrax that was clearly produced by someone who knew what he was doing." The Federal Bureau of Investigation ("FBI") reported to the USPS Inspection Service which, in turn, notified [Postmaster General John] Potter that the letter had contained a "potent" strain of anthrax. Despite these developments, USPS officials allegedly instructed Brentwood supervisors "to provide false safety briefings ... representing to the employees that there was no evidence any anthrax contaminated letter or mail had come through the facility at any time, including the letter that was sent to Senator Daschle's office." Plaintiff Ossie

Alston, a supervisor at Brentwood, asserts that he refused to deliver this message. ...

On Wednesday, October 17, 2001, the United States House of Representatives was shut down after it appeared that thirty-one (31) staff members had tested positive for exposure to anthrax. Anthrax spores were found in a mail room at the Dirksen Senate Office Building, through which the letter to Senator Daschle had passed ... USPS ordered that the Brentwood facility be tested for anthrax spores on that day, as well, although no one advised employees of any possible danger.

On Thursday, October 18, 2001, all buildings on Capitol Hill were closed and quarantined. USPS officials, including Brentwood Plant Manager Timothy Haney and USPS Senior Vice President Deborah Willhite, met that morning with Senate representatives. According to notes kept by Mr. Haney, he privately advised Ms. Willhite that "'the mail was leaking and that we were affected.'" During that same morning, USPS was notified that the Centers for Disease Control ("CDC") had confirmed that a letter carrier in New Jersey, where the Daschle letter had been mailed, was suffering from cutaneous anthrax. However, during a morning press conference at the White House, Postmaster General Potter assured the public that the mail was safe.

In the early afternoon, the Postmaster General held a second press conference in an unused section of Brentwood, where he again told the news media and employees in attendance that Brentwood was safe. When Plaintiff Vincent Gagnon attempted to ask a question at the press conference, a Postal Inspector prevented him from doing so. Mr. Gagnon – who had clocked out to attend the press conference – then returned to work, where his supervisor informed him that "she had been directed [by Plant Manager Haney] to initiate proceedings to fire him for going to the press conference and trying to ask questions."

Plant Manager Haney held a series of "floor" meetings with Brentwood employees on Thursday, October 18, 2001, to inform them that there was no anthrax in the building. He also mentioned that the CDC would be conducting tests in *protective gear (i.e., "moonsuits"). ... Mr. Haney apparently told employees that they would lose their jobs if they did not report for work, noting that "it would cost the USPS $500,000 a day if the Brentwood facility were shut down." At another "floor" meeting, Mr. Haney allegedly refused to answer questions about why the machines and the building were being tested but employees were not.*

Also on Thursday, October 18, 2002, USPS contacted the Fairfax County (Virginia) HAZMAT Team to have an on-site field test for anthrax spores conducted at Brentwood. Two HAZMAT Team members and inspectors from a private consulting firm came to Brentwood in moonsuits that afternoon, to begin testing for contamination while postal employees continued their normal duties. At least by sometime that evening, the test results apparently showed that some of the Brentwood equipment "'[a]gain ... tested hot.'" Testing continued until 2:30 a.m. on October 19, 2001.

Notes from Plant Manager Haney indicate that, by 11 a.m. on Friday, October 19, 2001, USPS officials had determined that the DSBC # 17 had been used to sort the mail that included the letter to Senator Daschle. The CDC arrived at Brentwood that afternoon and began its analysis. In the meantime, USPS officials asked the District of Columbia Department of Health to place all Brentwood employees on antibiotics for exposure to anthrax. On that same day, Mr. Potter told a television interviewer that early reports of testing showed no anthrax contamination at Brentwood; this same information was posted on all employee bulletin boards at the Brentwood facility. Similarly, Mr. Haney held another series of "floor" meetings to assure employees that Brentwood was safe and that he was doing everything in his power to protect them.

Despite Messrs. Potter's and Haney's representations, rumors began to circulate throughout Brentwood on Friday afternoon that DBCS # 17 was contaminated with anthrax spores. [Supervisors gave conflicting information about the safety of DBCS # 17. One] supervisor allegedly advised Mr. Alston that gloves and masks were available for employee use, but that he should not pass them out to employees unless they specifically asked for them. At some point on Friday, October 19, 2001, DBCS # 17 was taken off-line.

At approximately 11:30 p.m. on Friday, October 19, 2001, a Brentwood manager "insisted that [DCBS # 17] was not contaminated and ordered [technicians] to clean DCBS # 17 by 'blowing it out' with compressed air and to get it on-line immediately." Brentwood employees reportedly heard managers state that they needed DBCS # 17 on-line because another DBCS machine had broken down. As a result, DBCS # 17 was re-activated.

Also on Friday, October 19, 2001, Brentwood employee Leroy Richmond entered the emergency room at Fairfax Inova Hospital with symptoms of inhalation anthrax. Doctors determined from blood tests that Mr. Richmond was suffering from inhalation anthrax. Mr. Richmond's wife called Plant Manager Haney and left a voicemail message describing her husband's condition and telling Mr. Haney to shut down Brentwood.

During an early-morning meeting with the Mayor's Office of Emergency Response on Saturday, October 20, 2001, it is alleged that USPS officials – including Mr. Haney – discussed Mr. Richmond's illness, and "'confirmation that the facility tested positive; and that more testing was on the way.'" Nonetheless, Mr. Haney conducted "floor" meetings at Brentwood throughout the day on Saturday and allegedly told employees, "'We have made it this far and we do not have any positive test results for anthrax.'" ...

At 4:39 a.m. on Sunday, October 21, 2001, Brentwood employee Thomas Morris, Jr., called 911 complaining of anthrax-like symptoms. Mr. Morris died of inhalation anthrax several hours later.

At approximately 11:00 a.m. on Sunday, a CDC representative told Plant Manager Haney that Brentwood needed to be closed. Mr. Haney then ordered all employees to gather at noon in the cafeteria, where he told them that a postal worker was in the hospital with a confirmed case of anthrax exposure and that Brentwood was being closed as a "'precautionary measure.'"

The employees in attendance were directed to go to a ... government facility, for medical evaluation and treatment.

... [A] group of eight to ten workers was directed to report to a manager's office [rather than being allowed to attend the cafeteria meeting]. They were told that they were needed to "round up all of the mail at Brentwood and move it to the loading dock/platform so that it could be loaded onto trucks" and removed from the building. ... Plaintiff Jeffrey Butler ... worked until 5:00 p.m. and then, upon driving out of the parking lot, received a flyer that was being distributed to incoming workers. Only upon receiving the flyer did Mr. Butler learn that Brentwood was closed and the postal workers were being directed [elsewhere] for medical evaluation and treatment. Plaintiff Vincent Gagnon continued to work inside Brentwood until approximately 7:00 p.m. to turn off fans and air and dust-handling equipment. Brentwood was finally closed at approximately 7:00 p.m. on Sunday, October 21, 2001, although truckers continued to handle the mail that had been in Brentwood and was being moved for processing to other facilities.

On Monday, October 22, 2001, Brentwood employee Joseph Curseen went to the hospital with flu-like symptoms. Mr. Curseen died that evening of inhalation anthrax. Two other Brentwood employees were hospitalized and nine became ill with anthrax-like symptoms.

■ ■ ■ ───────────────────────────────────

It was the next day – October 23 – when the postal workers in Miami filed their grievance.

─────────────────────────────────── ■ ■ ■

... [O]ne of the mid-level managers allegedly [stated] that the mid-level managers had been instructed by senior management to lie to the floor supervisors and employees about Brentwood being contaminated with anthrax.

When the complaint [in this case] was filed in October of 2003, Brentwood was still closed due to anthrax contamination. It has now reopened. ...

... Plaintiffs assert:

> *once Defendants affirmatively acted to provide Plaintiffs with information regarding the safety of the Brentwood facility and whether the facility was contaminated with anthrax, they had a constitutional duty, under the well-established State/Government Endangerment Theory, not to enhance or make Plaintiffs more vulnerable to the danger of anthrax contamination (a) by lying to them and misleading them with information Defendants knew to be false, and (b) by preventing Plaintiffs from learning of their exposure to anthrax and preventing them from getting medical treatment.*

... [W]hether Defendants can be held liable under the theory of State Endangerment requires a two-part analysis, which raises the following questions: (1) has there been an affirmative act by Defendants to create or increase the danger that resulted in harm to Plaintiffs and, if so, (2) does that act shock the conscience? ...

Defendants argue that Plaintiffs have failed to allege that Defendants acted affirmatively to create or enhance a dangerous situation. They contend that Plaintiffs' substantive due-process claim is based on Defendants' inaction ...

Defendants are correct that in light of [earlier case law], their mere failure to warn Plaintiffs about a danger of anthrax contamination does not expose them to constitutional liability. [Other laws would apply.] However, Plaintiffs' allegations are not premised upon the notion that Defendants violated their ... rights solely by failing to warn them of a known risk or to provide them with a safe working environment. Instead, Plaintiffs allege that Defendants made affirmative misrepresentations about the safety of the facility. While it is clear that Plaintiffs do not allege that Defendants created the danger at Brentwood, Plaintiffs contend that by providing false safety briefings and representing to employees that there was no evidence of anthrax contamination at the facility (despite alleged actual knowledge to the contrary), Defendants increased the risk that Plaintiffs would be exposed to deadly anthrax spores and made Plaintiffs more vulnerable to such danger. ...

The Court has given considerable thought to Plaintiffs' arguments. If the facts are as alleged, the conduct of USPS managers would appear commendable for their dedication to getting the mail out but deplorable for not recognizing the potential human risk involved. ... [T]hese alleged actions demonstrated a gross disregard for a dangerous situation ... It is alleged that Defendants "had been put on notice of the serious consequences that could result" from Plaintiffs' exposure to anthrax yet, despite such knowledge, Defendants engaged in a campaign of misinformation designed to keep the employees at work. ... The Court therefore finds that Plaintiffs have sufficiently alleged that Defendants' conduct amounted to deliberate indifference, which violated their substantive due-process rights under the State Endangerment theory. ...

... Plaintiffs here are not seeking constitutional redress based on Defendants' failure to protect them from a hazard that was "inherent" in their occupation. While it is true that Defendants did not force Plaintiffs to become postal workers, potential exposure to anthrax is not a danger that one would reasonably anticipate when accepting employment at a post office. ...

Figure 8.1 shows a chest radiograph 22 hours prior to death showing widened mediastinum due to inhalation anthrax.

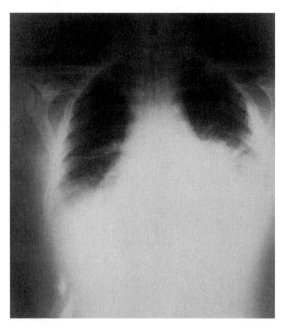

FIGURE 8.1 Chest x-ray shows distortion of central thoracic cavity caused by inhalation anthrax
Source: Photo Courtesy of CDC/Public Health Image Library PHIL ID#1118

■ ■ Critical Thinking ■

In the *Miami Area Local* case, the court was being asked to order immediate action (by granting an injunction) to prevent harm. In *Briscoe*, the harm had already occurred and the court was considering whether plaintiffs had a valid cause of action for damages. What kinds of concerns were foremost for the judges in each situation? Should the judges' concerns have been different, and if so, how?

Workplaces and Mass Quarantine

Depending on which infectious agent was involved, it is possible that a bioterrorist act or a pandemic such as influenza could necessitate a public health intervention that would mandate various social distancing techniques for weeks or even months. We analyzed this situation from the perspective of government power in Chapter 7. Here, we consider the impact of such an order on individual workers and the private sector, especially the employment law questions that would immediately arise.

Job Protection

Persons who need to absent themselves from work for any form of quarantine should not be penalized for cooperating with public health agencies in efforts to impede the spread of disease. As a practical matter, however, the great majority of people will not be able to simply stay home without risking the loss of their job. For employees, even if an income replacement system was in place, the dislocation from losing one's job would be enormous. Similarly, most employers will be unable to afford such a loss of productivity without some form of government assistance. (As you read Chapter 9, consider how the Stafford Act might apply in this situation.)

In the United States, there is no federal law guaranteeing that a person's job will be preserved if he or she is absent during an emergency for these reasons. Very few states provide job protection for persons under quarantine, and even in those states, the laws are not adequate. New Mexico law, for example, extends job protection to "a person who is placed in isolation or quarantine pursuant to the provisions" of its state law. (N.M. Statutes § 12-10A-16) However, in a widespread outbreak or pandemic, health officials may have to rely on voluntary self-quarantine as was done in Toronto during SARS. Individuals who acted as good citizens in response to the request would not have their jobs protected by a law such as New Mexico's.

The most extensive protections in state law exist in New Jersey:

a. Any person who has been placed in isolation or quarantine pursuant to an order of the commissioner [of health] and who at the time of quarantine or isolation was in the employ of any public or private employer, other than a temporary position, shall be reinstated to such employment or to a position of like seniority, status and pay, unless the employer's circumstances have so changed as to make it impossible or unreasonable to do so, if the person:

(1) receives a certificate of completion of isolation or quarantine issued by the department or the authorized local health department;

(2) is still qualified to perform the duties of such position; and

(3) makes application for reemployment within 90 days after being released from isolation or quarantine.

b. If a public or private employer fails or refuses to comply with the provisions of this section, the Superior Court may, upon the filing of a complaint by the person entitled to the benefits of this section, specifically require the employer to comply with the provisions of this section, and may, as an incident thereto, order the employer to compensate the person for any loss of wages or benefits suffered by reason of the employer's unlawful action. A person claiming to be entitled to the benefits of this section may appear and be represented by counsel, or, upon application to the Attorney General, request that the Attorney General appear and act on his behalf. If the Attorney General is reasonably satisfied that the person so applying is entitled to the benefits, he shall appear and act as attorney for the person in the amicable adjustment of the claim, or in the filing of any complaint and the prosecution thereof. No fees or court costs shall be assessed against a person so applying for the benefits under this section. Attorney fees shall be awarded to the Attorney General or to the counsel for a person entitled to benefits under this section, who prevails in the proceeding.

c. The Attorney General may apply to the Superior Court and the court may grant additional relief to persons placed in isolation or quarantine ...

(New Jersey Statutes 26:13-16)

If an employer does not voluntarily offer special leave in an emergency, many workers could use existing medical leave to cover an absence. The Family Medical Leave Act (FMLA) guarantees up to 12 weeks of unpaid leave for persons who have a "serious health condition" or persons who need the time off to care for a newborn or newly adopted child, or for a child, spouse, or parent with a serious health condition (29 U.S. Code § 201 et seq.). "Serious health condition" is defined as one involving inpatient care or continuing outpatient treatment.

Here, too, however, there are gaps in coverage. The FMLA applies only to entities with 50 or more employees, leaving small employers and self-employed workers uncovered. Workers must have been employed for at least one year and must work a certain number of hours per year, which averages to slightly more than three days a week. Caring for anyone not included in the statutory list – such as a grandchild, domestic partner, or neighbor – would disqualify the worker from using leave under the FMLA. Although an already-infected person would meet the criteria for having a "serious health condition," someone who had been exposed but was not ill, or who was taking precautions against exposure, would not qualify.

Laws that prohibit discrimination based on disabilities could be useful in some emergency situations, but not all. The Americans with Disabilities Act (ADA) prohibits firing an individual because he or she *has* a disability, or once *had* a disability, or is *perceived* to be disabled, or *associates* with someone who is disabled (42 U.S. Code § 12101 et seq.). Disability is defined for purposes of discrimination law as a physical or mental impairment that substantially limits a major life activity. One major life activity is working.

The ADA would apply if, for example, an employee was fired because she had been infected with smallpox virus but was now recovered so that she could safely work, or because a false rumor had circulated that she was infectious. However, imagine that same person were fired for absenteeism, which happened because she could not be vaccinated because of contraindications to smallpox vaccine (such as pregnancy), which in turn necessitated her staying away from public spaces until the epidemic passed. In that situation, the ADA might not apply. If a healthy person voluntarily stayed home, even at the request of health officials, he would not be protected by the ADA if he were fired. There is a substantial and complex body of case law interpreting the ADA, and its possible application would have to be assessed in each individual case.

Without a specific statute such as job protection laws or the ADA, employees have little recourse. Under what is known as the employment-at-will doctrine, companies usually do not have to identify a specific reason for firings. Employers have the freedom to terminate workers at will, with or without good cause, unless a statute (such as an antidiscrimination law), an employment contract, or a collective bargaining agreement applies, and in essence changes the terms of the employer–employee relationship. The legal adage is that employers can fire workers for any reason or for no reason, but not for a prohibited reason.

In certain rare instances, courts will bar firings if they find that the employer's reason seriously undermines public policy. Examples have included firing an employee for refusing to perform an unlawful act or for filing a complaint with a regulatory agency (*Sabine Pilot Service, Inc. v. Hauck*, 1985). It is possible that courts would use this doctrine to invalidate a firing if the employee had an emergency-related reason to not report for work, although this relief would come only after the fact, if the employee sued.

Income Replacement

Even if an individual's job was preserved, an employer might well furlough workers during an extended emergency because of the financial hardship of paying them while at least parts of the business were closed. The most obvious model for income replacement in existing American law is our unemployment compensation benefits system. As a threshold matter, however, persons who did not lose their jobs, but who received unpaid leave, would not generally qualify for unemployment compensation.

Other nations have handled this issue differently. All the countries most affected by the SARS outbreak in 2003 adopted laws that provided some form of monetary compensation to persons who were under quarantine or who had been advised to remain at home (Rothstein et al. 2003) and (Rothstein and Talbott 2007). There is precedent in international law. The International Labour Organization, which is affiliated with the United Nations and the World Health Organization, adopted a recommendation 40 years ago that sickness benefits should include a cash award to compensate for loss of earnings caused by an individual being quarantined (ILO Medical Care and Sickness Benefits Recommendations, 1969 (No. 134, Art. 8)).

Health Care

Virtually all Americans younger than 65 who have health insurance receive it through a workplace group plan. This fact creates another reason why preserving one's job is essential. Termination from employment also means termination of health insurance. More than 45 million Americans, however, have no health insurance, nor are they covered by public programs such as Medicare or Medicaid. In a disaster or lengthy emergency, their health needs will require substantial additional assistance.

In the wake of September 11, eligibility criteria for Medicaid were loosened for those who lost their homes or jobs in lower Manhattan. Normally, only indigent persons qualify for Medicaid. The Disaster Relief Medicaid program allowed delivery of medical care to thousands of uninsured persons, primarily in New York (Public Law 107-242). A similar response could be necessary in the event of another terrorist attack or major disease outbreak.

■ ■ Critical Thinking ■

Perhaps the biggest problem with the kinds of laws now available to address issues of job protection, income replacement, and access to medical care during a lengthy emergency is that even if all of them could be used to the maximum, people would have no assurance in advance that their interests – as both employees and employers – would be protected. At best, their usefulness would be extremely uneven. Should America's legal system prepare now for this kind of eventuality and if so, how? Alternatively, are there advantages to waiting to see if such needs arise? Which do you think is the better course?

Important Terms

- Active endangerment
- Americans with Disabilities Act
- Cutaneous anthrax
- Employment-at-will doctrine
- EMTALA
- Family and Medical Leave Act
- Inhalational anthrax
- Injunction
- Medicaid

Review Questions

1. Design a chart mapping all the ways that a four-week-long public health emergency would disrupt normal functioning of the government and the economy. How should these costs be allocated? Who should bear which costs? How might the law operate to carry out policy decisions about the distribution of burdens?

2. Imagine that you are the head of a large urban hospital. Since hospitals are workplaces, you have a duty under OSHA to develop a contingency plan for emergencies. What issues would your plan address?

3. Why would the law set such a high standard – irreparable injury – before a judge can grant an injunction as sought in the *Miami Area Local* case?

4. Why would the law provide that the government's action could meet the criteria for "active endangerment" only in the limited circumstances described in *Briscoe*?

PART III

Disaster Management

▪▪▪ 9
▪▪▪
▪▪▪
The Stafford Act

What You Will Learn

- How federal law governing disaster relief evolved from a hodge-podge of programs into today's system
- The ways in which the Stafford Act treats "major disasters" and "emergencies" differently, both in how they are declared and in which specific benefits they trigger
- The different kinds of aid that individuals and state and local governments can obtain from federal officials
- The circumstances under which furnishing disaster relief is a federal obligation, not just an option

Introduction

By far, the most important federal law in the area of disaster management is the Robert T. Stafford Disaster Relief and Emergency Assistance Act, commonly known as the Stafford Act. Its stated goal is "to provide an orderly and continuing means of assistance by the Federal Government to State and local governments in carrying out their responsibilities to alleviate the suffering and damage which result from such disasters" (42 U.S. Code § 5121). The agency responsible for implementing the Stafford Act is the Federal Emergency Management Agency (FEMA). Through FEMA, tens of millions of dollars are distributed each year to help individuals and communities recover from natural or human-caused disasters.

The Stafford Act and the case law interpreting it have raised a number of legal questions that control how, when, and whether relief activities can go forward. This chapter will focus on the act's definitions, the declaration process, eligibility for various types of assistance, and when the act creates duties on the part of government. These issues are both weighty and frequent; in a typical year, dozens of events give rise to declarations under the Stafford Act.

History

Until the 1930s, disaster aid was a responsibility of state and local government. The federal government began its involvement in the field with New Deal programs that provided assistance primarily for flood control or economic emergencies. The 1950 Disaster Relief Act provided that the federal government could provide a broader range of assistance to states and localities. Throughout the 1960s and 1970s, Congress enacted a series of bills that continued to expand federal aid in multiple categories and created an uncoordinated tangle of agency responsibilities. In 1979, President Carter consolidated more than a hundred programs into FEMA (Department of Homeland Security, 2009; Sar, 1996).

In 1988, Congress passed the Stafford Act, named after the Vermont senator who was its chief sponsor. The Stafford Act revised and streamlined an earlier disaster relief law. In 2002, as part of the creation of the Department of Homeland Security (DHS), FEMA lost its independent agency status and was made part of DHS (see Chapter 3). After the dismal federal response to Hurricane Katrina, Congress passed new legislation in 2006 making FEMA a more distinct entity but keeping it within DHS. FEMA's director was given a direct reporting line to the DHS secretary and to the President during times of emergency. The change of administrations in 2009 reignited debates over whether FEMA should once again become a fully independent agency.

Conflicting Voices

Table 9.1 lists the arguments for keeping FEMA part of DHS and for making FEMA an independent agency again.

Table 9.1   Arguments for Keeping FEMA Part of DHS and for Making FEMA an Independent Agency Again

Keep FEMA in DHS	Make FEMA Independent again
Retention of FEMA would enable better coordination with other entities, such as the Coast Guard, which will definitely remain in DHS	An independent agency is more nimble in its responses, with fewer steps up the chain of command needed to reach the White House
Retention of FEMA would avoid the need to recreate a separate bureaucratic structure	FEMA could control its own budget and determine its own strategic direction
Moving FEMA back to independent status would create more instability, and sap time and energy better spent on program implementation	Restoring independence would lift morale in an agency badly harmed by its performance in Katrina
Retaining FEMA in DHS would enhance the overall effectiveness of DHS	FEMA's removal would enable DHS to concentrate on national security threats

Definitions

The Stafford Act enables multiple forms of federal assistance to flow to states and localities and to individual victims of catastrophic loss. It creates two primary categories of events that qualify for such aid: "major disasters" and "emergencies," each with a specific definition. Depending on the category, different forms of assistance are available.

A "major disaster" is:

> any natural catastrophe (including any hurricane, tornado, storm, high water, winddriven water, tidal wave, tsunami, earthquake, volcanic eruption, landslide, mudslide, snowstorm or drought), or, regardless of cause, any fire, flood, or explosion, in any part of the United States, which in the determination of the President causes damage of sufficient severity and magnitude to warrant major disaster assistance under this Act to supplement the efforts and available resources of States, local governments, and disaster relief organizations in alleviating the damage, loss, hardship, or suffering caused thereby.
>
> (42 U.S. Code § 5122(2))

An "emergency" under the Stafford Act is:

> any occasion or instance for which, in the determination of the President, Federal assistance is needed to supplement State and local efforts and capabilities to save lives and to protect property and public health and safety, or to lessen or avert the threat of catastrophe in any part of the United States.
>
> (42 U.S. Code § 5122(1))

Some events will fit into one category but not another. Some events could fit into both. How would a bioterrorist attack accomplished by the release of smallpox virus be classified? Could a computer virus that paralyzed the nation's financial and telecommunications infrastructure qualify as either a major disaster or an emergency? What about radiological contamination? Is actual damage necessary prior to a declaration?

The Declaration Process

There can be no declaration of a major disaster unless the governor of the affected state(s) submits a request for a declaration to the President. (The request is actually submitted through the regional FEMA office, which makes a preliminary damage assessment.) The governor's request must include several components:

- A statement that the disaster is of such severity and magnitude that effective response is beyond the capabilities of the state and local governments and that federal assistance is necessary
- Confirmation that the state's emergency plan has been activated
- Information on the nature and amount of state and local resources that are being committed to response efforts, together with a commitment to meet the state's share of the cost of federal assistance
- An estimate of the amount and severity of damage and of the amount and type of federal assistance that is needed. (This last requirement may be waived for "catastrophes of unusual severity and magnitude.")

(42 U.S. Code 5170)

The emergency declaration process is similar but less strict. Governors must execute the state's emergency plan and identify the federal aid they seek, but they do not have to specify exactly which state and local resources that have been committed. The President also has discretion to declare an emergency (but not a disaster) without a gubernatorial request if the emergency condition is primarily or solely a federal responsibility. The impetus to do this may originate in the White House, or a regional FEMA director may recommend it to the President. The first exercise of independent presidential authority came in 1995, after the bombing of the federal building in Oklahoma City.

The text of the declaration itself will specify which counties within a state are covered by it, which specific federal programs are being activated by the declaration, and whether the federal share of the cost of the emergency measures will be increased from the default amount of 75%. If a particular county is omitted from the text of the declaration, it cannot be eligible for any assistance; likewise, if a federal program is not mentioned, it cannot be utilized (Abbott, 2005).

Although the declaration process may seem like a formality, courts insist that the formalities be followed, as we see from the following case:

State of Kansas v. United States
U.S. District Court for the District of Kansas, 1990.

> *... On July 26, 1989, an explosion occurred at the Day and Zimmerman Ammunition Plant near Parsons, Kansas. As a result of this explosion, the ammunition plant was shut*

down and 604 of the 1,422 workers were laid off. The laid-off employees were paid state unemployment benefits for 26 weeks. Upon the exhaustion of state unemployment benefits, 480 employees remained unemployed. Because of needed repairs to plant facilities, it was anticipated that these workers would remain laid off until February of 1990.

On December 27, 1989, Governor Mike Hayden ("Governor Hayden") submitted a request to FEMA for the Parsons Area to be declared a "major disaster" area. Such a declaration would make federal unemployment benefits available to the laid-off employees. … By letter dated January 30, 1990, Robert H. Morris, Acting Director of FEMA ("Morris"), notified Governor Hayden that his request for declaration of "major disaster" was denied. On February 15, 1990, Governor Hayden directly appealed the denial to President George Bush ("The President"). Governor Hayden's appeal was denied and notification of the denial was again sent by a letter signed by Mr. Morris, dated March 21, 1990.

For purposes of [this] motion, the only controverted facts concern whether the decision to deny the "major disaster" declaration was made by the President or by Morris. …

In his complaint, [Governor Hayden] asserts that defendant, Federal Emergency Management Agency ("FEMA"), through its Acting Director, Robert H. Morris, made an erroneous interpretation of law; considered facts outside the record without giving the plaintiff an opportunity to respond; and unfairly allowed the same person who denied Governor Hayden's request (i.e., Morris) to deny the appeal. …

President Bush is the only person with the statutory power to deny such a request. … Section 5141(b) [of the Stafford Act] provides in relevant part:

Based upon such Governor's request, the President may declare that a major disaster exists, or that an emergency exists.

By [this] express language…, the President is the sole person empowered to deny or grant a request for declaration of major disaster. … Thus, any decision to not submit a request [to the President] which allegedly complies with procedural

*requirements would be a decision which FEMA and its offi-
cials have no discretion to make, and would therefore, be
subject to judicial review. Thus, the court finds that it has ...
jurisdiction over the plaintiff's claim that its request for declaration of relief was not presented to the President for acceptance or denial, [and the Plaintiff is allowed to proceed with
the case] ...*

FEMA's organizational chart is presented in Figure 9.1.

■ ■ Critical Thinking ■

Diagram the differences in the declaration process for major disasters and emergencies. What functions are served by the creation of
these two categories?

Overview of Federal Assistance

As a practical matter, the biggest distinction between major disasters
and emergencies is the difference in federal assistance that each triggers.
In short, many more forms of aid are available if there is a disaster declaration than an emergency declaration. Categories of aid that may be
deployed in response to a disaster – but not for an emergency – include
unemployment benefits, transitional housing assistance, individual and
family cash grants, food stamps, access to Small Business Agency (SBA)
loans, and assistance to public service agencies. For either a disaster
or emergency, federal assistance offers short-term emergency food and
shelter and the deployment of federal employees to assist state and local
relief teams in such activities as the restoration of public services and
debris removal.

General Federal Assistance

General federal assistance is available for both major disasters and
emergencies. Under these provisions, any federal agency can be directed
to deploy its personnel, equipment, supplies, and services to support
state and local relief efforts. Federal entities or assets can be used to
disseminate information and to distribute medicine, food, and other
forms of emergency assistance (42 U.S. Code § 5170a).

The Stafford Act also authorizes the use of Department of Defense
resources "for the purpose of performing on public and private lands
any emergency work which is made necessary by such incident[,] which
is essential for the preservation of life and property," and which state

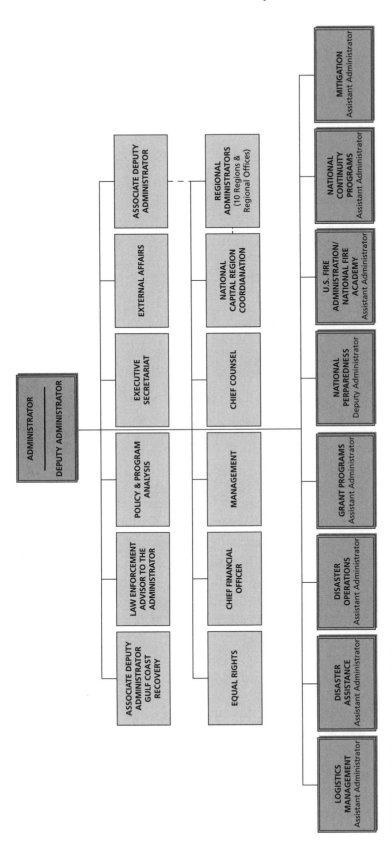

FIGURE 9.1 FEMA's Organizational Chart

and local governments cannot provide (42 U.S. Code § 5170b(c)(1) and 44 C.F.R. § 206.34(a)). Does this provision create an appropriate exception to the Posse Comitātūs Act (see Chapter 4)? Does it matter that deployment of military personnel must be requested by a governor?

Assistance to Individuals and Households

When a major disaster is declared, individuals in the affected counties become eligible for a wide range of specific federal assistance programs in addition to the general assistance described above. Individuals contact FEMA directly to apply. One caveat for all Stafford Act benefits is that they are available only to individuals who lack insurance coverage or benefits from other sources that cover these needs (42 U.S. Code § 5155). Because of that principle, Stafford Act benefits effectively provide the greatest assistance to those most in need.

DISASTER UNEMPLOYMENT ASSISTANCE

One commonly used category of individual assistance under the Stafford Act is Disaster Unemployment Assistance:

The President is authorized to provide to any individual unemployed as a result of a major disaster such benefit assistance as he deems appropriate while such individual is unemployed for the weeks of such unemployment with respect to which the individual is not entitled to any other unemployment compensation … [It] shall be available to an individual as long as the individual's unemployment caused by the major disaster continues or until the individual is re-employed in a suitable position, but no longer than 26 weeks after the major disaster is declared. [The amount] shall not exceed the maximum weekly amount authorized under the … law of the State in which the disaster occurred. …

(42 U.S. Code § 5177)

In general, the courts view benefits decisions as "discretionary," which means that FEMA officials are given broad leeway to interpret and administer the program (see Chapter 13 for a fuller analysis of the discretionary function exception to liability). In the two opinions that follow, both emerging from a lawsuit filed by victims of Hurricane Katrina, the court analyzed which of FEMA's decisions were discretionary and ruled that the agency was liable for some of its nondiscretionary actions.

McWaters v. FEMA I
U.S. District Court for the Eastern District of Louisiana, 2005

... On August 29, 2005 at around 6:10 a.m. Hurricane Katrina devastated the Gulf Coast of the United States. Striking in the early morning, Hurricane Katrina initially made landfall in southeastern Louisiana before moving across Mississippi and Alabama, leaving a swath of destruction in excess of 250 miles. As a result of the storm, there were three significant separate levee breaches in New Orleans and the surrounding area, submerging up to 80% of the greater metropolitan in water as deep as twenty feet. This water did not recede completely for several weeks thereafter, and a majority of the homes and structures in Orleans Parish and the parishes surrounding it were destroyed or washed away. ...

As a result of the storm and the ensuing floods, many people, especially those in the city of New Orleans, were required to evacuate their homes, some literally swimming to safety. Most of those who, for a variety of reasons (mainly a lack of resources) failed to evacuate prior to the storm were either rescued or removed via a combination of local, state, and federal government ... officials dispatched from all [over] the country, including the National Guard. Most of these rescued citizens were placed on buses or airplanes out of New Orleans and bound for shelters, hotels, and motels in various parts of the country, with most not knowing their final destinations. Parts of the city remained flooded for weeks, and citizens were forbidden from returning by local and state officials working in connection with the federal government. Over 1,200 Americans died, with over 1,000 of these deaths in Louisiana alone, many from drowning. For those who did get out, the vast majority of their homes were destroyed or rendered uninhabitable or inaccessible as a direct result of the storm, and in some cases residential areas remained closed to homeowners for over three months.

Notably, more than 90,000 people in the affected areas had incomes of less than $10,000 per year. In Orleans Parish alone, more than 40% of children affected by Katrina lived in households with incomes below the federal poverty line.

According to the Center on Budget and Policy Priorities, of the 5.8 million individuals who lived in those states struck hardest by Katrina, over one million lived in poverty prior to the storm. In New Orleans, 28% of the city's residents were living in poverty prior to Katrina, and those who were poor commonly lacked their own means of transport. For instance, 65% of poor elderly households in New Orleans did not have a vehicle, making it more difficult for them to escape the storm and its effects. About one of every three people who lived in areas hit hardest by Katrina were African-American; in contrast, one of every eight people in the nation is African-American. More than one in three black households in New Orleans (35%), and nearly three in five poor black households (59%) lacked a vehicle.

As a result of the destruction, evacuees were dispersed to forty-five states, with more than 250,000 people ending up in shelters, most with nothing left. Others were placed by the Red Cross into its "Direct Payment Hotel/Motel Program." This program allowed evacuees with few resources to stay in hotels and motels paid for by the Red Cross until such time as evacuees were able to find more permanent housing. On October 24, 2005 the Federal Emergency Management Agency ("FEMA") took over the hotel/motel program and it became known as the "Short-Term Lodging Program." FEMA is the federal agency responsible for providing disaster victims with temporary housing assistance, either in the form of financial assistance to pay for rental housing, or a trailer or mobile home. FEMA's obligations arise pursuant to the ... Stafford Act. ...

On November 15, 2005 FEMA announced that as of the close of business on November 30, 2005, it would cease funding the Short-Term Lodging Program ... Subsequently this deadline was extended by FEMA directive to December 15, 2005, or January 7, 2006, with extensions being granted on a state-by-state basis and depending upon the number of evacuees in hotels or motels in each state. Only those ten states that were currently housing the greatest number of evacuees were eligible to apply for the January 7, 2006 extension. As of December 9,

2005, FEMA again modified this date with a letter stating that those individuals staying in hotels in any State that have yet to receive a decision on their application for individual assistance by December 9, 2005 or have been approved but not yet received that assistance, would have their current hotel subsidy extended to January 7, 2006. FEMA ... informed the Court that the states of Louisiana, Mississippi, and Texas have applied for and been granted the January 7, 2006 state extension.

Plaintiffs ... have applied for and, as of the date of filing [of this case], had failed to receive, any disaster assistance from FEMA. ...

[Temporary Housing Assistance Payments]

... [T]he Stafford Act provides: "[A]n individual or household shall not be denied assistance under paragraph (1) [Temporary Housing] ... of subsection c [Types of Housing Assistance] solely on the basis that the individual or household has not applied for or received any loan or other financial assistance from the Small Business Administration or any other Federal Agency."

Despite this provision, plaintiffs have provided declarations showing that individuals with FEMA have either misinformed or not fully informed applicants for Temporary Housing Assistance [that an SBA loan application] is only necessary if "Other Needs Assistance" (medical, dental, and the like) is required. FEMA has also not made it clear that even if Other Needs Assistance is sought, one may still receive the Temporary Housing Assistance in the meantime or without applying for an SBA loan.

Therefore ... the Court finds that FEMA has violated a mandatory duty through the mis-communication or inartful communication of the protocol for receiving Temporary Housing Assistance by causing some applicants to believe that an SBA loan application is a necessary prerequisite to receiving Temporary Housing Assistance. Thus the Court will grant plaintiffs' requested relief as to this claim ...

[Pending Applications]

With regard to the 84,470 applications still deemed "pending" almost three months after the storm, the Court is keenly aware of the immediate needs of those applicants. The Court is also keenly aware of the admonition of Congress for Courts not to unduly interfere in administrative decisions and procedures. Plaintiffs have requested that the Court order all pending applicants to be considered presumptively eligible and/or order FEMA to act on these applications on or before January 1, 2006. The Court notes that the method of proceeding with applications does involve an element of discretion on the part of FEMA ... The Stafford Act and the regulations pursuant to it are unclear as to when FEMA should be mandated to act on these pending applications. The Court is aware that this catastrophe has stretched everyone's resources, and both Congress and FEMA have made substantial efforts to increase FEMA's resources in particular. The Court will not issue an order setting forth a timetable at this point; nor will the Court declare all pending applications as presumptively eligible. However, if requested by plaintiffs, the Court will reexamine the necessity of establishing such a timetable at a later date should FEMA not make extremely substantial progress in processing these pending applications. ...

[Short Term Lodging]

FEMA's actions in reference to its subsidy of hotels and motels has been notoriously erratic and numbingly insensitive. Persons who have lost their jobs, their homes, their cars, all their worldly possessions, and in some cases, family members, have been living in hotel rooms for many months. At the hearing, plaintiff Leonora Bartley testified that she is four months pregnant, estranged from her husband, and living in San Antonio, Texas with her 8-year-old son in a FEMA-paid room at a Motel Six. Hers is one of more than at least 37,000 hotel and motel rooms that FEMA is currently subsidizing. Bartley was a nursing home rehab technician before Katrina struck, and as a result of the storm, was displaced first to Gonzales, Louisiana and eventually ended up in San Antonio because she had no luck finding a place to live in Gonzales.

When asked by the Government whether living in a tempo-
rary apartment instead of a motel wouldn't be better, Bartley
said, "Of course. I'd have a stove. I'd have a refrigerator. I
wouldn't be living out of an ice chest." Ms. Bartley further
testified that despite her own diligent efforts, including the
use of a FEMA provided 1-800 number, she has been unable
to find adequate housing (either public or private) in San
Antonio for herself and her son. Ms. Bartley's story is only
one of thousands [of] very similar stories, and these victims
have been told by FEMA that they would have to leave their
respective hotels or motels on November 30, 2005, then
December 15, 2005. They were then told that some would
have to leave on December 15, 2005 whereas others would
have until January 7, 2006. As of December 9, 2005, the
date of the hearing, FEMA provided a letter which in essence
stated that in the event an applicant had not received his or
her funds by December 15, 2005, the applicant could remain
at their hotel or motel. It is unimaginable what anxiety and
misery these erratic and bizarre vacillations by FEMA have
caused these victims, all of whom, for at least one point
in time, had the very real fear of being without shelter for
Christmas. When Michael Hirsch, Individual Assistance
Branch Chief of FEMA's Recovery Division, was asked as
to the rationale for this termination of benefits, he seemed
as bewildered as this Court and basically stated he did not
know.

It is very evident to the Court that the majority of the persons
affected by the January 7, 2006 deadline are the most disad-
vantaged of our citizens and/or the persons who lost virtu-
ally all of their property, economic livelihood, and in some
cases, family members as a result of Hurricane Katrina and
its aftermath. Congress, in enacting the Stafford Act clearly
mandated that "... relief and assistance activities shall be
accomplished in an equitable and impartial manner without
discrimination on the grounds of ... economic status." The
arbitrary January 7, 2006 termination of benefits is directly
aimed at those who have virtually no resources, economic or
otherwise. Nor is this termination equitable or impartial as
mandated by the statute. Many of the persons who already
received Temporary Housing Assistance have a place to
reside, either in their own home, the homes of friends or

relatives, or resources to afford replacement housing. The plaintiffs ... did not choose to live in hotel rooms and, by definition, [none] was homeless prior to the hurricane. Clearly the hurricane did not discriminate based on economics, as the wealthy as well as the poor were substantially affected; however those persons with resources and access have generally found alternate housing and are not living in a hotel or motel or shelter. Clearly the economic status of those in the hotels is in general far less than those victims not in hotels.

The Government has stated on at least two occasions at the hearing that citizens have come to think of every problem in the United States as a federal problem and that the federal government is responsible for them. While the Court has no empirical evidence of this statement (or that it is true), certainly in this instance, by law and mandate, the federal government is responsible. This refrain by FEMA clearly indicates an insensitivity to their Congressional mandate ...

Although FEMA made some effort to extend the deadline for all persons to January 7, 2006, this does not resolve the underlying economic discrimination. In the event a victim receives their benefits on January 6, 2006, it would be virtually impossible to find housing in one day. Moreover, according to the testimony of Ms. Bartley, without funds in hand it is impossible to find housing, and even with funds in hand, it will be extraordinarily difficult in some areas. Of course, FEMA could provide a person with a trailer and that would resolve the issue if it could be done in a timely fashion. FEMA has admitted that it cannot process all of the pending applications by January 7, 2006, and FEMA has taken the position that a Court cannot order them to do so. ... Although the Court commends FEMA for modifying its position [and delaying the cut-off], it is simply not enough. ...

[Relief]

... [1][D]efendants are hereby temporarily restrained and enjoined from requiring applicants for Temporary Housing Assistance to complete an SBA loan application or apply for an SBA loan as a prerequisite to applying for or receiving temporary housing assistance, or from inquiring into the

income of applicants in connection with processing applications for Temporary Housing Assistance, or from miscommunicating the nature of [the Stafford Act requirement] to any Applicant so inquiring.

[2] It is further ordered that defendants must notify those applicants who, as a result of any past mis-communication, filled out an unnecessary SBA loan application, or may not have pursued assistance because they were told that an applicant must apply for a SBA loan in order to obtain temporary housing assistance. Defendants must notify applicants and potential applicants that no such requirement exists and that no applications will be held up for Temporary Housing Assistance processing due to an SBA Loan application not being filled out, or being filled out incorrectly, unnecessarily, and/or superfluously. Defendants must publicize the rule that only those applications requesting Other Needs Assistance as defined by the Stafford Act and determined by FEMA will be required to fill out an SBA Loan Application, and in no cases will such a Loan Application be required for Temporary Housing Assistance.

[3] It is also ordered that ... defendants are hereby temporarily restrained and enjoined from terminating the Short-Term Lodging Program as to any person in any state earlier than January 7, 2006 even if that person receives Temporary Housing Assistance ... or a denial of their Application prior to that time.

[4] It is further ordered that the Short-Term Lodging Program shall terminate no later than February 7, 2006 unless ordered by this Court or if FEMA chooses to extend the deadline established by this Court.

[5] It is further ordered that every evacuee currently participating in the Short-Term Lodging program shall have two (2) weeks from the time of receiving a determination of their application for Assistance, namely either (a) approval for and receipt of Assistance, or (b) a denial determination, to remain in their present FEMA-subsidized hotel or motel before their participation in the Short-Term Lodging program is terminated ...

McWaters v. FEMA II
U.S. District Court for the Eastern District of Louisiana, 2006

[Plaintiffs returned to court asserting, among other claims, that FEMA still had failed to provide the Temporary Housing Assistance for which they are eligible.]

... FEMA admits that all persons meeting the [statutory] eligibility criteria ... are entitled to assistance, and all of them will receive it. In fact, most cases are automatically determined eligible or ineligible by the [agency's] computer system, requiring no human intervention or approval, such that eligible applicants essentially "automatically qualify" for assistance and are then automatically paid via either computer generated check or an electronic funds transfer. Furthermore, [FEMA makes no claim that it] has insufficient resources to provide assistance to all eligible applicants ... As such the Court finds that the mandatory and non-discretionary policies and regulations under the Stafford Act which require FEMA to automatically provide assistance to all applicants deemed eligible creates a reasonable expectation of the benefit of federal disaster assistance in these applicants, and this expectation rises to the level of a property interest protectable under the Due Process Clause. ...

However, despite FEMA's lack of discretion in providing Temporary Housing Assistance, as well as the seemingly interminable delays in provision of such assistance, and despite the fact that a protected interest under the Due Process Clause in receiving such assistance exists in recipients, ... [e]vidence adduced throughout the course of this litigation reveals that FEMA was definitely unprepared to quickly and efficiently deal with the multitude of applications for temporary housing assistance stemming from Hurricane Katrina. ... [D]espite FEMA's lack of preparation, and regardless of the property interest implicated, having heard all of the evidence presented, the Court must find that the delay faced by FEMA in processing the voluminous number of Katrina-related housing applications was inevitable due to the sheer practicalities of the circumstances wrought by the aftermath of the storm. ... FEMA did and is taking action, albeit at a rather excruciatingly slow place. Accordingly, ... the Court finds no actionable violation of the constitutional standard applicable to this claim ...

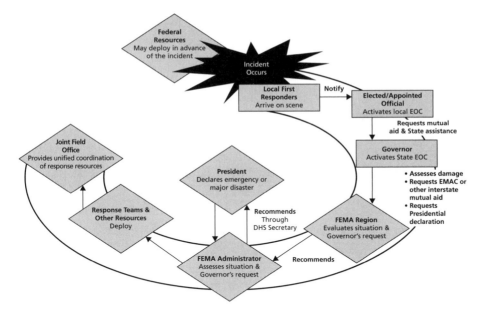

FIGURE 9.2 The Stafford Act Process
Source: U.S. Department of Homeland Security

■ ■ Critical Thinking ■

The *McWaters* lawsuit illustrates how courts can come to the aid of those who are treated badly by disaster relief agencies. What other institutional reactions – other than litigation – are possible? Which do you think would be most effective? Why?

Public Assistance

First, be sure not to confuse "public assistance" in this portion of the Stafford Act with traditional welfare programs. Here, public assistance refers to programs to help state and local government agencies and some nonprofits. (Local governments include Indian tribes.) The goal is to assist with the repair, restoration, reconstruction, or replacement of facilities that provide goods or services to the public. If the entity is a private (nongovernment) nonprofit organization, it is eligible only if it provides essential, government-type services and is open to the general public without exception. As with individual and household benefits, aid will be provided only for damages not covered by insurance.

FEMA relies primarily on three factors to determine eligibility and grant amounts under this portion of the Stafford Act:

- Whether the organization is eligible for relief
- Whether the proposed action is eligible
- Whether the costs incurred were reasonable

As you will see from the following two examples, agency officials have wide latitude to certify which expenses in the Public Assistance category qualify for reimbursement.

California-Nevada Methodist Homes, Inc. v. FEMA
U.S. District Court for the Northern District of California, 2001

> *... Plaintiff is a non-profit organization that owns and operates Lake Park, a retirement community in Oakland. Lake Park is a 12-story L-shaped building, divided into two wings. One floor on one of the wings contains a skilled-nursing facility, which provides 24-hour nursing care to residents who require assisted living. In 1989, Lake Park was damaged in the Loma Prieta earthquake. Plaintiff subsequently sought disaster-relief funds. [Figures 9.3 and 9.4 show the location and impact of the Loma Prieta earthquake.]*

> *The Stafford Act and FEMA's regulations establish different regimes for the provision of federal relief to victims of natural disasters. In general, the Act and accompanying regulations define who is eligible to obtain aid from FEMA and what types of costs are eligible for recovery. Under the regime at issue here, the Public Assistance Project, once the president declares an area to be a "major disaster," victims of the disaster can apply for federal assistance through a state agency (the Governor's Office of Emergency Services in California), which forwards the request to FEMA. Either a FEMA inspector, state representatives, or both then prepare a project worksheet for each discrete project for which the applicant (subgrantee) seeks funding. The project worksheet must specify the damage caused by the disaster and "must identify the eligible scope of work and must include a quantitative estimate for the eligible work." Before FEMA obligates any funds to the state agency (grantee), FEMA must approve the final project worksheet ...*

> *Pursuant to this regime, between 1989 and 1996, FEMA granted plaintiff more than $10 million. On July 10, 1997, however, FEMA refused to approve an additional $573,364 in relief that plaintiff requested. This money, plaintiff claimed, was necessary to construct separate utilities for the skilled-nursing*

facility. According to plaintiff, state authorities mandated the construction of separate utilities, because this was required by the California Building Code. FEMA regulations, plaintiff argues, define eligible costs to include costs necessary to meet code standards in effect as of the date of the disaster. Even though the Building Code at the time of the earthquake required separate utilities, plaintiff contends, because plaintiff's skilled-nursing facility was built under an older, less-stringent version of the building code, it shared common utilities with the rest of the building.

... FEMA denied plaintiff's request to fund the utility work ... because [according to FEMA] the work was required "as a result of the subgrantee's failure to plan for and schedule required inspections. Because this work was not required as a direct result of the disaster or by an applicable code, it is not eligible for "funding." ...

... Section 5172 of the Stafford Act provides that the President "may make contributions" to eligible entities, such as plaintiff. The "Grant Approval" section of FEMA's regulations pertaining to the Public Assistance Project does not contain any requirement that FEMA approve eligible costs or any standard for their approval. No regulation under the Public Assistance Project requires FEMA to approve any funding request. Rather, these regulations simply refer to costs that are "eligible," i.e., expenses that FEMA could choose to pay. Whether to approve requests for eligible costs is a matter of agency discretion ...

Although it is not reported in a published decision, former FEMA General Counsel Ernest Abbott has described a case arising from Tropical Storm Allison in 2001, when the Texas Medical Center (TMC) electricity plant was flooded. The plant had previously been part of TMC's organizational structure, but to facilitate joint financing of expansion projects, TMC had transferred the plant to a separate nonprofit corporation, which supplied electricity to a number of nonprofit hospitals in the area. Although the plant was a nonprofit corporation and it sold electricity only to other nonprofit entities, it did not serve the general public. As a result, FEMA decided that repairs to the plant were ineligible for reimbursement with Stafford Act funds (Abbott, 2005).

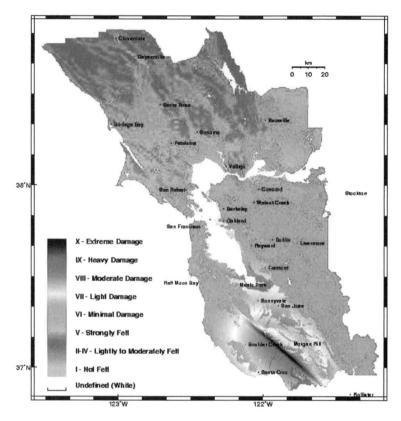

FIGURE 9.3 Geological Map of Damage Caused by Loma Prieta Earthquake
Source: http://quake.usgs.gov/research/strongmotion/intensity/1989.html

FIGURE 9.4 Aftermath of the Loma Prieta Earthquake
Source: http://pubs.usgs.gov/dds/dds-29/

Important Terms

- Disaster unemployment assistance
- Emergency
- Major disaster
- Public assistance
- Short-term lodging
- Temporary housing assistance

Review Questions

1. What are the essential elements of the content of a Stafford Act declaration?
2. How do the procedures required under the Stafford Act illustrate the dynamics of federalism?
3. The incident that gave rise to the *State of Kansas v. United States* case was an explosion that left more than 600 people out of work. The lawsuit did not directly challenge the decision that this did not qualify as a major disaster, nor could it have – that decision was clearly within the discretion of officials. But imagine that you were a FEMA staffer responsible for recommending whether it should qualify as a disaster. What factors would you consider? How would you set minimal levels for what would qualify?
4. The judge in the *McWaters* case wrestled with whether and when he should issue orders directing how FEMA should conduct its relief efforts after Hurricane Katrina. The case is a good example of how courts and agencies play different roles in the process of creating law. How would you evaluate the way in which a court acted as a check and balance against improper government action in that case?

10

The Powers of State and Local Governments

What You Will Learn

- The legal frameworks for how state and local governments respond to emergencies and disasters (other than public health emergencies, covered in Chapter 6)
- The role of structural constitutional issues, such as separation of powers, at the state level
- The division of authority between states and localities
- How a state emergency management agency is organized

Introduction

In Chapter 1, we analyzed some of the fundamental aspects of how the Constitution structures American government, including the principle of separation of powers between the three branches of government and the principle of federalism, under which states retain a substantial measure of sovereignty. The fact that divided powers and federalism are built into government provides checks and balances against the risk that excessive power will be concentrated in one location. Emergencies pose some of the biggest challenges to this protection.

A similar dynamic operates within each state government. Each state has its own constitution, and there is significant variance in details among these 50 charters of government. Although the exact text varies, however, each state constitution also separates powers among the three branches. As we will see from the cases below, the pressure to expand the authority of the executive – i.e. the governor – is enhanced during emergencies at the state level as well. Moreover, although local units of government within a state do not retain the same level of authority that the states do within the United States, there is usually some degree of local independence of action. State statutes set the parameters for the scope of state versus local power.

STATE AND LOCAL VIEWPOINTS

*In times of natural catastrophe or civil disorder, imme-
diate and decisive action by some component of state
government is essential. The legislative ... power can of
course be exercised ... In practice, however, the ravages of
nature ... usually necessitate prompt governmental response.
Since the executive is inherently better able than the legislature to provide this immediate response, state chief execu-
tives have frequently been given substantial discretionary
authority in the form of emergency powers to deal with
anticipated crises. Consequently, when public emergencies
arise, the center of governmental response is usually the
governor's office.*

Cougar Business Owners Ass'n v. State (1982)

Even though Grand Forks [North Dakota] had experienced periodic flooding of the Red River of the North, the
City Attorney's office had only minimal involvement with
prior flood activities. All of that changed in April of 1997.
Following a fierce winter which thrust eight blizzards upon
the community, including a severe ice storm and blizzard
during the first week of April, while flood fighting efforts
were well under way, the Red River continued to rise past
its predicted crest of 49 feet. [It] ultimately crested at 54.11
feet, but not until its flood waters had rendered the municipal water treatment plant inoperable, breached dikes and
flood walls, flooded thousands of homes, destroyed businesses and memories alike, and caused the evacuation of virtually the entire population of two sister communities, East
Grand Forks, Minnesota, and Grand Forks, North Dakota,
having a combined population of approximately 60,000
residents. As if the destruction of the flood was not enough,
the downtown business district in Grand Forks lost eleven
buildings to a major fire ...

... [T]he realization of the need for city attorney involvement
and coordination in disaster planning and response became
painfully obvious. Like most city attorneys, I was aware of
an ordinance contained within the city code that authorized
certain emergency powers, and I was generally aware of the

State's emergency and disaster statutes. Not having had a prior reason to rely upon them, my knowledge was limited at best. The delicate art of practicing municipal law under conditions of hell and high water became reality.

Swanson (2000)

Separation of Powers in an Emergency: The Governor and the Legislature

Worthingon v. Fauver
Supreme Court of New Jersey, 1982

To alleviate the potentially disastrous overcrowding of inmates in state and county correctional institutions, the Governor issued Executive Order No. 106 on June 19, 1981. In promulgating the order, the Governor invoked his emergency powers under the ... Disaster Control Act. This temporary emergency measure granted to the Commissioner of Corrections the authority to direct that county correctional facilities house prisoners sentenced to state institutions. The Commissioner was also given the power to redistribute such prisoners among the county facilities.

Atlantic County challenges the statutory and constitutional validity of this emergency measure. We hold that the Governor's Order is authorized by the Disaster Control Act and does not violate the constitutional principle of separation of powers.

I

It is commonly acknowledged that overcrowding in prisons causes grave problems. Rehabilitative programs and recreation become disrupted or nonexistent. As crowding increases, frustration and anger emerge, causing tempers to flare and fights to erupt. Lack of space makes it difficult if not impossible to segregate prisoners for disciplinary and other purposes. Overcrowding can contribute to riots.

According to the Commissioner of Corrections, prison over-crowding first became a serious problem in New Jersey in 1975. Although ameliorated somewhat from 1978 to 1980, the problem lately has reached crisis dimensions. This has been caused in large part by an increase in the number and length of custodial sentences. ...

At the time this suit was filed, the state prison population was well in excess of the system's capacity. This necessitated housing approximately 480 offenders sentenced to state prison in county facilities because the overcrowded state institutions were physically unable to receive them. This in turn has created overcrowding in many county jails. ...

... Declaring overcrowding in state prisons to be an emergency, the [Executive] Order explained that the Department of Corrections "is physically unable to accept from the Sheriffs of the various counties the custody of inmates sentenced to the custody of the Commissioner of the Department of Corrections, as mandated by [New Jersey statute]." The Governor invoked the emergency powers of the Disaster Control Act on the grounds that

"these unusual conditions endanger the safety, welfare and resources of the residents of this State, and threaten loss to and destruction of property, and are too large in scope to be handled entirely by regular operating services of either the counties or the New Jersey Department of Corrections."

Because of the "need to efficiently allocate inmates of state and county penal and correctional institutions to those institutions having available space in order to alleviate overcrowding," the Order designated the Commissioner of Corrections as the sole authority empowered to allocate inmates among the various county facilities, and when possible, to move those prisoners to state institutions. ...

II

... [W]e initially decide whether the Governor has the statutory power to issue [the executive order]. This involves a

determination as to (1) whether the current crisis constitutes an emergency within the meaning of the Disaster Control Act, and (2) whether the means chosen by the Governor to address the emergency are authorized by the statute.

A

The challenged executive orders rely on the authority of the Disaster Control Act ... The purpose of the act and the broad powers conferred on the Governor are clearly stated in [the New Jersey Code]:

The purpose of this act is to provide for the health, safety and welfare of the people of the State of New Jersey and to aid in the prevention of damage to and the destruction of property during any emergency as herein defined by prescribing a course of conduct for the civilian population of this State during such emergency and by centralizing control of all civilian activities having to do with such emergency under the Governor and for that purpose to give to the Governor control over such resources of the State Government and of each and every political subdivision thereof as may be necessary to cope with any condition that shall arise out of such emergency and to invest the Governor with all other power convenient or necessary to effectuate such purpose.

The Governor's ample powers are further elaborated ...

The Governor is authorized to utilize and employ all the available resources of the State Government and of each and every political subdivision of this State, whether of men, properties or instrumentalities, and to commandeer and utilize any personal services and any privately owned property necessary to avoid or protect against any emergency subject to the future payment of the reasonable value of such services and privately owned property as hereinafter in this act provided.

Finally, the scope of the Governor's authority to issue emergency orders is defined ...:

In order to accomplish the purposes of this act, the Governor is empowered to make such orders, rules and regulations as may be necessary adequately to meet the various problems *presented by any emergency and from time to time to amend or rescind such orders, rules and regulations, including among other[s] the following subjects:*

i. On any matter that may be necessary to protect the health, safety and welfare of the people or that will aid in the prevention of loss to and destruction of property.

j. Such other matters whatsoever as are or may become necessary in the fair, impartial, stringent and comprehensive administration of this act.

These sweeping provisions reveal three general, pertinent features of the act. First, the act vests the Governor with broad powers to provide for the health, safety and welfare of the people of the State during any "emergency." Second, these powers include the authority to centralize control over the resources of the State government and its subdivisions, including the counties, "whether of men, properties or instrumentalities." Third, a significant purpose of the act is the prevention of harm to life and property.

B

We now address whether the current prison overcrowding in New Jersey constitutes an "emergency" within the meaning of the Disaster Control Act. Section 33.1 of the act defines "emergency" and "disaster" as used in the statute.

(1) "Disaster" shall mean any unusual incident resulting from natural or unnatural causes which endangers the health, safety or resources of the residents of one or more municipalities of the State, and which is or may become too large in scope or unusual in type to be handled in its entirety by regular municipal operating services.

(4) "Emergency" shall mean and include "disaster" and "war emergency" as above in this section defined.

Plaintiffs argue that prison overcrowding is not an "unusual incident." It is not "unusual" because it has been recognized as a major problem as early as 1977. It is also not an "incident" because it is not a sudden or unforeseen event.

We reject this overly narrow interpretation of the scope of the act. Any grant of executive authority must be construed to accomplish the Legislature's purpose. This is especially true when those statutes operate to protect the public health, safety and welfare, especially during emergencies. ... [T]he Disaster Control Act ... has permitted the Governor to handle a wide variety of crises, including storms, energy shortages, labor strikes, factory explosions, and water shortages.

The Disaster Control Act must be understood in light of its purposes. It sought to protect the public by centralizing control over local government resources in situations whose remedies were beyond the authority and power of local government. A crisis can arise because of a failure to take action. Thus, it is not a necessary component of an "emergency" that it be sudden or unforeseen. Prison overcrowding is closely analogous to the recent water shortages, which arose over time and which were appropriately ameliorated by an emergency executive order. The question is not whether the incident emerged suddenly, but whether the scope of the present crisis prevents local governments from safeguarding the people, property and resources of the State. ...

Recent disruptions in prisons across the country graphically illustrate the destructive potential inherent in prison overcrowding. They entail substantial loss of property and often loss of life. The record below demonstrates that our state and county facilities may be dangerously close to producing such a disaster. The prevention of such an occurrence is clearly a proper subject of executive emergency action under the statute. ...

There is sufficient evidence in the record to sustain a finding that the problem of prison overcrowding in New Jersey has reached dangerous proportions, and that there is a substantial likelihood of a disastrous occurrence in the immediate future. We therefore hold that the current crisis of prison overcrowding is an "emergency" under the Disaster Control Act and is a proper subject of emergency executive action. We now consider whether the measures taken by the Governor to alleviate that crisis are authorized by the statute.

C

In reviewing executive actions undertaken pursuant to delegated emergency powers, we must determine whether the actions are authorized by the statute. This involves, first, a determination of whether the Executive Order bears a rational relationship to the legislative goal of protecting the public. Second, the executive action must be closely tailored to the scope of the current emergency situation. The nature of the (statutory) power determines what may be done and the nature of the emergency restricts the how of its doing, i.e., the means of execution.

The executive orders in question empower the Commissioner of Corrections to allocate state prisoners to county correctional facilities and to redistribute such prisoners among the counties. These remedial measures are specifically authorized by the Disaster Control Act. The act gives the Governor emergency power to issue orders and centralize control over the resources of the political subdivisions of the State government. It further authorizes him "to utilize and employ all the available resources of the State Government and of each and every political subdivision of this State, whether of men, properties or instrumentalities." County jails are certainly "resources" of "political subdivisions" of the State within the meaning of the act. The plain language of the statute clearly authorizes the Executive Orders issued in the current emergency. ...

D

We next consider whether the measures prescribed by these orders are rationally related to the legitimate governmental interest in protecting the public and whether they are closely tailored to the magnitude of the current emergency.

There can be no question that centralization of power to allocate prisoners among the various state and county facilities is a rational means of alleviating the problem of overcrowding in our prisons. Since it is undisputed that some county jails have significant excess capacity, it is rational to empower the Commissioner to make use of those facilities to relieve the overburdened prisons. Thus, the measures imposed by the executive orders are clearly related to the statutory ends of protecting life and property.

We must determine, therefore, whether the executive orders are tailored to the magnitude of the current crisis. While the Disaster Control Act grants broad authority to the Governor to deal with an emergency, his powers under that statute are not without limit. These emergency powers represent an extraordinary delegation of authority by the Legislature to the Executive. Because of the extraordinary nature of that authority, the executive orders must not only bear a rational relationship to the goal of protecting the public, but their scope must not exceed the extent of the emergency. The statutory validity of executive actions pursuant to emergency power will depend on the nature of the emergency and the gravity of the threat to the public. Thus, a more serious emergency may justify greater responsive measures. ...

[Here, as] the threat of damage is extensive and the exercise of emergency power rather limited, it can hardly be disputed that the measures authorized by the executive orders are properly tailored to the magnitude of the current emergency. ...

IV

The final issue is whether the executive orders violate the constitutional principle of separation of powers under the State Constitution. This involves consideration of (1) whether the orders represent a usurpation of legislative power by the executive branch; (2) whether the enabling legislation represents an unconstitutional delegation of legislative power to the executive; and (3) whether the legislative delegation of power or the executive implementation of the orders impermissibly encroaches on the proper sphere of the judiciary. ...

The purpose of the constitutional separation of powers is to prevent oppressive action by the government. Its premise is that the concentration of unlimited power inevitably results in tyranny. Separation serves to maintain the balance between the three branches of government, preserve their respective independence and integrity, and prevent the concentration of unchecked power in the hands of any one branch. The doctrine thus represents a fundamental and indispensable bulwark against despotism.

The purpose of the doctrine is to restrain public power, not to restrict the legitimate operation of representative democracy. Rigid classification of the duties and powers of each branch is therefore neither possible nor desirable. ... [T]he delegated authority [under the Disaster Control Act] includes the power to utilize the available resources of the counties. Thus, the executive action is not in derogation of the authority of the Legislature. ...

In this case, the Legislature has specifically delegated the authority to the Governor to utilize the resources of the counties to protect the public in emergencies. The Legislature retains the power to amend the Disaster Control Act to take away executive power to utilize the county jails in the current crisis. It may also enact legislative solutions to the current problem. Because the Legislature has not relinquished this corrective power, there is no reason to believe that the executive orders have impaired its essential functions. ...

■ ■ Critical Thinking ■

How is the delegation of legislative power related to the separation of powers principle?

At one point, the court finds that the prison overcrowding problem presents "a substantial likelihood of a disastrous occurrence in the immediate future." Do you agree that the facts as described in the opinion satisfy that standard? Even if they arguably do not, why might the court apply a lenient standard of review? Does the statutory language permit this approach?

Separation of Powers in an Emergency: The Governor and the Courts

The National Tax-Limitation Committee v. Schwarzenegger
California Court of Appeal, 2003

... Under the California Emergency Services Act, the Governor is empowered to proclaim a state of emergency when he finds that certain conditions exist. The [California Emergency Services] Act further provides: "The Governor shall proclaim the termination of a state of emergency at the earliest possible

date that conditions warrant. All of the powers granted the Governor by this chapter with respect to a state of emergency shall terminate when the state of emergency has been terminated by proclamation of the Governor or by concurrent resolution of the Legislature declaring it at an end."

On January 17, 2001, pursuant to his powers under the Act, former Governor [Gray] Davis proclaimed a state of emergency to exist based on the following findings:

"[S]hortages of electricity available to California's utilities have today resulted in blackouts affecting millions of Californians; and

"[U]nanticipated and dramatic increases in the price of electricity have threatened the solvency of California's major public utilities, preventing them from continuing to acquire and provide electricity sufficient to meet California's energy needs; and

"[T]he California Public Utilities Commission, the Independent Systems Operator and the Electricity Oversight Board have advised that the electricity presently available from California[']s utilities is insufficient to prevent widespread and prolonged disruption of electric service within California; and

"[T]his energy shortage requires extraordinary measures beyond the authority vested in the California Public Utilities Commission; and

"[T]he imminent threat of widespread and prolonged disruption of electrical power to California's emergency services, law enforcement, schools, hospitals, homes, businesses and agriculture constitutes a condition of extreme peril to the safety of persons and property within the state which, by reason of its magnitude, is likely to be beyond the control of the services, personnel, equipment, and facilities of any single county or city; ..."

In an exercise of his emergency powers, former Governor Davis then ordered the Department of Water Resources (the Department) to "enter into contracts and arrangements for the purchase and sale of electric power with public and private entities and individuals as may be necessary to assist in mitigating the effects of this emergency." In connection with this order, the Governor suspended "the provisions of the Government Code and the Public Contract Code applicable to state contracts, including but not limited to, advertising and competitive bidding requirements."

On June 13, 2002, [Lewis] Uhler, the president of The National Tax-Limitation Committee, wrote to the Governor and asked that he "proclaim the termination of [his] emergency powers immediately" because "[t]he energy crisis has long since subsided." The Governor refused to do so.

Accordingly, on October 9, 2002, plaintiffs filed a petition for a writ of mandate against the Governor and the

■ ■ ■ ▬▬▬▬▬▬▬▬▬▬▬▬▬▬▬▬▬▬▬

A writ of mandate or mandamus is a court order issued to a government official directing him to take action required by law, but which he has failed or refused to do.

▬▬▬▬▬▬▬▬▬▬▬▬▬▬▬▬▬▬▬ ■ ■ ■

Department, alleging that "California is no longer in the midst of a 'power crisis' and [the Governor] is mandated to terminate his emergency powers, relating thereto, as a matter of law." Plaintiffs requested a writ of mandate "requiring [the Governor] to terminate his declaration of an energy emergency and the exercise of all powers flowing therefrom, including, but not limited to, the purchase of electricity or the negotiation of contracts therefore."

The Governor ... [argued that] the Act provides for termination of a state of emergency only by the Governor or the Legislature, and therefore the court was barred by the separation of powers doctrine from granting the requested relief. The trial court agreed, stating that "this is not the type of case that is appropriate for judicial review. ... [¶] ... [I]t is ... a legislative [decision] or a decision of the Governor as to ... whether or not there is still an emergency situation due to an energy shortage." ...

The California Emergency Services Act recognizes and responds to a fundamental role of government to provide broad state services in the event of emergencies resulting from conditions of disaster or of extreme peril to life, property, and the resources of the state. Its purpose is to protect and preserve health, safety, life, and property. A state of emergency may be proclaimed by the Governor under the conditions prescribed for any area affected. The act confers broad powers on the Governor to deal with emergencies.

For example, during a state of emergency, the Governor may suspend any regulatory statute or statute prescribing the procedure for conduct of state business, or suspend the orders, rules or regulations of any state agency, if these would prevent, hinder or delay the mitigation of the effects of the emergency. The Governor may command or utilize private property or personnel deemed by him necessary in carrying out his responsibilities, paying for its reasonable value. ... The state is not liable for any claim based upon discretionary functions. The Governor is empowered to make expenditure from any fund legally available to deal with the conditions of a state of emergency. ...

... [T]he Governor has the power to proclaim a state of emergency when he finds: (1) that a rapid, unforeseen shortage of energy has caused the existence of conditions of disaster or of extreme peril to the safety of persons and property within the state; (2) that the energy shortage requires extraordinary measures beyond the authority vested in the California Public Utilities Commission; and (3) that local authority is inadequate to cope with the emergency. ...

It follows, as a matter of parity, that the Governor likewise is entitled to exercise his discretion in later determining whether and when "conditions warrant" termination of the state of emergency – for example, because one or more of the conditions prerequisite to declaring the state of emergency in the first place has ceased to exist. In other words, the Governor's duty to terminate a proclaimed state of emergency arises only when the Governor has determined that "conditions warrant" termination of the state of emergency. That foundational determination is committed to the sound discretion and judgment of the Governor under the Act.

Arguing that "mandamus cannot lie to control an exercise of discretion, i.e., to compel an official to exercise discretion in a particular manner," the Governor contends his "authority to declare the ... end of a state of emergency" cannot be controlled by a writ of mandate because he [alone] has the discretion to determine when conditions warrant termination of the state of emergency. ...

[The discretion is broad, but not limitless. To successfully challenge its exercise, plaintiff] must show the official acted arbitrarily, beyond the bounds of reason or in derogation of the applicable legal standards. Where only one choice can be a reasonable exercise of discretion, a court may compel an official to make that choice.

It follows ... that while the Governor may have no ... duty to terminate a state of emergency until he determines, in the exercise of his discretion, that conditions warrant such an action, mandamus will lie to correct an abuse of discretion by the Governor in making that foundational determination. If, under the facts, the only choice that would be a reasonable exercise of the Governor's discretion would be to determine that conditions warrant termination of the state of emergency, then a writ of mandate can compel him to make that choice. ...

Under the foregoing analysis, the question here is whether, based on the facts plaintiffs alleged in their petition, the only reasonable choice before the Governor was to determine that conditions warrant terminating the state of emergency. We conclude the answer to that question is "yes." ...

This statute provides immunity from tort liability; it does not "immunize" the Governor from a writ of mandate properly issued to compel him to correct an abuse of his discretion under the Act. ...

■ ■ ■ ▬▬▬▬▬▬▬▬▬▬▬▬▬▬▬▬▬▬▬▬▬▬▬▬

Tort is the body of law that establishes the principles under which a person may recover damages for having suffered harm, whether caused intentionally or by negligence.

▬▬▬▬▬▬▬▬▬▬▬▬▬▬▬▬▬▬▬▬▬▬▬▬ ■ ■ ■

Thus, while the Governor could not be sued for [monetary] damages alleged to have resulted from his discretionary decision not to terminate the state of emergency, it does not follow that his decision cannot be reviewed for abuse of discretion under the court's traditional power to issue writs of mandate. Accordingly, the Governor's immunity argument fails. ...

■ ■ Critical Thinking ■

The *Schwarzenegger* case illustrates that courts, as well as legislatures, have a role to play in containing the expansive scope of a governor's powers during a state of emergency. If the state legislature believed that this decision gave the courts too much power, what options would the legislature have to redress the balance?

State Government v. Local Government in an Emergency

State of Missouri v. Pruneau
Missouri Court of Appeals, 1983

> *... The facts and legal history of this case are unusual, to say the least, and raise serious questions as to who has the authority and responsibility to take lawful emergency measures, including commandeering, seizing, and using property not their own, to alleviate the effects of disasters, either natural or man-made.*
>
> *On December 4, 1982, Kenneth J. Rothman, Acting Governor of Missouri, [issued Executive Order 82-23, which] declared Wayne, Bollinger and Butler counties to be disaster areas by reason of heavy rainfall followed by severe flooding. The order recited that the safety and welfare of the citizens of those counties required an invocation of ... the powers of the governor during an emergency, the definition of which term includes a natural disaster, such as a flood of major proportions. Those emergency powers include the right, during the period that the state of emergency exists or continues, to "seize, take or requisition to the extent necessary to bring about the most effective protection of the public" certain things, such as communications systems, fuel, and facilities for housing, feeding, and hospitalization of the people. The statute also authorizes the governor to enforce and put into operation any plan relating to disasters, to assume direct operational control of all emergency forces and volunteers, and to take action and give direction to state and local agencies as*

"may be reasonable and necessary for the purpose of securing compliance with the provisions of this law and with the orders, rules and regulations made pursuant thereof."

Executive order 82-23 went on to authorize that the approved "Missouri Comprehensive Emergency Preparedness and Disaster Relief Plan" be activated, and authorized the use of "such agencies, personnel and equipment of the State as may be necessary for the preservation of life, property and the restoration of public facilities in those counties." It also specifically authorized and ordered several state agencies, including the [Missouri Highway and Transportation] Commission, to utilize the personnel and equipment of their agencies "in support of local government as may be deemed appropriate under the circumstances" during the period the order was in effect ...

On December 10, 1982, Wayne County ..., filed a petition in the Circuit Court of Wayne County asking for relief consisting of a court order in the nature of mandamus directing nine defendants, who were members or employees of the Commission "for their cooperation and for the loan of 3 motor graders, 3 dump trucks, and 1 front end loader, together with their operators, for utilization by plaintiff for the ensuing five-day period or until further Order of this Court, and for such other and further relief as the Court deems proper and just in the circumstances." The petition recited that the state of Missouri owned, and that the Commission operated, certain equipment for the use and benefit of the people of Missouri, and that a part of that equipment, including motor graders, dump trucks and front end loaders, and operators for the same, were in Wayne County. It further recited that because of the flood, much of the county-maintained road system was unusable, and that Wayne County did not have the equipment and personnel to repair the roads for evacuation and rescue purposes, and to permit the Wayne County residents served by the roads to travel them to obtain food, water, and other supplies. The petition stated that "Plaintiffs have requested assistance through the District Engineer, who has responsibility for the Wayne County area regarding defendants' equipment, but defendants, through their District Engineer, have failed and refused and continue to fail and refuse to provide said equipment [the motor graders, dump trucks, and front end loaders] and operators, in violation of law." The petition did not state what law defendants were violating, and did not state what … duty defendants had, if any, to furnish the demanded equipment and operators to Wayne County or its county court. The petition closed by stating the county had no adequate remedy at law except the requested court order, and that it needed the equipment and operators "for the purposes of emergency repairs of public and county roadways and thoroughfares, as to plaintiff seems necessary in its discretion."

The filing of the petition triggered a series of events which, in retrospect, seem incredible. On the same day that the petition was filed, before service was obtained upon defendants, and without notice to them, Judge Pruneau … ordered the defendants, upon receipt of the writ and petition, to provide County Judge Boyer, as the chief executive officer of Wayne County, with three motor graders, three dump trucks, one front end loader and competent operators for the equipment, for utilization by Wayne County "untill [sic] further Order of a Court of competent jurisdiction is entered disolving [sic] this Order or until a peremptory Writ of Mandamus may be entered after a hearing to resolve the issues which affect the rights of all parties." …

On Saturday, December 11, armed with the order, Boyer, Bearden, and an accompanying entourage of deputy sheriffs, newsmen, and county employees, without notice to any of the defendants, proceeded to two storage sheds north of Piedmont, Missouri, entered the buildings by means of acts that would constitute felonies if not committed under legal authority (breaking latches of locked doors), and removed two motor graders, two dump trucks, and a front end loader, the property of the Commission, from the sheds. Boyer, Bearden, and their associates evidently used the equipment that day in repairing county roads, and returned it to the sheds that evening. During the night, Commission employees removed the equipment from the county, fearing a repetition of the incident. …

The only real question here is whether the trial judge had jurisdiction to issue the preliminary order and peremptory writ of mandamus, under which the members of the county court claimed authority to commandeer, seize and use property which did not belong to Wayne County. ...

Seizure of property by the government, or any political subdivision thereof, has always been looked upon with deep suspicion by our people, and, in fact, is constitutionally prohibited, unless done under the auspices of due process of law.

Respondents claim that they were justified in taking the Commission's property for their own use because such action was necessary, due to the existence of an emergency. This argument has been used down through the history of mankind to justify every sovereign act which in the bright light of reason and calm debate might be said to be excessive or repressive. Such sovereign acts have included the imposition of martial law, establishment of curfews, and suspension of the writ of habeas corpus, but never have any of such acts been justified in this country, after the establishment of the constitutional guarantees of due process, unless such acts are specifically authorized by the constitution and laws of the sovereign state.

The general assembly of Missouri, recognizing that there must be a coordinated effort to cope with natural and man-made disasters, passed into law the Civil Defense Act. As a part of this act, the governor, as the chief executive officer of the state, has general direction and authority over disaster control operations and may assume direct control over all or part of a disaster response if local capabilities are exhausted. He is generally authorized to direct the cooperation of state agencies and officials and local political subdivisions in performing emergency functions. Under specified conditions, the governor or the legislature may declare the existence of a state of emergency. In the event that he does so, the governor, under emergency powers granted him by law, may, as mentioned earlier, put emergency response plans into operation, control emergency forces and operations, and seize certain types of property. No such power is given to a political subdivision such as Wayne County. The powers of political subdivisions ... do not include the right to seize the property of others for their own use. The provision that political subdivisions may "expend funds, make contracts, obtain and distribute equipment, materials, and supplies for civil defense purposes" may not possibly be construed as an authorization to seize property.

Furthermore, the contention ... that because a state of emergency existed, ... the county was entitled to the equipment in question on demand ... is not supported by either law or logic. No right is given a county to commandeer the Commission's employees and equipment for use in repairing the county roads. There is nothing in the statute relied on which could even be remotely construed to justify the seizing and use of Commission property by Wayne County officials on the basis of a unilateral decision by the county court that such action was "necessary." The statute in question directs the officers and personnel of all state agencies to cooperate with and extend their services and facilities regardless of their usual functions and services "to the governor and to the disaster organizations of the state upon request." It alters neither the discretionary evaluation of the emergency situation to be made by the governor or his designated agents under the guidelines of the regulations heretofore referred to, nor the need for a specific directive to be given to the appropriate state agency as to the extent of aid to be given to political subdivisions. Local government is authorized to utilize the services, equipment and supplies of the agency so directed to combat the emergency, but there is nothing in the statute that permits, even by implication, a political subdivision to commandeer and use property as was done here. ...

STATUTORY GRANT OF MUNICIPAL AUTHORITY

Despite the facts of *Pruneau*, most local government officials don't resort to weekend raids to respond to emergencies. The special powers that municipalities have during emergencies are usually specified in state statutes. For example, the North Carolina state code provides in § 14-288.12:

(a) The governing body of any municipality may enact ordinances designed to permit the imposition of prohibitions and restrictions during a state of emergency.

(b) The ordinances authorized by this section may permit prohibitions and restrictions:

(1) Of movements of people in public places;

(2) Of the operation of offices, business establishments, and other places to or from which people may travel or at which they may congregate;

(3) Upon the possession, transportation, sale, purchase, and consumption of alcoholic beverages;

(4) Upon the possession, transportation, sale, purchase, storage, and use of dangerous weapons and substances, and gasoline; and

(5) Upon other activities or conditions the control of which may be reasonably necessary to maintain order and protect lives or property during the state of emergency.

■ ■ Critical Thinking ■

The President and governor can commandeer property; local officials cannot (unless a state statute gives them that power). Would you favor enactment of a law that allows local governments to seize private property during an emergency, rather than state government property, as occurred in *Pruneau*? Why?

Maryland as a Case Study

Since every state is different, the following section describes how the laws of a typical state have established institutions and procedures for emergencies.

Under the Maryland Emergency Management Act, the governor has the authority to declare "that an emergency has developed or is impending due to any cause" (§ 14-107(a)(1)). The Act defines an "emergency" as

the threat or occurrence of a hurricane, tornado, storm, flood, high water, wind-driven water, tidal wave, earthquake, landslide, mudslide, snowstorm, drought, fire, explosion, and any other disaster in any part of the State that requires State assistance to supplement local efforts in order to save lives and protect public health and safety; or an enemy attack, act of terrorism, or public health catastrophe.

(§ 14-101(c))

The state of emergency continues until the governor

(i) finds that the threat or danger has passed or the emergency has been dealt with to the extent that emergency conditions no longer exist, and (ii) terminates the state of emergency by executive order or proclamation.

(§ 14-107)

A state of emergency may not continue for longer than 30 days without renewal by the governor, and the General Assembly may terminate a state of emergency by joint resolution at any time. (There is a separate statute providing for gubernatorial powers in a "public emergency," which includes civil disturbances and energy emergencies, and also a catastrophic public health emergency act.)

The Maryland Emergency Management Act requires that a declaration of emergency by the governor contain "the nature of the emergency, the area threatened, and the conditions that have brought about the state of emergency or that make possible the termination of the state of emergency" (§ 14-107(b)(1)).

The Governor of Maryland has various powers under Article II of the state constitution: he or she is the chief executive of the state, commander-in-chief of the Maryland National Guard, and responsible for insuring the faithful execution of state laws. A declaration of a state of emergency provides the governor with these additional powers:

- To suspend statutes, rules or regulations of state agencies or of local governments
- To compel evacuations
- To authorize state use of private property
- To provide temporary housing
- To appropriate and manage funds necessary to respond to the emergency

Responsibility for implementation of the state's emergency plan lies with the Maryland Emergency Management Agency (MEMA), which is part of the Maryland Military Department. The adjutant general, who is appointed by the governor, is the head of the department. During emergencies, however, the director of MEMA reports directly to the governor. Together with other units in the Military Department, MEMA operates the Maryland Joint Operations Center (MJOC), which monitors events in the state for signs of natural or other emergencies and functions as a communications hub during an emergency. Figures 10.1 and 10.2 illustrate the division of responsibilities and the internal organization of MEMA.

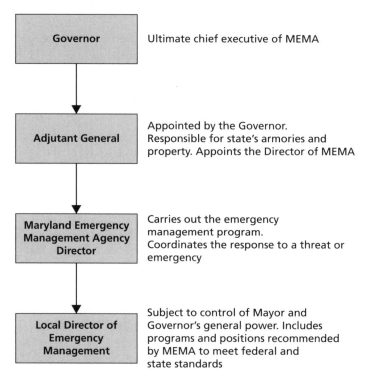

FIGURE 10.1 MEMA Chain of Command

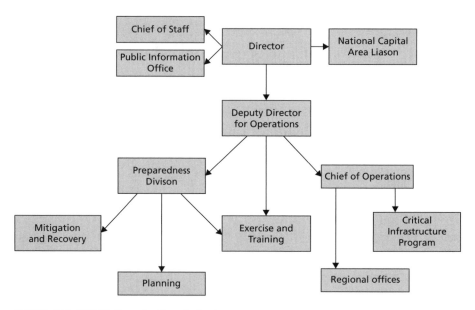

FIGURE 10.2 MEMA Organizational Chart

Important Terms

- Commandeer property
- Delegation of legislative power
- Immunity from tort liability
- Political subdivision of a state
- Writ of mandate or mandamus

Review Questions

The bedrock policy question raised in this chapter is how to balance the powers needed by a governor during an emergency with sufficient checks and balances against abuses of that power. Do you agree with the following argument?

> The constitutional case for a presumption of executive authority is stronger at the state level than at the national level. At a minimum, such a presumption should encompass broader lawmaking powers (including [suspension of statutes and] agency rulemaking), and generally should be sufficiently triggered by all interstate crises, not just attacks. Such executive authority would include not only general authority to issue executive orders but also broad rulemaking authority (subject to a state's administrative process) that exceeds extant legislative delegations to the executive. This presumption would both stand to enhance political legitimacy during times of crisis and have a strong legal basis in state constitutions.
>
> Rossi (2006)

11
Who Does What

What You Will Learn

- The legal rules and operational structures that govern how multiple agencies and levels of government work together in disaster relief
- How the federal government's system for organizing assistance has evolved into an all-hazards approach
- How the distinctive system of state-to-state assistance works
- Legal issues concerning vulnerable populations that affect emergency response work

Introduction

So far in this book, we have been examining different areas of law one by one, as well as various structures and functions of government at the federal and state levels. This chapter will start the process of putting it all together, by looking at how the pieces should synchronize in real time when emergency and disaster responses are underway. For example, we have discussed the mechanism under several laws for declaration of an emergency and the kinds of powers and resources that each declaration triggers. As you read the next section, which describes how all the pieces came together in the response to the attacks on New York on September 11, consider how the multiple declarations of emergency combined to produce a massive response to a devastating event.

The September 11 Response

In re: World Trade Center Disaster Site Litigation
U.S. District Court, Southern District of New York, 2006

> *In the aftermath of the attacks, government leaders at the local, state and federal levels took immediate action to secure physical assistance and funding for the recovery effort at the World Trade Center site. The Mayor of the*

City of New York, the Governor of the State of New York, and the President of the United States all declared states of emergency, authorizing and directing government agencies and officials to undertake those measures necessary to assist the City of New York in its process of recovery.

Pursuant to the authority granted him under [state law], the Mayor of the City of New York, Rudolph W. Giuliani, issued a Mayoral Order on September 11, 2001, proclaiming a local state of emergency based on the danger to public safety posed by the attacks. In declaring a state of emergency, the Mayor directed "the Police, Fire and Health Commissioners and the Director of Emergency Management to take whatever steps are necessary to preserve the public safety and to render all required and available assistance to protect the security, well-being and health of the residents of the City." In subsequent proclamations, and pursuant to [state law] allowing for suspension of local laws and regulations during states of emergency, the Mayor directed that local regulations governing the leasing of real property to the City be suspended so as to "permit the immediate leasing of office and other space for use by City agencies in order to continue to provide essential services and critical functions of the City." The Proclamation of Emergency was renewed by Mayoral Order every five days, as mandated by [state law], throughout the duration of the recovery and cleanup efforts at the World Trade Center site, through the end of June 2002.

A disaster emergency was also declared for the State of New York by Executive Order of Governor George E. Pataki on September 11, 2001, pursuant to the authority granted him under the New York State and Local Natural Disaster and Man-Made Disaster Preparedness Law ("Disaster Act"). Noting the "unspeakable atrocities" that occurred in New York City, Washington D.C., and Pennsylvania, Governor Pataki "direct[ed] the implementation of the State Disaster Preparedness Plan and authorize[d]" various state agencies to take "all appropriate actions to assist in every way all persons killed or injured and their families, and protect state property and to assist those affected local governments and individuals in responding to and recovering from this disaster, and to provide such other assistance as necessary to protect the public health and safety[.]"

On September 14, 2001, President George W. Bush, acting pursuant to the National Emergencies Act, declared the existence of a national state of emergency "by reason of the terrorist attacks at the World Trade Center ... and the Pentagon, and the continuing and immediate threat of further attacks on the United States." The declaration was deemed effective as of September 11, 2001. The declaration served also to activate provisions of the Stafford Act. Pursuant to the Presidential declaration of a national emergency, the Director of the Federal Emergency Management Agency ("FEMA"), Joe M. Allbaugh, declared that a national emergency existed in the State of New York and, in the interest of ensuring the provision of federal assistance, authorized FEMA "to allocate from funds available for these purposes, such amounts as [are] necessary for Federal disaster assistance and administrative expenses."

The City Asserts Control and the Recovery Operation Commences

The City response began mere moments after the terrorist attacks on New York City. American Airlines Flight 11 crashed into One World Trade Center at 8:40 a.m. By 8:50 a.m. on September 11, the City, initially through the Fire Department, had established its Incident Command Post and had asserted control over the World Trade Center complex and the surrounding areas. The rescue and recovery efforts at the site were thereafter coordinated through the City Office of Emergency Management ("OEM"), with the Fire Department designated as the incident commander for the site, and with the City Department of Design and Construction ("DDC") assuming total control over all aspects of safety, construction, demolition, and cleanup activities at the site.

On September 12, 2001, the DDC set up a temporary command center at Public School IS 89 in lower Manhattan, immediately to the north of the World Trade Center site, and commenced daily meetings to organize rescue and recovery efforts. Of utmost concern to the DDC was securing the World Trade Center site and limiting access to the area. Together with other City agencies, including the OEM, the DDC established stringent protocols determining "not only who would have access to the site, but also how that access would take place and under what constraints." The City further enlisted the Port Authority of New York and New Jersey (the "Port Authority") to assist in maintaining the security of the perimeter and to report observed safety protocol discrepancies.

The City also engaged private contractors for the recovery effort. On September 15, 2001, FEMA confirmed that contracts could be awarded without need for competitive bidding under the emergency conditions existing after September 11. Requirements for competitive bidding having been waived, and pursuant to the Declarations of Emergency issued at the City, State and Federal levels, the DDC engaged [several construction companies] to provide the work necessary for removal and demolition services. ... The efforts of [these] contractors were coordinated, and supervised, through the DDC at twice daily meetings held at the temporary command center, and by numerous visits to the worksite. By September 14, 2001, the DDC had divided the site into four quadrants with a primary contractor assigned as a "construction manager" for each individual quadrant. The primary contractors acted as supervisors for their individual quadrants, with responsibility for enforcing applicable regulations and ensuring compliance. ...

In the initial days and weeks following September 11, the City and its contractors, together with public utilities, worked also to restore essential services to the City. The September 11 attacks resulted in the immediate loss of power to all of lower Manhattan and in the destruction of critical components of the gas and steam infrastructure. The Con Edison substations, which had been located directly beneath World Trade Center Seven, were destroyed by fire and by the building's ultimate collapse, resulting in a critical disruption of services to Lower Manhattan. Con Edison assumed sole responsibility for restoring electric, gas and steam services and related facilities that were damaged or destroyed due to the events of September 11. The Verizon Building, located at 140 West Street, also sustained severe structural damage, crippling the phone system. Other critical services, such as the transportation system running through the World Trade Center site, were also destroyed and disrupted.

The Development of Health and Safety Standards at the Site

Conditions at the World Trade Center site, particularly the hazards posed by the dust and contaminants that enveloped lower Manhattan for weeks following the attacks, posed significant dangers to the rescue and recovery workers. In the months following September 11, and continuing to the close of operations at the site in June of 2002, the Occupational Safety and Health Administration ("OSHA") reported levels of various contaminants, including dioxin and asbestos, in excess of OSHA's permissible exposure limits. The debris pile itself, containing what remained of two 110-story towers of concrete and steel, created its own volatile, unstable, and inherently dangerous worksite. Implementation and enforcement of viable and responsive health and safety standards was therefore essential. The workers at the site were presented with a dangerous environment, below and surrounding their work activities, threatening their health and safety. ...

The Role of Federal Agencies

The enormity of the task necessitated the involvement of, and cooperation with, federal agencies. Although the City, through the DDC, assumed primary control over the site, several federal agencies, including FEMA, OSHA, the EPA and the United States Army Corps of Engineers ("Army Corps"), participated in the rescue and recovery effort. These various agencies would ultimately play an active role in the efforts at the World Trade Center, most particularly through their attendance at meetings addressing overall concerns of worker health and safety and through their assistance in developing and enforcing appropriate health and safety protocols responsive to such concerns.

The Activation of Federal Assistance

[President Bush's September 14 declaration of a state of emergency activated the Stafford Act.] Activation of the Stafford Act ... allowed for implementation of the course of federal assistance provided pursuant to the framework outlined in the Federal Response Plan ("FRP").

The FRP, an agreement among twenty-seven federal agencies, "establishes a process and structure for the systematic, coordinated, and effective delivery of federal assistance to address the consequences of any major disaster or emergency declared under the [Stafford Act]." Specifically, the FRP sets forth a "Basic Plan," presenting "the policies and concept of operations that guide how the Federal Government will assist disaster-stricken State and local governments." The Basic Plan provides that, upon exhaustion of local resources and at the request of the affected local government, FEMA shall operate as the lead federal agency for coordinating an appropriate federal response, providing for both technical and financial assistance.

The FRP further coordinates the structure and nature of federal assistance by grouping the types of federal assistance most likely to be utilized by overwhelmed state and local governments into twelve separate Emergency Support Functions ("ESFs"). Each individual ESF is headed by a primary agency "designated on the basis of its authorities, resources, and capabilities in the particular functional area," and assisted by one or more other federal agencies acting in a supporting capacity. As the lead agency in charge of coordinating any federal response pursuant to a declaration of emergency, FEMA is authorized to activate "some or all of the ESFs, as necessary."

Pursuant to activation of the FRP, and FEMA's subsequent activation of the relevant ESFs, OSHA, the EPA and the Army Corps each provided technical and physical assistance to the City of New York in their respective areas of expertise and authority. Federal financial assistance was also provided throughout the duration of the recovery effort with FEMA promising to cover the cost of all operations at the World Trade Center Site ...

The Rescue and Recovery Effort Comes to a Close

From the time that the rescue and recovery operation began at the World Trade Center site in the moments following the September 11 attacks, to the close of operations in June of 2002, work at the site never ceased, continuing twenty-four hours a day, seven days a week, including holidays, with the exception only of Veteran's Day 2001. Despite the enormity of the task, however, work progressed at a rate that many could not have imagined and, as early as April of 2002, the transition of control over the site from the DDC to the Port Authority was being designed and implemented.

On May 10, 2002, control over Seven World Trade Center was returned to the Port Authority. The turnover of control as to the remainder of the World Trade Center complex followed shortly thereafter, on June 30, 2002, with the Port Authority once again assuming complete responsibility for the site. Although control has officially been returned to the Port Authority, work at the site continues to this day with efforts now turned to the completion of all steps necessary to rebuilding. ...

■ ■ Critical Thinking ■

Identify the actions and resources made available by each of the multiple declarations that followed the attack.

Developing a Comprehensive Response Plan

After September 11, Congress and the President sought to enhance national preparedness to respond to disasters of all sorts. One outcome was the creation of the Department of Homeland Security (DHS; see Chapter 3), which merged a number of agencies from different departments, each of which had been responsible for some aspect of preparedness or response. The following Presidential Directive set forth the lines of command and communication in light of the new bureaucratic structure.

Homeland Security Presidential Directive (HSPD) 5
The White House, February 28, 2003

Subject: Management of Domestic Incidents

Policy

... (3) To prevent, prepare for, respond to, and recover from terrorist attacks, major disasters, and other emergencies, the United States Government shall establish a single, comprehensive approach to domestic incident management. The objective of the United States Government is to ensure that all levels of government across the Nation have the capability to work efficiently and effectively together, using a national approach to domestic incident management. In these efforts, with regard to domestic incidents, the United States Government treats crisis management and consequence management as a single, integrated function, rather than as two separate functions.

(4) The Secretary of Homeland Security is the principal Federal official for domestic incident management. Pursuant to the Homeland Security Act of 2002, the Secretary is responsible for coordinating Federal operations within the United States to prepare for, respond to, and recover from terrorist attacks, major disasters, and other emergencies. The Secretary shall coordinate the Federal Government's resources utilized in response to or recovery from terrorist attacks, major disasters, or other emergencies if and when any one of the following four conditions applies: (1) a Federal department or agency acting under its own authority has requested the assistance of the Secretary; (2) the resources of State and local authorities are overwhelmed and Federal assistance has been requested by the appropriate State and local authorities; (3) more than one Federal department or agency has become substantially involved in responding to the incident; or (4) the Secretary has been directed to assume responsibility for managing the domestic incident by the President.

(5) Nothing in this directive alters, or impedes the ability to carry out, the authorities of Federal departments and agencies to perform their responsibilities under law. All Federal departments and agencies shall cooperate with the Secretary in the Secretary's domestic incident management role.

(6) The Federal Government recognizes the roles and responsibilities of State and local authorities in domestic incident management. Initial responsibility for managing domestic incidents generally falls on State and local authorities. The Federal Government will assist State and local authorities when their resources are overwhelmed, or when Federal interests are involved. The Secretary will coordinate with State and local governments to ensure adequate planning, equipment, training, and exercise activities. The Secretary will also provide assistance to State and local governments

to develop all-hazards plans and capabilities, including those of greatest importance to the security of the United States, and will ensure that State, local, and Federal plans are compatible.

(7) The Federal Government recognizes the role that the private and nongovernmental sectors play in preventing, preparing for, responding to, and recovering from terrorist attacks, major disasters, and other emergencies. The Secretary will coordinate with the private and nongovernmental sectors to ensure adequate planning, equipment, training, and exercise activities and to promote partnerships to address incident management capabilities. ...

Tasking

(14) The heads of all Federal departments and agencies are directed to provide their full and prompt cooperation, resources, and support, as appropriate and consistent with their own responsibilities for protecting our national security, to the Secretary, the Attorney General, the Secretary of Defense, and the Secretary of State ...

(15) The Secretary shall develop, submit for review to the Homeland Security Council, and administer a National Incident Management System (NIMS). This system will provide a consistent nationwide approach for Federal, State, and local governments to work effectively and efficiently together to prepare for, respond to, and recover from domestic incidents, regardless of cause, size, or complexity. To provide for interoperability and compatibility among Federal, State, and local capabilities, the NIMS will include a core set of concepts, principles, terminology, and technologies covering the incident command system; multi-agency coordination systems; unified command; training; identification and management of resources (including systems for classifying types of resources); qualifications and certification; and the collection, tracking, and reporting of incident information and incident resources.

(16) The Secretary shall develop, submit for review to the Homeland Security Council, and administer a National Response Plan (NRP). The Secretary shall consult with

appropriate Assistants to the President (including the Assistant to the President for Economic Policy) and the Director of the Office of Science and Technology Policy, and other such Federal officials as may be appropriate, in developing and implementing the NRP. This plan shall integrate Federal Government domestic prevention, preparedness, response, and recovery plans into one all-discipline, all-hazards plan. The NRP shall be unclassified. If certain operational aspects require classification, they shall be included in classified annexes to the NRP.

■ ■ ■ ────────────────────────────

The NRP replaced the Federal Response Plan mentioned in the September 11 case. In 2008, the National Response Framework (NRF) replaced the NRP.

──────────────────────────── ■ ■ ■

(a) The NRP, using the NIMS, shall, with regard to response to domestic incidents, provide the structure and mechanisms for national level policy and operational direction for Federal support to State and local incident managers and for exercising direct Federal authorities and responsibilities, as appropriate.

(b) The NRP will include protocols for operating under different threats or threat levels; incorporation of existing Federal emergency and incident management plans (with appropriate modifications and revisions) as either integrated components of the NRP or as supporting operational plans; and additional operational plans or annexes, as appropriate, including public affairs and intergovernmental communications.

(c) The NRP will include a consistent approach to reporting incidents, providing assessments, and making recommendations to the President, the Secretary, and the Homeland Security Council. ...

(18) The heads of Federal departments and agencies shall adopt the NIMS within their departments and agencies and shall provide support and assistance to the Secretary in the development and maintenance of the NIMS. All Federal departments and

agencies will use the NIMS in their domestic incident management and emergency prevention, preparedness, response, recovery, and mitigation activities, as well as those actions taken in support of State or local entities. The heads of Federal departments and agencies shall participate in the NRP, shall assist and support the Secretary in the development and maintenance of the NRP, and shall participate in and use domestic incident reporting systems and protocols established by the Secretary. ...

(20) Beginning in Fiscal Year 2005, Federal departments and agencies shall make adoption of the NIMS a requirement, to the extent permitted by law, for providing Federal preparedness assistance through grants, contracts, or other activities. The Secretary shall develop standards and guidelines for determining whether a State or local entity has adopted the NIMS. ...

■ ■ Critical Thinking ■

Based on what you have learned, identify the sources of law that give the President the authority to issue this directive.

The National Incident Management System

After Hurricane Katrina, the White House issued a report descrbing the template for emergency response:

The National Incident Management System (NIMS) establishes standardized incident management protocols and procedures that all responders – Federal, State, and local – should use to conduct and coordinate response actions. It sets forth a "core set of doctrine, concepts, principles, terminology and organizational processes to enable effective, efficient, and collaborative incident management at all levels" of government. The NIMS provides a common, flexible framework within which government and private entities at all levels can work together to manage domestic incidents of any magnitude. In March 2004, the Secretary of Homeland Security approved the NIMS and sent a memorandum to officials at all levels of the government asking for continued cooperation and assistance in further developing and implementing the NIMS.

The central component of the NIMS is the Incident Command System (ICS).

■ ■ ■ ▬▬▬▬▬▬▬▬▬▬▬▬▬▬▬▬▬▬▬▬▬▬▬▬

The ICS grew out of conflicts between federal, state, and local firefighting units when responding to wildfires in the western United States in the 1970s.

▬▬▬▬▬▬▬▬▬▬▬▬▬▬▬▬▬▬▬▬▬▬ ■ ■ ■

... The ICS provides a means to coordinate the efforts of individual responders and agencies as they respond to and help manage an incident. The ICS organization, the structure and size of which can be tailored to the complexity and size of any given incident, comprises five major functional areas – Command, Planning, Operations, Logistics, and Finance/ Administration. ...

ICS requires that a command system be established from the onset of incident operations, thereby ensuring a unified command and the efficient coordination of multi-agency and multi-jurisdictional efforts. Recognizing that most incidents are managed locally, the command function under ICS is set up at the lowest level of the response, and grows to encompass other agencies and jurisdictions as they arrive. Some incidents that begin with a single response discipline (e.g., fire or police department) within a single jurisdiction may rapidly expand to multi-discipline, multijurisdictional incidents requiring significant additional resources and operational support.

The concept of unified command is both more important and more complicated when local, State, and Federal commanders are required to coordinate their efforts. ICS clarifies reporting relationships and eliminates confusion caused by multiple, and potentially conflicting, directions and actions. The National Response Plan requires senior officials from multiple levels of government to come together at a single location to establish a common set of objectives and a single incident plan. This group, referred to as the "Unified Command," provides for and enables joint decisions on objectives, strategies, plans, priorities, and public communications. ...

[Federal-State-Local Coordination]

After a Stafford Act declaration, FEMA, on behalf of the Federal government, receives State requests for assistance and fulfills them by tasking other Federal departments or agencies with the appropriate expertise or resources to meet the specific needs. This is often referred to as a "pull" system for Federal assistance because local and State governments must identify needs and make specific requests for assistance before the Federal government can deliver – they "pull" assistance from the Federal government. Equally important to understanding the current "pull" system is the method in which Federal assistance is delivered to those in need – relying on the State as an intermediary between the Federal government and any other entity. In many cases, the Federal government will satisfy a State request by providing commodities or assets to the State. In so doing, the Federal government is helping the State meet the needs of their local governments and first responders, as well as various operational components of the State. The Federal government does not always directly deliver its assistance to local governments or others in need. The State's role has been compared to retail sales in terms of organization, delivery, and management. Under this description, the Federal government's role is comparable to wholesale. This generally works well and should continue in the majority of instances.

However, in some instances the State and local governments will be overwhelmed beyond their ability to satisfy their traditional roles in this system. Indeed, in some instances, State and local governments and responders may become victims themselves, prohibiting their ability to identify, request, receive, or deliver assistance. This is the moment of catastrophic crisis – the moment when 911 calls are no longer answered; the moment when hurricane victims can no longer be timely evacuated or evacuees can no longer find shelter; the moment when police no longer patrol the streets, and the rule of law begins to break down.

Hurricane Katrina – Lessons Learned (2006)

■ ■ Critical Thinking ■

As we learned from Katrina, a system based on all pull and no push does not always work. Is there any constitutional barrier to assigning more responsibility and initiative to the federal government? If not, what factors produce such reluctance?

DEFENDING THE NATIONAL RESPONSE PLAN

The first test of the National Response Plan came in 2005, when Hurricane Katrina devastated New Orleans and much of the Gulf Coast. Whatever else went wrong – and many things did – the federal response was poorly managed. Professor Michael Greenberger argues that the fault lay not in the plan, but in how it was executed:

> It is now widely acknowledged that the NRP was triggered quite belatedly during Katrina. On a practical basis, however, there is every indication that it was never implemented as intended, i.e. there was almost certainly no central federal operations unit composed of cabinet or sub-cabinet level representatives sitting in an executive operations center communicating on a real-time basis with state and local government. Instead, the federal response, even after the NRP was enacted, was mostly ad hoc, and to the extent it was centralized, the federal representatives were not sufficiently high level. ...

> [T]he NRP is a well-thought-out, all-hazards plan that addresses the necessity of a delicate balance between different levels of government. If implemented as intended, with true coordination between stakeholders from all levels of government in a classic war room-like setting, the NRP should end the false dichotomy about whether state and local units or the federal government supervises the response and recovery effort.
>
> Greenberger (2006)

The National Response Framework

In March 2008, the Department of Homeland Security replaced the NRP with a new and very similar document that it calls the National Response Framework (NRF) in part to emphasize that the set of priorities and functions it outlines is less of a specific plan than a framework to guide operations in many different types of situations. The NRF is designed to be fully or partially implemented, depending on the scale of the event. Like the NRP before it, it is geared toward translating the NIMS template into specific allocations of responsibility. The HSPD-5 is still in effect.

Drawing on lessons from Katrina, the NRF modified the NRP's heavy emphasis on the secondary nature of federal responsibilities, as compared to state and local relief activities. Official policy still includes "a basic premise … that incidents are generally handled at the lowest jurisdictional level possible." However, DHS guidance on the NRF also states:

> Following a catastrophic event, segments of State, tribal, and local authorities as well as NGOs [non-governmental organizations, such as the Red Cross] and the private sector may be severely impacted. The Federal Government will employ a proactive Federal response to expedite resources to the impacted area. In rare instances …, the Federal Government may temporarily assume certain roles typically performed by [other levels of government]. For example, … the Federal Government may establish a unified command structure … As soon as State, tribal or local authorities reestablish the incident command structure, the Federal Government will transition to its normal role [of] support[] …
>
> (DHS, NRF: Frequently Asked Questions)

Because a massive catastrophe could impede the ability of a governor to follow the normal process for seeking federal assistance, the NRF has created a new category of event: "catastrophic incident."

> A catastrophic incident is defined as any natural or manmade incident, including terrorism, that results in extraordinary levels of mass casualties, damage or disruption severely affecting the population, infrastructure, environment, economy, national morale, and/or government functions.
>
> NRF (2008)

Once the DHS Secretary determines that a catastrophic incident has occurred or is likely to occur, federal resources can be immediately sent to the area.

The NRF also designates lead federal agencies for various functions and types of events. (These are called "emergency support functions.") For example, FEMA is the lead agency for emergency management, emergency assistance, mass care, and search and rescue. The Army Corps of Engineers is the lead agency for public works and engineering, and DHS is in charge of communications. Law enforcement responsibility rests with the Department of Justice.

If military troops are used, they retain their separate chain of command and are not subject to direction by the officials operating under the NRF and NIMS.

On the Ground

Although the overall approach to disaster response can quickly start to sound like alphabet soup, it is not that complicated. The ICS is simply a standardized management system that is built on modular units, the complexity of which can be scaled up or down depending on the extent of the problem. It establishes a common structure and vocabulary for all the agencies at all levels of government that are involved in a response. It can be used in a situation as simple as one involving several agencies from a single jurisdiction – for example, local police and fire departments. Or it can be scaled up to accommodate multiple agencies from multiple jurisdictions, as in a large-scale emergency. The NIMS is essentially one kind of an ICS.

Central to the ICS/NIMS approach is the concept of unified command. Unified command, another standardized management approach, means that, rather than a silo-like approach in which each agency or jurisdiction operates independently, a collaborative structure is set up. For example: if police, fire, and social services departments were all responding to a plane crash, representatives from each of those agencies would literally work together in the same location (an incident command post) and make decisions jointly, rather than having each agency issue directions for the workers within its control without consultation with the other agencies. The lead person on site in charge of an agency's operations would be the agency's incident commander. Together, the incident commanders would make decisions. If no other level of government was involved, then the mayor, for example, might appoint one overall incident commander.

In response to a large-scale disaster, the modular approach would scale up to accommodate the greater complexity and larger number of persons and entities involved. For example, all local agency leaders would report to the local incident commander; all state agency leaders would report to the state incident commander, and so forth. The incident commanders representing federal, state, and local operations would collaborate in the unified command. However, each agency would retain its full scope of legal authority and responsibility.

State-to-State Assistance Agreements

In 1992, Hurricane Andrew devastated Florida. Then Governor Lawton Chiles sought assistance not only from FEMA, but also from neighboring states. To make the process easier in the future, he led the Southern Governors Association in creating a formal mechanism to simplify the sharing of resources between states. This agreement among states evolved into the Emergency Management Assistance Compact (EMAC) and was ratified by Congress in 1996.

The EMAC system is a streamlined and effective mutual assistance network. In 2005, resources deployed through EMAC accounted for more than 50 percent of out-of-state personnel sent to the Gulf Coast in the wake of Katrina. The categories of personnel who were mobilized through EMAC included search and rescue teams, healthcare professionals, fire and hazmat personnel, law enforcement officers, and animal rescue workers (National Emergency Management Association, 2008).

To join EMAC, a state must adopt legislation to ensure that all EMAC members are operating under the same rules. All 50 states plus the District of Columbia, Puerto Rico, the Virgin Islands, and Guam have enacted this legislation. Maryland's EMAC law, for example, can be found in Section 14-602 of its Public Safety Code. The model for EMAC legislation consists of 15 articles, each of which sets forth a binding obligation between the states.

One of the most important provisions of EMAC, Article 5 of the model, deems persons who are licensed professionals in one member state to be licensed when rendering assistance during an emergency in another member state:

> Whenever any person holds a license, certificate or other permit issued by any state evidencing the meeting of qualifications for professional, mechanical or other skills, such person may render aid involving such skill in any party state to meet an emergency or disaster; and such state shall give due recognition to such license, certificate or other permit as if issued in the state in which aid is rendered.

An important caveat: EMAC does *not* provide for recognizing the licensure of individuals who travel on their own, without being sent as part of the EMAC process.

Other articles cover compensation, benefits, and liability. Article 8 makes each state responsible for payment of compensation and death benefits relative to the members of its own team, on the same terms as if the injury or death had occurred in the home state. Article 6 provides that persons providing aid and assistance are considered employees of the state where the aid is rendered for purposes of tort liability. (See Chapter 13 for more detail on liability.)

What about the use of military personnel? Recall from Chapter 4 that National Guard units can be deployed for law enforcement purposes if they are acting under the command of the state's governor, but not if they have been federalized and are operating under command of the President. Into what category does the National Guard fall when it has been sent from one state into another pursuant to an agreement between governors? Under EMAC, National Guard units sent interstate can be used only for humanitarian purposes, not for law enforcement or military functions.

The EMAC process requires two steps for activation. First, a governor must formally declare a disaster or emergency pursuant to state law. Second, that state (the "requesting state") must request assistance through EMAC's national coordinating group. "Assisting states" deploy resources, and, after the crisis is over, the requesting state will reimburse certain expenses of the assisting states. While the operation is underway, the NIMS/ICS system functions as the operational template.

■ ■ Critical Thinking ■

The legal framework underlying the EMAC system guarantees that some issues are handled uniformly by all the states, in all emergencies. However, it doesn't prevent states from entering into additional agreements with each other. What other sorts of arrangements might states want to make with other states?

WHAT EXACTLY IS THE AMERICAN RED CROSS?

In 1905, Congress chartered the American Red Cross, a humanitarian organization founded to provide relief and aid to survivors of war and disasters. Clara Barton founded the American Red Cross Society in 1881, modeling it on the original international association established in Geneva in 1863. In its early years, the Red Cross primarily served military service members and their families; today it coordinates volunteers and donations and distributes aid of various sorts.

The Red Cross is a private organization and not an agency of the government, but it works closely with federal, state, and local governments during times of crisis. It has more than 1,000 chapters throughout the United States. Officials often suggest that Americans wanting to help disaster victims can donate to the Red Cross.

Human Rights during an Emergency

The human and civil rights dimensions of assistance efforts have received relatively little attention until recently. Any disaster relief activities undertaken by government agencies (at any level of government) are bound by the constitutional principles protecting individual rights and liberties that we examined in Chapter 2. In addition, the Stafford Act contains its own more specific nondiscrimination provision:

> [T]he distribution of supplies, the processing of applications, and other relief and assistance activities shall be accomplished in an equitable and impartial manner, without discrimination on the grounds of race, color, religion, nationality, sex, age, or economic status.
>
> (42 U.S. Code § 5151)

The plaintiffs in the *McWaters* case (Chapter 9) invoked this part of the Stafford Act in their lawsuit, but the court found that there had been no intentional discrimination in the chaos of the Katrina aftermath. Its rulings for the plaintiffs were based on other provisions in the law. Three states – Connecticut, North Carolina, and Utah – have laws prohibiting disaster relief agencies from discrimination based on race, sex, and economic status (Hoffman, 2009).

A federal law of particular relevance to emergency response work is the Americans with Disabilities Act (ADA), which both prohibits discrimination based on disabilities and also requires agencies to accommodate disabled people, unless doing so would create an undue burden on their activities (42 U.S. Code §§ 12101 et seq.). In 2006, the Department of Justice issued "An ADA Guide for Local Governments: Making Community Emergency Preparedness and Response Programs Accessible to People with Disabilities." The guidance document covers a number of practices that may need to be adjusted to adapt policies to persons with mobility or other impairments, including notification, evacuation, transportation, and sheltering (Hoffman, 2008).

DISASTER RELIEF EFFORTS AND DISCRIMINATION

Hurricane Katrina was not the first time that disaster relief reinforced rather than alleviated the impact of social stratification and discrimination. After catastrophic flooding along the Mississippi River in 1927, government and Red Cross workers segregated the evacuees, placed African–Americans in uninhabitable camp locations, and cut their food rations (Barry, 1997). As University of South Carolina Professor Susan Cutter has written, "Disasters are income neutral and color-blind. Their impacts, however, are not" (Cutter, 2006).

The effects of disasters like Katrina are not gender neutral either:

> It was ... women more than men who were evacuated from nursing homes, and women more than men whose escape of sorts was made with infants, children and elders in tow. ... In the dreary months ahead, ... the burdens on women will be exceptional and exceptionally invisible. Imagine cleaning just one flooded room, helping just one toddler or teen to sleep well again, restoring the sense of security to a widowed mother's life. The basic chores of "homemaking" ... are vastly more difficult in a FEMA trailer, a friend's apartment or the basement of a church – and parents will call upon daughters more than sons for help. ...Women across the nation are also the lifeblood of voluntary organizations of all descriptions ... Long after we think Katrina over and done with, women whose jobs and professions in teaching, health care, mental health, crisis work, and community advocacy bring them into direct contact with affected families will feel the stress of "first responders" whose work never ends.
>
> Enarson (2006)

Important Terms

- Americans with Disabilities Act
- Catastrophic Incident
- Domestic incident management
- Emergency Support Functions
- Incident Command System

- National Incident Management System
- National Response Framework
- Unified Command

Review Questions

1. See if you can diagram the structures for ICS, NIMS, and the NRF. How does the idea of unified command fit into these?
2. What kinds of complications might arise from this arrangement because military units like the National Guard are under a separate command structure?
3. How does the NRF's category of "catastrophic incident" compare to the Stafford Act's categories of "emergency" and "major disaster"? To the National Emergency Act? To the declaration of a public health emergency? What function does the NRF category serve?

::: 12
Searches, Seizures, and Evacuations

What You Will Learn

- How the Fourth Amendment constrains the ability of public officials to conduct searches
- When and for what purposes an emergency provides an exception to the normal Fourth Amendment rules
- When the Takings Clause of the Fifth Amendment might require the government to compensate for property seized or destroyed during an emergency
- The ways in which *state* emergency laws address these issues

Introduction

In this chapter, we will be examining how two amendments in the Bill of Rights limit the actions of public officials and how those limitations might alter the range of permissible responses to a public emergency. The Fourth Amendment imposes restrictions on searches of both individuals and property. Although these restrictions are most commonly applicable in the context of criminal prosecutions, they can also affect how emergency officials respond to an emergency. The Fifth Amendment provides a general rule, known as the Takings Clause, that the government must pay just compensation whenever it "takes" private property for a public use. During an emergency, the Takings Clause could be triggered by such things as forced closures or evacuations and the commandeering of health institutions for purposes such as quarantine. An emergency official must be aware of the normal scope of, and the exceptions to, these rules when planning responses to an emergency.

> ### THE FOURTH AND FIFTH AMENDMENTS
>
> "The Fourth and Fifth Amendments to the U.S. Constitution apply only to government-sponsored actions; therefore public health officials, like all government agents, must conform their investigations to constitutional standards." (Goodman et al., 2003) As a general rule, these amendments will apply to any government official as well as any individual acting as an agent of the government. Any actions by private sector entities or ordinary citizens are not covered by the Fourth and Fifth Amendments.

The Fourth Amendment

The Fourth Amendment reads:

> The right of the people to be secure in their persons, houses, papers, and effects, against unreasonable searches and seizures, shall not be violated, and no Warrants shall issue, but upon probable cause, supported by Oath or affirmation, and particularly describing the place to be searched, and the persons or things to be seized.

The protection afforded by this Amendment historically emanates from the home. The idea that the privacy of one's own home is somehow special is centuries old. It was in 1604 that an English court famously observed, "the house of every one is to him as his castle and fortress" (quoted in *Wilson v. Layne,* 1999). While the range of Fourth Amendment protections has increased over time, the home is still seen to a large extent as inviolable. As we will see, knowing when and why a private home can be entered can be very important during an emergency. Meanwhile, the "seizure" strand of the Fourth Amendment refers mainly to the detention and interrogation of individuals.

Reasonable Searches

Because the Fourth Amendment prohibits only those searches that are "unreasonable," the touchstone for analysis is reasonableness. Although testing for reasonableness may seem difficult, the Supreme Court has held that reasonableness is synonymous with the presence of a warrant. As a result, warrantless searches are presumed to be "unreasonable" and therefore in violation of the Fourth Amendment unless they conform to certain narrowly defined exceptions. We will soon be turning to some of these exceptions and how they might be relevant in emergency situations.

Before we do, note that the Amendment also demands that warrants can only be issued "upon probable cause." Probable cause has come to require that the official(s) have some individualized suspicion as to the person or place to be searched. One way of understanding probable cause is that officials must show a "likelihood to believe that evidence of a crime will be found in the area to be searched." (Goodman et al., 2003) Generally, with or without a warrant, searches are only valid when based on probable cause.

Seizures are subject to slightly different rules. Arrests usually require a warrant issued on probable cause, unless the circumstances make this both impractical and dangerous. Interrogations, on the other hand, normally only require probable cause.

HOW IS THE FOURTH AMENDMENT ENFORCED?

The most powerful mechanism for enforcing the Fourth Amendment is the principle that if the police violate an individual's rights by engaging in an unlawful search, they are prohibited from using whatever they find against the person in a criminal prosecution. This so-called exclusionary rule will not usually be relevant in emergencies that typically involve no wrongdoing and therefore no need for criminal prosecution – for example, a naturally occurring epidemic or a flood. Of course, in the case of bioterrorism, this rule could prove very important, as the desire to hold someone responsible might strongly conflict with the need to prevent the spread of the disease or future attacks.

Community Caretaking

The Fourth Amendment is primarily concerned with public officials operating pursuant to criminal law enforcement needs for example, chasing a suspect or investigating a crime. There are a number of different exceptions to both the warrant and probable cause requirements, and most of these exceptions arise when officials are acting for purposes other than law enforcement. Because the nature of an emergency is frequently outside the criminal law context, these exceptions might often be of great use to emergency officials.

Perhaps the most important of the exceptions arises when the police are acting in their "community caretaker" function. When acting in that role, the police are generally not bound by the normal warrant and probable cause requirements (Decker, 1999). The difference between the community caretaking and normal law enforcement functions is one of motivation:

> The law enforcement function includes conduct that is designed to detect or solve a specific crime, such as making arrests, interrogating suspects, and searching for evidence. Community caretaking on the other hand, is based on a service notion that police serve to ensure the safety and welfare of the citizenry at large. For example, this may involve approaching a seemingly stranded motorist or lost child to inquire whether he or she needs assistance, assisting persons involved in a natural disaster, or warning members of a community about a hazardous materials leak in the area.
>
> Decker (1999)

One court colorfully summed up the exception as follows:

> *Police are required to serve the community in innumerable ways, from pursuing criminals to rescuing treed cats. While the Fourth Amendment's warrant requirement is the cornerstone of our protections against unreasonable searches and seizures, it is not a barrier to a police officer seeking to help someone in immediate danger.*
>
> *People v. Molnar (2002)*

How does the community caretaking exception alter the normal rules of the Fourth Amendment? "When an officer is pursuing a community caretaking function that in no way involves a 'seizure' of a person, no 'particularized and objective justification' for his actions is required" (Decker, 1999). In other words, so long as no one is detained or interrogated, neither a warrant nor probable cause are necessary in this context.

While the Supreme Court has never explicitly defined this as an "emergency" exception, the caretaking functions listed above suggest that it is commonly triggered by emergencies, both large (a hazardous materials leak) and small (a cat in a tree). The Supreme Court has connected this exception with public health emergencies. In fact, in a case mentioning "inspections, even without a warrant, that the law has traditionally upheld in emergency situations," the Court offered this list: exposure to unwholesome food, smallpox and other contagious diseases, and tubercular cattle (*Camara v. Municipal Court of City and County of San Francisco*, 1989).

Although there are few cases that specifically address public health or other emergencies as such, the decisions that do exist clarify how acting out of public health and welfare concerns can at least partially trump the warrant and probable cause requirements.

Firefighting, for example, is a caretaking function. Firemen entering a house to fight a fire are generally not subject to Fourth Amendment strictures. So long as they are not specifically looking for evidence of a crime, any evidence they might find while fighting the fire would be admissible in court. Meanwhile, police officers would similarly be operating outside the Fourth Amendment to the extent that they were helping put out or investigate the cause of the fire, subject again to the limitation that they cannot be looking for evidence of a crime.

Case Study 1 – The Furniture Store Fire

[F]irefighters were dispatched around midnight to a furniture store to extinguish a fire. While fighting the fire, firefighters came across two containers of flammable liquid and summoned the police, who seized the containers as possible evidence of arson. Police and firefighters then briefly scanned the rest of the building in an attempt to determine the exact cause of the fire. Due to darkness and smoke, the officials were not able to establish the fire's origin and, consequently, evacuated the premises around 4:00 a.m. after verifying that the fire was completely extinguished.

Later that morning, police and firefighters re-entered the premises without a warrant several times to further investigate the cause of the fire. During those entries, police seized pieces of a rug and bits of the stairway as evidence suggestive of a fuse trail. More than three weeks later, police again made repeated visits to the scene to investigate and to obtain evidence against the defendants, the owners of the store, who were charged with conspiracy to commit arson.

■ ■ ■ ─────────────────────────────────

When does the community caretaking function end and evidence collection begin?

─────────────────────────────── ■ ■ ■

The police had neither a warrant nor consent for any of these various entries. At trial, the defendants moved to suppress all evidence obtained after the initial entry as the fruits of illegal warrantless searches.

The Supreme Court noted that a fire in progress, of course, was an obvious emergency permitting immediate governmental action. However, the Court pointed out that owners of fire-damaged premises, whether commercial or residential, which are not completely destroyed, continue to have a reasonable expectation of privacy in their premises even after the exigency of the fire has passed. Thus, the Fourth Amendment is applicable in this context, and government officials must obtain a warrant to conduct a search of the premises for origin of the fire or evidence of arson in the absence of either consent or an applicable exception to the warrant requirement.

Decker (1999) (describing *Michigan v. Tyler*)

Imagine that instead of a fire, the house had been partially damaged by a flood or wholly contaminated by the release of a biological agent. What limitations would there be on entries by public health officials and other emergency workers? In the latter scenario, what happens if or when it becomes clear that the release of the agent was intentional and probably criminal?

Two other cases might provide some answers. In one, a 911 call alerted the police about a "strange odor" coming from an apartment, so strong and putrid that some neighbors had to vacate their apartments. Police officers arrived and knocked on the door, but no one answered. After concluding there was no alternative, they forced their way into the apartment. The apartment was covered with vermin and a dead body was protruding from a closet. The evidence seen and collected by the officers was admitted into court because "[t]he police were not functioning in a criminal arena, but acting as public servants in the name of protecting health and safety" (*People v. Molnar*, 2002). In the other, a police officer, who had received tips that the defendant kept the manufacturing ingredients for narcotics in his car, approached the defendant's car only to smell an odor of ether "so strong that it made his eyes water" (*People v. Clements*, 1983). Concerned the ether might explode, the officer opened the trunk and found the ether in a glass whiskey bottle. The court held that the search was permissible because the smell of ether presented an emergency.

Although there are few clear lines in this area, there appears to be a space in which an emergency official can be acting primarily out of his caretaking obligation while at the same time clearly engaged in more traditional law enforcement efforts.

FACTORS THAT TRIGGER COMMUNITY CARETAKING OR EMERGENCY EXCEPTIONS

What is required to trigger the community caretaking or emergency exception?

Law professor John F. Decker has identified three factors.

- *First*, there must be some identifiable emergency. In other words, the circumstances must suggest that the "officer could have reasonably believed that there was an immediate need for his or her community caretaking assistance." Recognized examples include the following: a burning building, a person in need of medical treatment, missing persons, kidnapping, a child in danger, report of an assault in progress, the odor of a dead body, and the presence of volatile chemicals.
- *Second*, the officer must be motivated by some caretaking instead of law enforcement concern.
- *Third*, the action must fall within the scope of the emergency, both in terms of time and place.

Decker (1999)

Administrative Searches

Another exception to the normal warrant requirement has been established for administrative authorities charged with ensuring public health and safety compliance. Such "[a]dministrative searches have been described generally as a means of ensuring compliance with such matters as occupancy permits and proper wiring standards" and have generally been permitted because they "normally involve only a minimal invasion of privacy" (Gould and Stern, 2004). Administrative searches are not excused from the warrant requirement altogether, but rather are subjected to a lower standard of probable cause than law enforcement searches. As opposed to the traditional "likelihood that evidence will be found," in the administrative context "probable cause is satisfied by 'reasonable legislative or administrative standards for conducting an area inspection ... with respect to a particular dwelling'"

(Goodman et al., 2003). In other words, ensuring compliance can be done in a more systematic way than criminal searches, which require individualized suspicion.

Generally, routine (what we might call nonemergency) searches conducted by public health officials will qualify as administrative searches:

> [C]ommon purposes of public health investigations include, for example, detecting and remediating biological, chemical, or other threats to community health; developing information regarding risk factors for the occurrence of diseases, injuries and disabilities; and providing a scientifically rational basis for implementing prevention and control measures. These purposes may require public health officials to make entries to obtain samples of substances that pose a threat to public health, conduct inspections, or to alleviate hazardous conditions. Entry may also be sought in response to a complaint, in furtherance of a regulatory scheme, or pursuant to an enforcement provision in a statute or ordinance.
>
> Goodman et al. (2003)

■ ■ Critical Thinking ■

What types of administrative searches might be necessary during or after a pandemic? A flood or earthquake? To what extent do you think administrative searches might be inapplicable in the event of a bioterrorist attack?

Case Study 1 *Continued* – The Furniture Store Fire Revisited

We can locate a primary example of how the administrative search doctrine functions by revisiting the scene of a fire:

> *If the primary object [of a search] is to determine the cause and origin of a recent fire, an administrative warrant will suffice. To obtain such a warrant, fire officials need show only that a fire of undetermined origin has occurred on the premises, that the scope of the proposed search is reasonable and will not intrude unnecessarily on the fire victim's privacy, and that the search will be executed at a reasonable and convenient time.*
>
> *Michigan v. Clifford (1984)*

Recall the furniture store fire in *Michigan v. Tyler* described above. In that case, the firefighters and police officers entered the building at three different times and for three different purposes: *first*, while the fire was burning, to put it out; *second*, later that morning, to further investigate the cause of the fire; and *third*, more than three weeks later, to look for evidence of arson.

The first entry was permissible without a warrant on the grounds of the emergency or community caretaking exception. For obvious reasons, we do not want to make firefighters wait for a warrant before putting out a fire. Accordingly, there was no Fourth Amendment violation, and although the firefighters could not actively look for evidence of a crime, any evidence they came across in the course of putting out the fire would be admissible.

The second entry presents a harder case, coming so soon after the fire was put out. Remember that the scope of the emergency exception is limited to the timeframe of the emergency. In *Michigan v. Tyler*, the fire had already been extinguished, so the Supreme Court would have required a warrant. Because they were only looking for the cause of the fire – then unknown – the firefighters probably would have needed only an administrative warrant. Under slightly different circumstances, however, we might imagine a court ruling that the emergency was still ongoing and therefore not requiring a warrant; or alternatively taking a stricter view of the Fourth Amendment and requiring a traditional warrant supported by individualized probable cause.

The third entry, however, was conducted for the purpose of finding evidence of arson. This search would not fit the administrative search or community caretaking exception, and an ordinary warrant accompanied by probable cause would have been necessary.

THE SCOPE OF AN ADMINISTRATIVE SEARCH

It is important to realize that administrative warrants provide "no wholesale right to do a thorough search of the house, such as opening drawers or cabinets" (Goodman et al., 2003). Rather, the search is limited to its purpose: a public health official testing for chemical agents, for example, might only need access to a main room and the water supply, but would have little reason to rifle through a desk. Searches that exceed their purpose are often found to violate the Fourth Amendment. Items in "plain view," however, are fair game. So if the health inspector, while testing the tap water, sees contraband in the sink, the contraband can be admitted into evidence in court.

Now, consider *Florida Department of Agriculture v. Haire*. In that case, citrus tree growers challenged search warrants permitting area-wide searches to find trees infected with citrus canker. Any infected trees and any trees within 1,900 feet of an infected tree were to be removed and destroyed. Although the court would have allowed warrants that included multiple properties, it found the area-wide warrants invalid. The probable cause requirement, whether in a criminal or administrative warrant, requires "particularity in the description of the property to be searched" (*Florida Department of Agriculture v. Haire*, 2003).

Special Needs

There is one other relevant exception to the general rules of the Fourth Amendment. The special needs exception applies "[o]nly in those exceptional circumstances in which special needs, beyond the normal need for law enforcement, make the warrant and probable cause requirement impracticable" (*New Jersey v. T.L.O.*, 1985). Generally, the common thread tying such searches together is the presence of a "safety concern of sufficient magnitude to outweigh the particular privacy interests involved" (*American Federation of Teachers v. Kanawha County Board of Education*, 2009). Although such special needs searches may sound similar to the emergency or caretaking exception, they usually do not involve actual emergency situations. Instead, the special needs doctrine has been used to uphold systematic, suspicionless searches, such as routine drug tests of students, government employees, and railway employees (Gould and Stern, 2004). In other words, the special needs exception applies when warrants would present an undue administrative burden given the safety concerns involved, not because those safety concerns are time-sensitive. This doctrine has also been used to permit the search of probationers' homes on individualized suspicion less than the normal probable cause.

One law review article considered this doctrine in a hypothetical involving a small atomic bomb – for which we might substitute a dirty bomb – smuggled into a city and tracked to an area comprising 100 private homes (Gould and Stern, 2004). In a normal criminal search, the one-in-100 chance afforded by the tracking would not amount to probable cause as to any house. And as we discussed above, warrants generally cannot be used to conduct area-wide sweeps. Could the special needs doctrine work here?

> Because the special-needs rationale has been used to permit a search of the home [of a probationer], and given that protecting the public is one of the concerns allowing such searches, it might appear that our hypothetical search, aimed at protecting homes in an entire urban area, fits neatly within this exception ... [But unlike probationers], all citizens have a broad and cherished expectation of privacy in their homes and have no relation to the police that would give the latter any right to intrude on the home.
>
> Gould and Stern (2004)

The special needs doctrine would probably not work under this scenario. The needs here are too closely aligned with normal law enforcement. Could you argue, however, that these searches ought to be permitted under the emergency exception?

■ ■ Critical Thinking ■

Jacobson Revisited (Again)

Briefly read over the facts of *Jacobson* in Chapter 1. *Jacobson* involved forced vaccinations. Consider for a moment the fact that the Supreme Court has allowed numerous systematic drug-testing programs under the special needs theory.

Now, imagine the sudden outbreak of a highly contagious and deadly disease in a major U.S. city. Public health officials want to conduct mandatory blood testing on all of the city's residents. What problems would the Fourth Amendment potentially present for this plan? How great do you consider the privacy invasion – the needle in the arm and the blood examined – for the individuals involved? Are there any hurdles the officials will have to clear before beginning the testing? Or will certain exceptions and limitations on the Fourth Amendment render the Amendment inapplicable in these circumstances?

The Fifth Amendment and the Takings Clause

The Fifth Amendment states:

> No person shall be held to answer for a capital, or otherwise infamous crime, unless on a presentment or indictment of a Grand Jury, except in cases arising in the land or naval forces,

or in the Militia, when in actual service in time of War or public danger; nor shall any person be subject for the same offense to be twice put in jeopardy of life or limb; nor shall be compelled in any criminal case to be a witness against himself, nor be deprived of life, liberty, or property, without due process of law; nor shall private property be taken for public use, without just compensation.

The last clause of the Amendment is commonly referred to as the Takings Clause. As demonstrated above by the special status given to the home, the law is very protective of private property: "It is a principle of universal law that wherever the right to own property is recognized in a free government, practically all other rights become worthless if the government possesses an uncontrollable power over the property of the citizen" (*House v. Los Angeles County Flood Control District*, 153 P.2d 950 [Cal. 1944]). The Takings Clause is one specific protection of private property.

Eminent Domain v. the Police Power

The general rule of the Takings Clause is that the government must pay just compensation for any property it has taken for public use. The government's power to take property for public use is called eminent domain.

Takings come in two forms. The first are physical occupations – or "real" takings – in which the government either physically damages or appropriates or occupies property. Such real takings are usually remedied by granting the property owner money damages for the market value of the property taken. An example might be the appropriation of a house or other private building to build some public structure in its place.

The other form is the regulatory taking, where some government action diminishes the owner's ability to use his property. For example, if a city rezones a parcel of land to prohibit almost all buildings or uses on that land, we might call this a regulatory taking. The government has not actually "taken" the land, but it has severely restricted its use. Regulatory takings are a confusing area of the law, but the rule of thumb is that they do not require compensation unless they deprive the property owner of all economically beneficial use of the land – a very high standard to meet (Salzberg, 2006).

Beyond the question of form, takings are defined by the motivation underlying them. Courts have strongly delineated between those takings that are effected for "public use" and those that occur for other purposes. One of the most important "other purposes" is the police power, which allows states to act in defense of the public health and safety. The line between public use and the police power is often a fine one, but it is very important because it separates those takings that require compensation from those that do not:

> *The distinction between an exercise of the eminent domain power that is compensable under the fifth amendment and an exercise of the police power [which is not compensable] is that in a compensable exercise of the eminent domain power, a property interest is taken from the owner and applied to the public use because the use of such property is beneficial to the public; and in the exercise of the police power, the owner's property interest is restricted or infringed upon because his continued use of the property is or would other-wise be injurious to the public welfare.*
> *Franco-Italian Packing Co. v. United States* (1955)

Put another way, the eminent domain power relates to public improvements and public works but does not cover emergency situations that threaten the public health (*Customer Company v. City of Sacramento*, 1995). One classic example of police power at work consists of those cases "in which buildings have been set on fire to prevent a larger fire from spreading" (Salzberg, 2006). In such a situation, the owners of the buildings set on fire are owed no compensation from the government.

Of course, this is not to say that in any situation the government can claim there was an emergency and be excused from paying compensation. The government must demonstrate that an emergency actually existed; in addition, the damage inflicted "cannot extend beyond the necessities of the case and be made a cloak to destroy constitutional rights" (*House v. Los Angeles County Flood Control District*, 1944). The government must also exercise the police power with reasonable care. When the government was the cause of the emergency compensation may be required (*Odello Brothers v. County of Monterey*, 1998).

■ ■ Critical Thinking ■

Do you think the distinction between taking property for public use and destroying property to protect the public health is a viable one? In the examples that follow, can you make the argument that the government should have been required to pay the property owner? Why might we consider this distinction a good one?

Public Health and Takings

What types of actions have been excused from the normal rule of compensation as exercises of the police power? Historically, the police power exception has been at its strongest during wartime. Compensation was denied for a tuna boat impounded off the coast of Costa Rica in the days after Pearl Harbor, an oil facility in Manila destroyed by the U.S. Army immediately prior to the Japanese invasion of the Philippines, and a bridge destroyed by Union forces to prevent a Confederate advance during the Civil War (*Franco-Italian Packing Company v. United States*, 1955; *United States v. Caltex, Inc.*, 1952; *United States v. Pacific Railroad*, 1887).

The historical record also provides a number of cases that deal directly with the public health. So, for example, the destruction of a herd of elk infected with contagious bovine tuberculosis did not require compensation (*South Dakota Department of Health v. Heim*, 1984).

Case Study 2 – The Smallpox Hospital

In 1896, Chicago built and began operating a smallpox hospital on the east side of Lawndale Avenue near West 33rd Street on a parcel of land the city owned. The owners of property on the west side of that same stretch of Lawndale Avenue sued the city, claiming that the smallpox hospital had rendered their property unsuitable for many investment purposes. The private property owners sought money damages under the Takings Clause. The court denied the property owners' claim, however, stating that it was within the city's police power to erect the hospital on its own land (*Frazer v. City of Chicago*, 1900).

What type of taking was involved in this case? How might the principles of the case be important during a public health emergency? Think specifically of quarantine and isolation. Note that 20 years later, a court granted compensation to a property owner who complained about "hospitals for the confinement and treatment of malignant, contagious, and infectious diseases" built adjacent to her land. One possible difference between these outcomes is that the property owner in the later case alleged that the city negligently maintained the "pest house" (*Oklahoma City v. Vetter*, 1919). What additional factors might that ruling require a public health official to consider in dealing with an epidemic?

Case Study 3 – The Nursing Home

In September 1976, the Woodland Nursing Home in Methuen, Massachusetts was facing serious budgetary issues. It told its staff that it could not longer pay them and informed the families and relatives of certain patients that they were advised to remove those patients immediately. The Massachusetts Commissioner of Public Health decided that the transfer of the patients would put them at serious risk, such that the situation constituted a public health emergency. As a result, the Governor of Massachusetts declared an emergency and ordered that the Department of Public Health take over the nursing home. The emergency declaration was revoked two days later, and the nursing home was turned back over to its owners.

The owners then sued Massachusetts for compensation under the Takings Clause. The court, however, held that no compensation was required:

> *We believe that the Commonwealth's action in these circumstances constituted an exercise of the State's police power and a regulation of or a restriction upon the plaintiff's use of its property "to prevent the use thereof in a manner that is detrimental to the pubic interest."*
>
> Davidson v. Commonwealth (1979)

Davidson deals with a somewhat limited emergency. How are the stakes changed when the situation is graver and potentially affects many more people? Think again about our example of a dirty bomb being detonated or other chemical agent being released in an urban area. Presumably, public health officials would need to use the existing health infrastructure – and hospitals in particular – to respond to the situation. This might well involve various degrees of appropriating hospitals, from using isolated wards for quarantine to taking over the entire operations of the facility. What types of claims might the hospital make once the emergency passed? Law professor Vickie J. Williams has suggested some possibilities:

> … Physical occupation of [a] hospital by the government would clearly involve interference with "property," since even a de minimus physical occupation of real property constitutes a compensable taking. An order establishing an isolation or quarantine center at a hospital could involve a physical occupation of the hospital by the government.

Nevertheless, it is far more likely to constitute a regulatory action directing the hospital to use its premises in a certain manner, thus disrupting the facility's day-to-day business. It is far from clear whether the hospital's contracts with insurers and other business associates, and day-to-day revenue-producing operations, are "property" within the meaning of the Takings Clause. Protecting these intangible interests would be of paramount importance to a hospital when considering whether to comply with an order designating it an isolation or quarantine center. The Supreme Court has found compensable takings when government action adversely affects intangible interests such as loss of repose, intellectual property, and monetary interest on pooled funds. Yet, hospital managers could not be certain whether the Takings Clause would protect the hospital's intangible business interests. Intangible business-related interests have been characterized as compensable "property" in some types of takings, but have been characterized as non-compensable losses in others.

Williams (2007)

Can you think of any other ways in which public health officials might "take" private property during such an emergency?

Takings and Emergencies – Statutory Response

In addition to the general concerns and issues involved with the application of the Takings Clause, many states have enacted legislation specifically expanding takings-type powers in times of emergency. New Jersey's law on takings and public health emergencies, based largely on the Model State Emergency Health Powers Act (MSEHPA; see Chapter 6), follows:

During a state of public health emergency, the commissioner may exercise, for such period as the state of public health emergency exists, the following powers concerning health care and other facilities, property, roads, or public areas:

a. Use of property and facilities. To procure, by condemnation or otherwise, subject to the payment of reasonable costs ..., construct, lease, transport, store, maintain, renovate or distribute property and facilities as may be reasonable and necessary to respond to the public health emergency, with the right to take immediate possession thereof. Such property and facilities include, but are not limited to, communication devices, carriers, real estate, food and clothing.

■ ■ ■ ═══════════════════════════════════════

Do you think reasonable costs are the same as just compensation?

═══════════════════════════════════════ ■ ■ ■

This authority shall also include the ability to accept and manage those goods and services donated for the purpose of responding to a public health emergency. The authority provided to the commissioner pursuant to this section shall not affect the existing authority or emergency response of other State agencies.

b. Use of health care facilities.

(1) To require, subject to the payment of reasonable costs ..., a health care facility to provide services or the use of its facility if such services or use are reasonable and necessary to respond to the public health emergency, as a condition of licensure, authorization or the ability to continue doing business in the State as a health care facility. After consultation with the management of the health care facility, the commissioner may determine that the use of the facility may include transferring the management and supervision of the facility to the commissioner for a limited or unlimited period of time, but shall not exceed the duration of the public health emergency. In the event of such a transfer, the commissioner shall use the existing management of the health care facility.

■ ■ ■ ═══════════════════════════════════════

How long might a health emergency last? Can a hospital challenge the state's determination of the duration of the emergency?

═══════════════════════════════════════ ■ ■ ■

(2) Concurrent with or within 24 hours of the transfer of the management and supervision of a health care facility, the

commissioner shall provide the facility with a written order notifying the facility of:

(a) the premises designated for transfer;

(b) the date and time at which the transfer will commence;

(c) a statement of the terms and condition of the transfer;

(d) a statement of the basis upon which the transfer is justified; and

(e) the availability of a hearing to contest the order, as provided in paragraph (3) of this subsection.

(3) A health care facility subject to an order to transfer management and supervision to the commissioner pursuant to this section may request a hearing in the Superior Court to contest the order.

(a) Upon receiving a request for a hearing, the court shall fix a date for a hearing. The hearing shall be held within 72 hours of receipt of the request by the court, excluding Saturdays, Sundays and legal holidays. The court may proceed in a summary manner. At the hearing, the burden of proof shall be on the commissioner to prove by a preponderance of the evidence that transfer of the management and supervision of the health care facility is reasonable and necessary to respond to the public health emergency and the order issued by the commissioner is warranted to address the need.

(b) If, upon a hearing, the court finds that the transfer of the management and supervision of the health care facility is not warranted, the facility shall be released immediately from the transfer order.

(c) The manner in which the request for a hearing pursuant to this subsection is filed and acted upon shall be in accordance with the Rules of Court.

■ ■ ■ ━━━━━━━━━━━━━━━━━━━━━━━━━━━━━━━━━

Why might the following section be very important to hospitals?

(4) A health care facility which provides services or the use of its facility or whose management or supervision is transferred to the commissioner pursuant to this subsection shall not be liable for any civil damages as a result of the commissioner's acts or omissions in providing medical care or treatment or any other services related to the public health emergency.

(5) For the duration of a state of public health emergency, the commissioner shall confer with the Commissioner of Banking and Insurance to request that the Department of Banking and Insurance waive regulations requiring compliance by a health care provider or health care facility with a managed care plan's administrative protocols, including but not limited to, prior authorization and pre-certification.

c. Control of property. To inspect, control, restrict, and regulate by rationing and using quotas, prohibitions on shipments, allocation or other means, the use, sale, dispensing, distribution or transportation of food, clothing and other commodities, as may be reasonable and necessary to respond to the public health emergency.

■ ■ ■ ▬▬▬▬▬▬▬▬▬▬▬▬▬▬▬▬▬▬▬▬▬▬▬▬▬▬

This section grants a great deal of leeway over most property. Is the "reasonable and necessary" requirement a serious limitation on this power?

▬▬▬▬▬▬▬▬▬▬▬▬▬▬▬▬▬▬▬▬▬▬▬▬▬ ■ ■ ■

d. To identify areas that are or may be dangerous to the public health and to recommend to the Governor and the Attorney General that movement of persons within that area be restricted, if such action is reasonable and necessary to respond to the public health emergency.

N.J. Stat. 26:13-9

Reasonable reimbursement, meanwhile, is determined and awarded by a State Public Health Emergency Claim Reimbursement Board (N.J. Stat. 26:13-24). How well does the New Jersey statute fit with what we already know about the Takings Clause and the limitations on it provided by the police power?

THE MAYOR OF DES MOINES DECLARES AN EMERGENCY

The massive floods of 1993 caused disruption throughout Des Moines, including the incapacitation of the city's water treatment facility. In response, the Mayor issued a proclamation of emergency that ordered businesses to provide their own sanitation facilities for employees. Most businesses complied, but some simply ignored the proclamation. The city began to receive complaints from employees that they were being forced to work in unsanitary conditions. The city's lawyers had to face the question of whether and how the proclamation could be enforced. The city's chief lawyer described the result:

> ... Iowa's state code provides for no specific penalty in this situation. Iowa statutes simply provide that in times of emergency the mayor may "govern the city by proclamation." The Legal Department reasoned that if the mayor can govern by proclamation, then the mayor can do by proclamation whatever the city council exercising the city's home rule powers can do by motion, resolution, amendment, or ordinance. We reasoned further that since the initial proclamation stated that all future proclamations were to have the force and effect of law, the proclamation requiring businesses to cease occupying their business premises had the same effect as an ordinance. Consequently, since the original proclamation provided that the violation of a proclamation would be considered a violation of law punishable as such, then a violation of a proclamation could be prosecuted as a simple misdemeanor under the Iowa Code and would be punishable as such.

> In the face of open defiance of the second proclamation by a small handful of businesses, the Legal Department advised the mayor and city staff to advise the public that violators would be prosecuted for misdemeanor violations. Fortunately for all concerned, the need to resort to such eventualities was avoided by the restoration of water service ...

> Nowadzky (1995)

Takings, Emergencies, and Public Policy

The Takings Clause is not merely an after-the-fact issue. From a policy standpoint, compensation for perceived takings could be a crucial issue both for the government and hospitals in preparing to react to emergencies:

> Because the availability, type, or amount of compensation under the Takings Clause is uncertain, the Clause is not an incentive for hospitals to comply with the orders of public health authorities during a pandemic. In the case of a wide-scale public health emergency requiring multiple isolation and quarantine centers capable of using sophisticated medical technology, the threat of massive amounts of litigation regarding the compensation due to hospitals is likely to cool the eagerness of hospitals to comply with the orders of public health authorities. It could also make the government think twice about designating hospitals as isolation and quarantine centers. This fear may dilute the response to the emergency, cause delay, and adversely affect the public's health. The undeveloped state of our Takings Clause jurisprudence in the context of public health emergencies encourages hospitals to protect themselves by resisting such orders in the first place. Resistance becomes far more attractive than taking the chance of complying and engaging in protracted litigation about the amount of compensation due afterward.

■ ■ ■ ▬▬▬▬▬▬▬▬▬▬▬▬▬▬▬▬▬▬▬▬▬

Do these concerns help explain or justify the distinction between eminent domain and "public use" on the one hand and the police power and protecting the public welfare on the other?

Are hospitals better off preparing to be unprepared?

▬▬▬▬▬▬▬▬▬▬▬▬▬▬▬▬▬▬▬▬▬ ■ ■ ■

> "Demoralization costs" are a less apparent danger to the viability and quality of our health care system from the uncertainty surrounding compensation for takings in public health emergencies. A "demoralization cost" is the loss in utility

that can be attributed to the likelihood that a property owner, knowing that the compensation she receives will be inadequate if her property is taken, will fail to maintain the property or use it properly. A hospital that knows that it is unlikely to receive adequate compensation for its losses if it is designated as an isolation or quarantine facility has little economic incentive to build additional capacity or invest in additional equipment in anticipation of a pandemic. In this context, demoralization costs may take the form of hospitals choosing to make themselves less attractive isolation or quarantine centers by channeling funds away from pandemic preparedness. Hence, hospitals that might have been well-prepared for a pandemic may consciously choose to under-prepare so that they can reap the financial benefits related to treating the more lucrative patients that isolation and quarantine centers will have to turn away. A perverse incentive to under-prepare such as this works to the severe detriment of the public's health by decreasing overall pandemic preparedness.

Williams (2007)

■ ■ Critical Thinking ■

How well do you think the New Jersey statute addresses the concerns identified by Professor Williams?

Important Terms

- Administrative search
- Community caretaking function
- Eminent domain
- Exclusionary rule
- Just compensation
- Plain view
- Probable cause
- Regulatory taking
- Special needs exception
- Taking for police power purposes
- Taking for public use
- Warrant

Review Questions

1. What are the usual requirements for conducting a search of a private home under the Fourth Amendment?

2. What exceptions to the normal Fourth Amendment rules might be triggered in the event of a public health emergency?

3. What is the difference between eminent domain and a taking effected under the police power? Which requires compensation to be paid to the property owner?

4. What policy reasons suggest that public health officials should be granted a good deal of leeway in both searching and taking private property during emergencies?

13

Sovereign Immunity and Government Liability

What You Will Learn

- The meaning of "sovereign immunity"
- The ways in which sovereign immunity law can determine issues of liability in emergency response and disaster management situations
- How the law measures whether negligence has occurred
- Why and how policymaking is an especially protected zone of government activity

Introduction

The focus of this chapter is on the question of whether and to what extent government should be required to pay damages to compensate persons who were injured by its actions. The debate over sovereign immunity, as the relevant doctrine is called, dates from English common law. As we will see, American law incorporates both a sovereign immunity defense to lawsuits and the allowance of damages in situations for which the defense has been waived. However, if the action being complained of was the formulation of policy rather than a failure by officials to adhere to clearly established rules, recovery can be blocked on that basis.

In other words, when plaintiffs seek money damages against the government, there must be a waiver of sovereign immunity for the lawsuit to be allowed. And even if there is a waiver, the lawsuit may be dismissed if the actions being complained of were discretionary or policymaking decisions by government officials.

The Sovereign Immunity Defense

Sovereignty is the defining characteristic of an autonomous, independent government. In *Federalist Paper No. 81*, Alexander Hamilton noted that it is inherent in the nature of sovereignty that lawsuits in which individuals seek monetary damages from the sovereign are barred unless the sovereign has waived its defense of immunity. The rationale for the defense is the common interest in efficient government and prudent management of government funds. Yet there is also the concern that citizens be able to bring meritorious claims if they have been injured.

> The legal uncertainties surrounding governmental responsibility for [injuries] committed by its agents reflect a number of ... values, includ[ing] society's interests in encouraging government to act vigorously without undue caution, deterring unreasonably risky conduct, avoiding judicial control of discretionary and policy decisions entrusted to the politically accountable branches, protecting the public fisc from excessive claiming attracted by government's uniquely deep pockets, and vindicating and exemplifying the rule of law. Striking a just balance among these goals has proven exceedingly difficult.
>
> Schuck and Park (2000)

As we know from Chapter 1, states are also considered sovereign entities. When the United States was created, each state retained much of its sovereignty, subject to the Supremacy Clause, which specifies that federal law will trump conflicting state law. One way that the Constitution recognizes this principle is reflected in the sovereign immunity provision of the Eleventh Amendment, which provides:

> The Judicial power of the United States shall not be construed to extend to any suit in law or equity, commenced or prosecuted against one of the United States by Citizens of another State, or by Citizens or Subjects of any Foreign State.

The Eleventh Amendment has a rich history: it was enacted in response to the Supreme Court's 1793 decision in *Chisholm v. Georgia*, which upheld the right of a South Carolina plaintiff to sue the state of Georgia over money that he claimed the state owed him for munitions supplied during the Revolutionary War. Georgia had argued that as a sovereign state, it could not be sued in court without its consent. The public outcry over the decision allowing the suit prompted the adoption of the Eleventh Amendment, which was meant to reassure those who feared a too-powerful national government.

■ ■ ■ ▬▬▬▬▬▬▬▬▬▬▬▬▬▬▬▬▬▬▬▬▬▬▬▬▬

Injunctions Are Treated Differently than Damages

Although the Eleventh Amendment immunizes nonconsenting states from suits for money damages, the Supreme Court has held that federal courts may *enjoin* state officials from violating federal law (*Ex parte Young*, 1908). An injunction is a legal order that directs a person to do or to refrain from doing a particular act. For instance, where a law is unconstitutional, a court may issue an injunction forbidding its enforcement.

▬▬▬▬▬▬▬▬▬▬▬▬▬▬▬▬▬▬▬▬▬▬▬▬▬ ■ ■ ■

The Eleventh Amendment bars lawsuits seeking money damages against the states only when the lawsuits are brought in federal courts. Each state's law incorporates the sovereign immunity defense covering actions filed in state courts, although the parameters of the defense vary by state. For example, most states include a provision regarding sovereign immunity in their disaster response laws. Some (such as Alabama) exempt from liability all emergency management activities, while others (such as Kansas) limit immunity to actions taken pursuant to a formal declaration of emergency (Lerner, 1991). Such provisions are also often included in health emergency statutes.

Statutory Waivers of Sovereign Immunity

Government immunity from suit is not absolute. Congress and all the state legislatures have enacted statutes that create waivers of the immunity defense for a certain category of lawsuits. These waiver laws play an important role in keeping government accountable. They allow government actors to be sued for the same acts that, if a private person committed them, would constitute negligence.

The primary waiver is in the Federal Tort Claims Act (FTCA), enacted in 1946, in which the federal government relinquishes its immunity for

> injury or loss of property, or personal injury or death caused by the negligent or wrongful act or omission of any employee of the Government while acting within the scope of his office or employment, under circumstances where the United States, if a private person, would be liable to the claimant in accordance with the law of the place where the act or omission occurred.
> 28 U.S. Code §1346(b)(1) (2000)

Each state also has a tort claims act, most of which are worded identically to the FTCA. Waivers can also be found in topic-specific statutes, such as civil rights laws or environmental laws.

Negligence

The scope of the waiver in the FTCA is for a "negligent or wrongful act or omission." Negligence – the fixing of responsibility for causing an injury – is a central legal concept in English and American law. In its simplest form, negligence can be defined as the failure to exercise appropriate care in circumstances in which the risk of harm is reasonably foreseeable. Defendants may be found negligent for their actions *or* for their failure to act.

For negligence law to apply, there must have been an actual injury and the injured person must be seeking to recover damages from the person who caused that injury. If a person behaves "negligently" but does not cause an injury – for instance, a drunk driver who makes it home without causing damage – there is no cause of action for negligence. If a drunk driver is stopped by the police, he or she may be charged with violating the law and face consequences for illegal behavior, but there cannot be a lawsuit for "negligent" behavior unless there is harm to other people or property.

To win a lawsuit for negligence, a plaintiff must establish several facts: that he or she suffered an injury; that the injury was caused by the defendant; that the defendant had a legal duty not to cause the injury; and that the defendant breached that duty. It is often relatively easy to establish an injury and damages. For example, a wrecked car and physical injury following a car accident can be proven by photographs, witnesses, doctor's reports, and in many other ways. Causation may be trickier – if the drunk driver was following the traffic laws while the sober driver ran a red light, for instance, the court could find that the drunk driver did not cause the accident.

The more complicated issue is usually establishing what the "duty of care" is in a given situation so that the jury can determine from the facts whether the defendant breached it. The duty of care is expressed as a failure to exercise "reasonable care," or to act as a reasonable person would in light of the risk that was foreseeable in the situation. In our drunk-driving example, for instance, the breached duty requirement might be expressed as follows: when a person drives a car, he or she has an obligation to the public, including other drivers, to exercise reasonable care in driving. This includes an obligation to use prescription lenses for eyesight problems, to obey traffic signals, to comply with the speed limit, and to take other normal precautions, certainly including the duty not to drive when intoxicated.

Judge Learned Hand offered a succinct summary of reasonable care in the 1947 case *United States v. Carroll Towing Co.* In what has become known as the Hand test for negligence, he concluded that a court can determine whether reasonable care was exercised by looking at three factors:

- The probability at the time of the action or failure to act of an accident occurring
- The gravity of the injury that resulted
- The burden on the actor of taking the necessary precautions to avoid the injury.

Generally, as the severity of possible injury increases, so does the required level of care to avoid that injury.

Statutes, regulations, building codes, and contracts also serve as sources of the standard of care (Binder, 2002). If a building's electrical system is not up to code, for example, that will constitute a breach of the duty of care owed by its owners to occupants. The same is true of professional standards. As the Supreme Court of Georgia wrote, "[t]he law imposes upon persons performing architectural, engineering, and other professional and skilled services the obligation to exercise a reasonable degree of care, skill, and ability, which generally is taken and considered to be such a degree of care and skill as, under similar circumstances, is ordinarily employed by their respective professions" (*Housing Authority of City of Carrollton v. Ayers*, 1955). In some situations, a statute or code will set the minimal standards for reasonableness, but more may be required to avoid liability.

Aslakson v. United States
U.S. Court of Appeals for the Eighth Circuit, 1986

> *Paul Aslakson [sued] the United States for the death of his son, Timothy Aslakson. Timothy was killed in a boating accident on Devils Lake, North Dakota, when the aluminum mast of his sailboat made contact with electrical power lines owned and operated by the Western Area Power Administration (WAPA), an agency of the United States government. Aslakson claims that the United States was negligent by failing to provide adequate vertical clearance between the power lines and the surface of the water. The United States denies any liability for the accident on the basis that its decision not to elevate the lines beyond*

the clearance provided is immune from a tort suit under the "discretionary function" exception to the Federal Tort Claims Act (FTCA). ...

WAPA transmits electrical power to fifteen central and western states. As part of its responsibility in the transmission of this electrical power, WAPA constructs and maintains its electrical power lines in accordance with the National Electric Safety Code (NESC). Rule 013B of the NESC states: "Existing installations, including maintenance replacements, which comply with prior editions of the Code, need not be modified to comply with these rules, except as may be required for safety reasons by the administrative authority." ...

WAPA inspects and maintains these lines on a routine basis. WAPA has a local maintenance crew at Devils Lake that carries out monthly aerial inspections of the transmission lines. Furthermore, ground inspections are conducted annually. As part of its responsibility, the maintenance crew is instructed to look for clearance problems caused by changed conditions and report any such clearance problems to the main office.

The particular power lines involved in this case were constructed in 1950 to comply with the 1948 edition of the NESC. As originally constructed, the power lines provided a vertical clearance of 28 feet and passed over land rather than water. Later the water level of Devils Lake rose to such an extent that the lines crossed over an area of Devils Lake called Creel Bay.

Motivated by a concern over what effect the rising water level of Devils Lake might have on WAPA's power lines, several WAPA employees conducted a field review of the lake in 1979. The review team did not inspect the lines over Creel Bay but focused its attention on the lines that crossed the main part of Devils Lake. After its inspection the review team concluded that the height of the conductors over the water surface "could be a hazard to tall-masted sailboats on the lake."

Although several long term solutions were suggested by the review team such as rerouting the lines and installing submarine cable, WAPA decided to elevate the existing lines over the main part of Devils Lake. Hence, in the spring of 1980 the power lines were retensioned to comply with the current edition of the NESC. The retensioned lines provided a vertical clearance of over fifty feet.

WAPA took no action, however, either to increase the vertical clearance or to warn boaters of the power lines over Creel Bay. According to Vernon Hartwick, WAPA's district manager of the Bismarck office, the power lines over Creel Bay were not considered a hazard, because of their remote location and because no reports or complaints had been received regarding their low vertical clearance.

The accident occurred on June 20, 1982, while Timothy was sailing a Hobie Cat sailboat on the north end of Creel Bay. Timothy was severely shocked when the sailboat's 26.5 foot mast made contact with WAPA's power lines. Timothy's body was later recovered in water that was approximately six feet deep. ...

In this case, the United States invokes the [discretionary function] exception on the basis that its policy required only that its power lines meet the standards of the 1948 edition of the NESC. Because the district court found that WAPA's power lines met the minimum vertical clearance requirements of the 1948 standards, the United States asserts that WAPA's power lines were within the requirements of its own policy. We disagree. ...

Under its policy, although WAPA is bound to the minimum vertical clearance requirements of the NESC in effect at the time of construction of its power lines, it must elevate those power lines to comply with revisions of the Code if safety reasons require such action. The United States claims that any decision by WAPA officials regarding the safety of its power lines is within the scope of the discretionary function exception. ...

We believe that such an expansive interpretation would result in the exception swallowing the rule. ...

WAPA's policy clearly required it to elevate its power lines if safety considerations compelled such action. Where the challenged governmental activity involves safety considerations under an established policy rather than the balancing of competing public policy considerations, the rationale for the exception falls away and the United States will be held responsible for the negligence of its employees.

For the government to show merely that some choice was involved in the decision-making process is insufficient to activate the discretionary function exception. The balancing of policy considerations is a necessary prerequisite. WAPA's determination that the power lines over Creel Bay were not a safety hazard did not involve an evaluation of the relevant policy factors; rather it was a decision made by WAPA officials charged with the responsibility of implementing an already established policy.

Furthermore, WAPA's policy does not allow its officials to choose a course of action they deem desirable if their power lines are dangerously low. The policy's mandate is clear; WAPA must raise its power lines if they constitute a safety hazard.

Although such a policy necessarily involves some degree of judgment on the part of government officials, it is not the kind of judgment that involves the weighing of public policy considerations. ...

Aslakson's challenge to the governmental activity involved here goes not to the policy itself or to the manner in which WAPA chose to implement that policy. Furthermore, the challenged conduct is neither regulatory in nature nor administrative decision-making grounded in social, economic, or political policy. Rather, Aslakson claims WAPA officials were guilty of failing to comply with their own safety policy in the maintenance of their electrical transmission lines. This claim smacks of ordinary 'garden-variety' negligence, and the meeting by WAPA officials of their responsibility under the safety policy does not come within the scope of the discretionary function exception.

*By fashioning an exception for discretionary governmental
functions, Congress took steps to protect the Government from
liability that would seriously handicap efficient government
operations. We conclude that holding WAPA responsible for
compliance with its own safety policy regarding its electrical
transmission lines will not undermine its governmental function. Hence, the conduct of WAPA officials must be reviewed
in accordance with North Dakota's tort law standards. ...*

■ ■ Critical Thinking ■

The sovereign immunity defense and the waivers of it create a seemingly all-or-nothing framework for plaintiffs seeking to recover damages from the government. Are there other ways that the law could
reflect the conflicting values underlying this debate that Schuck and
Park describe? One example would be by capping the amount of damages that a plaintiff could recover. Can you think of others? For each,
evaluate the pros and cons of whether they should be adopted.

Intentional Torts and Active Endangerment

In addition to the negligence standards discussed above, states also recognize claims for intentional ("wrongful") acts that cause injuries. One
category of intentional torts that has arisen in emergency situations is
called "active endangerment," or the intentional or knowing conduct
by government officials that places others in even greater danger than
what is already present.

The active endangerment theory was the basis for the lawsuit brought
by workers at the Brentwood mail processing facility in Washington, D.C.,
who alleged that the Postal Service intentionally misled them into believing
that their workplace was safe even after managers learned that some equipment was contaminated by anthrax. (This case is discussed in more detail in
Chapter 8.) Recall that two employees who worked there died from anthrax
inhalation and several others became ill. Here is how the court analyzed the
active endangerment doctrine:

*Plaintiffs allege here that Defendants acted with deliberate
indifference because they knew that Brentwood was contaminated with anthrax, yet, to keep the employees working,
they continued to make affirmative misrepresentations concerning the facility's safety. Plaintiffs also allege that by not
providing them with accurate information concerning the*

*safety of the Brentwood facility and by "threatening, intimi-
dating, and/or coercing" them to continue working at the
anthrax-contaminated facility, Defendants made Plaintiffs
more vulnerable to the danger of anthrax contamination.
In addition, Plaintiffs have alleged a series of events that
they argue demonstrate that Defendants were put on notice
"that anthrax spores sent through the mail could penetrate
the sides of a sealed envelope during processing at the
Brentwood facility and, thereby, cause serious injury and/or
death to Plaintiffs. ..."*

*The Court has given considerable thought to Plaintiffs'
arguments. If the facts are as alleged, the conduct of USPS
managers would appear commendable for their dedication
to getting the mail out but deplorable for not recognizing
the potential human risk involved. ... [T]hese alleged actions
demonstrated a gross disregard for a dangerous situation ...
It is alleged that Defendants had been put on notice of the
serious consequences that could result from Plaintiffs' exposure to anthrax yet, despite such knowledge, Defendants
engaged in a campaign of misinformation designed to keep
the employees at work. As noted by the Supreme Court ...
"[w]hen opportunities to do better are teamed with pro-
tracted failure even to care, indifference is truly shocking."*

Briscoe v. Potter (2004)

The Discretionary Function Exception

The discretionary function exception provides immunity for government officials' *policy* judgments, as opposed to actions they are
required by the law to carry out. In other words, the sovereign immunity defense is effectively reinstated by this exception to the waiver.
Under the FTCA, the discretionary function exception bars any claim
based on the "exercise or performance or failure to exercise or perform
a discretionary function or duty on the part of a federal agency or an
employee of the government, whether or not the discretion involved be
abused." (28 U.S. Code § 2680) This means that the sovereign has not
waived immunity for discretionary acts or policy decisions.

Although the rule is easy to state, it is not always clear which
actions are discretionary. In general, if a law clearly mandates that
officials perform specific acts, then the discretionary function exception
does not apply. But if a law places a broad requirement on an official

to meet an objective, are that official's independent decisions on how to reach the goal discretionary and immune, or are they mandated by law and therefore "fair game" for lawsuits under the FTCA if the actions cause injuries? The following case is the leading Supreme Court decision in this area of law.

The *Berkovitz* Case

The parents of a paralyzed infant sued the National Institutes of Health (NIH) under the FTCA after their child contracted polio from an oral polio vaccine. The Berkovitz family alleged that the Division of Biological Standards (DBS) within the NIH had been negligent in two of its actions: licensing the manufacturer of the vaccine, and then approving the specific vaccine lot in question. The government claimed that the decisions to license the manufacturer and to approve the vaccine lot were discretionary and therefore immune from suit.

Berkovitz v. United States
U.S. Supreme Court, 1988

> ... *The determination of whether the discretionary function exception bars a suit against the Government is guided by several established principles. This Court stated in [an earlier case] that "it is the nature of the conduct, rather than the status of the actor, that governs whether the discretionary function exception applies in a given case." In examining the nature of the challenged conduct, a court must first consider whether the action is a matter of choice for the acting employee. This inquiry is mandated by the language of the exception; conduct cannot be discretionary unless it involves an element of judgment or choice. See Dalehite v. United States (stating that the exception protects "the discretion of the executive or the administrator to act according to one's judgment of the best course"). Thus, the discretionary function exception will not apply when a federal statute, regulation, or policy specifically prescribes a course of action for an employee to follow. In this event, the employee has no rightful option but to adhere to the directive. And if the employee's conduct cannot appropriately be the product of judgment or choice, then there is no discretion in the conduct for the discretionary function exception to protect.*

Moreover, assuming the challenged conduct involves an element of judgment, a court must determine whether that judgment is of the kind that the discretionary function exception was designed to shield. The basis for the discretionary function exception was Congress' desire to prevent judicial 'second-guessing' of legislative and administrative decisions grounded in social, economic, and political policy through the medium of an action in tort. The exception, properly construed, therefore protects only governmental actions and decisions based on considerations of public policy. See Dalehite v. United States ("Where there is room for policy judgment and decision there is discretion"). In sum, the discretionary function exception insulates the Government from liability if the action challenged in the case involves the permissible exercise of policy judgment. ...

Petitioners' suit raises two broad claims. First, petitioners assert that the DBS violated a federal statute and accompanying regulations in issuing a license to Lederle Laboratories to produce Orimune [the oral polio vaccine]. Second, petitioners argue that the Bureau of Biologics of the FDA [Food and Drug Administration] violated federal regulations and policy in approving the release of the particular lot of Orimune that contained Kevan Berkovitz's dose. We examine each of these broad claims by reviewing the applicable regulatory scheme and petitioners' specific allegations of agency wrongdoing. ...

Petitioners' first allegation with regard to the licensing of Orimune is that the DBS issued a product license without first receiving data that the manufacturer must submit showing how the product, at the various stages of the manufacturing process, matched up against regulatory safety standards. The discretionary function exception does not bar a cause of action based on this allegation. The statute and regulations [governing the licensing of medical products] require, as a precondition to licensing, that the DBS receive certain test data from the manufacturer relating to the product's compliance with regulatory standards. The DBS has no discretion to issue a license without first receiving the required test data; to do so would violate a specific statutory and regulatory directive. Accordingly, to the extent that petitioners' licensing claim is based on a decision of the DBS to issue a license without having received the required test data, the discretionary function exception imposes no bar.

■ ■ ■ ▬▬▬▬▬▬▬▬▬▬▬▬▬▬▬▬▬▬▬▬▬▬▬▬▬

Note the importance of specific facts to the application of the legal principles in this case.

▬▬▬▬▬▬▬▬▬▬▬▬▬▬▬▬▬▬▬▬▬▬▬▬▬ ■ ■ ■

Petitioners' other allegation regarding the licensing of Orimune is difficult to describe with precision. Petitioners contend that the DBS licensed Orimune even though the vaccine did not comply with certain regulatory safety standards. This charge may be understood in any of three ways. First, petitioners may mean that the DBS licensed Orimune without first making a determination as to whether the vaccine complied with regulatory standards. Second, petitioners may intend to argue that the DBS specifically found that Orimune failed to comply with certain regulatory standards and nonetheless issued a license for the vaccine's manufacture. Third, petitioners may concede that the DBS made a determination of compliance, but allege that this determination was incorrect. Neither petitioners' complaint nor their briefs and argument before this Court make entirely clear their theory of the case.

If petitioners aver that the DBS licensed Orimune either without determining whether the vaccine complied with regulatory standards or after determining that the vaccine failed to comply, the discretionary function exception does not bar the claim. Under the scheme governing the DBS's regulation of polio vaccines, the DBS may not issue a license except upon an examination of the product and a determination that the product complies with all regulatory standards. The agency has no discretion to deviate from this mandated procedure. Petitioners' claim, if interpreted as alleging that the DBS licensed Orimune in the absence of a determination that the vaccine complied with regulatory standards, therefore does not challenge a discretionary function. Rather, the claim charges a failure on the part of the agency to perform its clear duty under federal law. When a suit charges an agency with failing to act in accord with a specific mandatory directive, the discretionary function exception does not apply.

If petitioners' claim is that the DBS made a determination that Orimune complied with regulatory standards, but that the determination was incorrect, the question of the applicability of the discretionary function exception requires a somewhat different analysis. In that event, the question turns on whether the manner and method of determining compliance with the safety standards at issue involve agency judgment of the kind protected by the discretionary function exception. Petitioners contend that the determination involves the application of objective scientific standards, whereas the Government asserts that the determination incorporates considerable "policy judgment." In making these assertions, the parties have framed the issue appropriately; application of the discretionary function exception to the claim that the determination of compliance was incorrect hinges on whether the agency officials making that determination permissibly exercise policy choice. The parties, however, have not addressed this question in detail, and they have given us no indication of the way in which the DBS interprets and applies the regulations setting forth the criteria for compliance. Given that these regulations are particularly abstruse, we hesitate to decide the question on the scanty record before us. ...

Notice that the Court has used a two-part test to determine whether the discretionary function exception applies.

- First, the action must be discretionary in that it involves some element of choice.
- Second, it must be a permissible use of discretion because it is based on considerations of social, economic, and political policies.

The Court's analysis of the first prong focused on whether there were specific rules and mandated actions that the agency was required to meet. If there were, the Court did not need to reach the second prong, i.e. whether a discretionary action was based on inappropriate considerations.

This was the standard relied on in a California case in which state employees who had been hired to install traps in a pest eradication program suffered injuries caused by exposure to a chemical in the traps. They alleged that their supervisors had concealed and misrepresented the dangers associated with the chemical. State law imposed strict notification requirements when pesticides were used. The government argued that its actions, taken during a declared state of emergency brought about by Medfly infestation, were exempt from a lawsuit because of the discretionary function exception. Here is how the court ruled:

> *We recognize in a state of emergency it is imperative the State must be able to act with haste in exercising its sovereign powers to protect the public. However, in exercising that power in situations in which the State is also obligated to provide accurate information to the public in the context of an eradication program, there can be no reason for the State to purposefully withhold health and safety information from persons most likely to be injured. The State cannot thwart plaintiffs' claims by labeling their actions as "discretionary acts" or acts which are but a "myriad of decisions regarding the implementation of the Medfly program." ... The State is required to use its best efforts to provide accurate and complete health and safety information; no decisionmaking is required. Thus, the [discretionary function exception] does not immunize the State.*
>
> *Adkins v. California* (1996)

THE DUTY THAT COMES WITH KNOWLEDGE

Discretionary immunity does not apply where state or federal officials *know* that their actions or omissions violate statutory or constitutional rights (*Harlow v. Fitzgerald*, 1982). Because no official is authorized to break the law, any decision to violate what are known to be protected legal rights is inherently outside the scope of authorized discretion.

A Hurricane Katrina Case

Now consider a case involving Hurricane Katrina and the failure of federal agencies and officials to provide enough aid, fast enough, to avert tragedy. The relatives of three deceased individuals, all of whom remained in New Orleans during Hurricane Katrina because of their impaired mobility, sued the federal government for its failure to deliver aid so as to prevent the deaths. Each person died in a separate incident.

Figure 13.1 shows a satellite image of Hurricane Katrina.

FIGURE 13.1 Hurricane Katrina
Source: http://www.nasa.gov/vision/earth/lookingatearth/h2005_katrina.html

Ms. Freeman died at the New Orleans Convention Center. After Hurricane Katrina made landfall, her home was flooded. Her son borrowed a boat to bring her, in her wheelchair, to higher ground. He was directed by local police to take her to the Convention Center. Once there, he notified police officers that she needed medical attention. They told him a bus would come to evacuate Ms. Freeman. The Convention Center was not equipped with food, medical supplies, clean water, blankets, medical assistance, triage, or transportation. Ms. Freeman died the day after her son brought her there.

The second decedent, Ms. Eleby, also died at the Convention Center. Ms. Eleby was bedridden. As Hurricane Katrina approached, her physician advised her to evacuate to a local hospital. Her caretaker contacted hospitals and was told that she could go to the Superdome but that no beds would be provided. As a result, she remained with her family who was trapped by the storm in their home. When the first rescue team arrived, they offered to take Ms. Eleby's family only if they left her behind because she was paralyzed and bedridden. A second boat took all of them to the Chef Menteur Highway where they spent the night without food, water, or shelter. The next day rescuers brought them to the Convention Center, and Ms. Eleby died the day following her arrival.

Finally, Mr. DeLuca died at Louis Armstrong International Airport on September 3, 2005. The storm had flooded the assisted living facility in which he resided. A helicopter crew rescued Mr. DeLuca and delivered him to the Pontchartrain Center. After that center flooded, another helicopter transferred him to the interchange of Interstate 10 and Causeway Boulevard (the "Cloverleaf"). The Cloverleaf was not equipped with medical supplies, food, water, shelter, or transportation – it was in the same squalid condition as the Convention Center. Although evacuation buses began arriving on August 31, 2005, a day after he was transferred, Mr. DeLuca was not evacuated. He remained on the Cloverleaf until September 2, 2005, when he collapsed from stress, heat exhaustion, hunger, and dehydration. A helicopter airlifted him to the airport, where he died the next day.

Shortly thereafter, the families of Ms. Freeman, Ms. Eleby, and Mr. DeLuca sued the federal government, alleging that the government failed to exercise due care in the provision of emergency aid pursuant to the National Response Plan (NRP), namely by failing to provide food, water, shelter, medical assistance, and transport to the Convention Center and to the Cloverleaf. The families' argument relied upon their characterization of the NRP as *mandating* the provision of relief. The government claimed that the NRP was a generalized plan that left much to the discretion of various officials and mandated no specific action, only goals. Who do you think prevailed?

Freeman v. United States
U.S. Court of Appeals for the Fifth Circuit, 2009

> *Under the first prong of the Berkovitz test, plaintiffs fail to identify any specific, nondiscretionary function or duty that does not involve an element of judgment or choice. To the*

contrary, plaintiffs cite a large number of NRP provisions that contain generalized, precatory, or aspirational language that is too general to prescribe a specific course of action for an agency or employee to follow. ...

Under the second prong of the Berkovitz test, we hold that the government's decisions about when, where, and how to allocate limited resources within the exigencies of an emergency are the types of decisions that the discretionary function exception was designed to shelter from suit. ... In light of the 'strong presumption' that, where permitted by the relevant statute or regulation, the exercise of choice or judgment implicates relevant policy, decisions regarding the feasibility, safety, and benefit of mobilizing federal resources in the aftermath of a natural disaster are grounded in social, economic, and public policy.

The court concluded:

The tragedies that gave rise to this litigation were compounded by the well-documented inability of all levels of government to provide timely relief to the hurricane's victims. The federal government has publicly admitted that it made many mistakes; however, even if those mistakes caused decedents' deaths, which we are presently in no position to determine, the federal government's negligence does not give rise to tort liability absent the United States' express waiver of sovereign immunity. For the above explained reasons, we conclude that the United States' has not waived sovereign immunity for the discretionary functions alleged in this case.

■ ■ Critical Thinking ■

Notice that all three of the decedents in *Freeman* had "impaired mobility." Without such extenuating circumstances those who disobey an evacuation order are disobeying a municipal ordinance and may be subject to criminal penalties, such as fines or detention. Do you think this should make a difference in whether a person may recover from the government for its actions during an emergency? Keep in mind the many able-bodied people who were trapped inside the Superdome and suffered physical and emotional injuries as a result. What if the evacuation order is the third in two weeks and both previous orders were issued for storms that missed the area completely?

Important Terms

- Active endangerment
- Discretionary function
- Duty of care
- Eleventh Amendment
- Federal Tort Claims Act
- The Hand test
- Negligence
- Sovereign immunity
- Tort

Review Question

Negligence and other bases for liability discussed in this chapter are independent of the issues that we have examined in previous chapters. Any one action by the government may be challenged in court on multiple grounds; each of those legal grounds will have separate components (like the elements of negligence) that a plaintiff must prove to succeed.

Imagine a scenario in which emergency management officials implement a plan for evacuation in advance of a hurricane, but they ignore how well its execution occurs in a neighborhood where most of the residents are low-income elderly persons. (In all other neighborhoods, the agency implements the plan extremely well.) Analyze what the possible legal liability could be for this differential treatment of one neighborhood. Draw on material from earlier chapters in this book as well as the law related to sovereign immunity. For each legal theory, identify the additional facts that you would need to know before you can reach a final conclusion.

14
Liability Issues for Individuals

What You Will Learn

- How liability rules for individuals differ from those that apply to government that we examined in Chapter 13
- How the law can transform nonemployees into employees for purposes of tort liability
- The degree to which individual volunteers do and do not have immunity from personal injury lawsuits
- The special laws and registration systems established to encourage health care professionals to volunteer for emergency assistance projects

Introduction

In the last chapter, we examined whether and when the government could be found liable for tortious acts committed in its name. In those situations, any monetary award to a plaintiff would be paid out of government funds. Could individual government employees be sued and forced to pay damages out of their own pockets? What about volunteers who assist the government in responding to an emergency? Are the rules different for physicians and other licensed professionals? These are the questions that we will explore in this chapter.

Government Responsibility for the Acts of Its Employees

In almost all instances, an employee of a government agency will be protected from *personal* liability for injuries that result from his or her performance of job duties. So long as the employee was carrying out his or her job responsibilities at the time of the incident, even if the employee's actions were negligent, plaintiffs will usually recover any damages to which they are entitled from the government rather than from the individual. (This assumes that the lawsuit would fit within the scope of a waiver of sovereign immunity – see Chapter 13.)

■ ■ ■ ──────────────────────────────

The government's obligation to pay arises from its role as employer. Under the English common law doctrine of *respondeat superior* (Latin for "let the superior answer"), an employer will generally be responsible for the wrongful acts of its employees, so long as those acts were performed in the normal course of business. This principle applies only to civilian government employees; other laws govern liability for acts committed by military personnel.

────────────────────────────── ■ ■ ■

If it is the employee who suffers an injury arising out of and in the course of employment, a workers compensation law will usually provide an automatic remedy. Workers' compensation systems are also the exclusive remedy for such an injury, meaning that the employee must give up the option to sue the employer for damages in return for this automatic entitlement (Cohn, 2005).

The umbrella that shields individual government employees does not, however, extend to situations in which the employee is acting outside the scope of his or her job. It also does not protect the individual from a lawsuit if the actions were unlawful or amounted to gross negligence or willful misconduct. To take a simple example, imagine that a government worker is driving a city-owned car while on the job and causes an accident. In most instances, any damages will be paid by the city (or, more likely, by its insurance company). However, if the employee was intoxicated or was using the car improperly – say, for personal trips – then the individual will be liable.

In some jurisdictions, the government chooses another option for shielding its employees. Rather than assume responsibility for employees' lawful actions as a threshold matter, the state or municipal government elects to indemnify any employees who are successfully sued for their activities on the job. "Indemnification" means that the government will reimburse the amount of damages that an employee is ordered to pay.

The Extension of Government Responsibility beyond Regular Employees

The federal government and many state governments have laws that deem persons who volunteer to assist in a government project, such as disaster relief, to be temporary government employees for the duration of that project. This ensures that those volunteers will receive the same protections from liability that regular government workers enjoy. The deeming approach may also apply when employees of one governmental entity are called in to assist another. For example, if employees of State A or County B assist the rescue efforts undertaken by State C, they may be deemed to be "special employees" of State C (Cohn, 2005).

Two deemer provisions in federal law are especially relevant to the law of emergencies. First, under the Stafford Act (see Chapter 9), the federal government may use nonfederal employees and may hire other emergency personnel:

> In carrying out the purposes of this Act, any Federal agency is authorized to accept and utilize the services or facilities of any State or local government, or of any agency, office or employee thereof, with the consent of such government. ...

> In performing any services under this Act, any Federal agency is authorized to appoint and fix the compensation of such temporary personnel as may be necessary, without regard to [Civil Service requirements] ...
>
> (42 U.S. Code § 5149)

The second example applies to health care workers. The Secretary of Health and Human Services is authorized to accept "services performed by individuals (hereafter called volunteers) whose services have been offered to the Government and accepted under a formal agreement on a without compensation basis for use in the operation of a health care facility or in the provision of health care" (45 Code § 57.2). One benefit accorded such "federalized" volunteers is that they receive the same immunity from tort claims that regular employees enjoy (45 Code § 57.5(a)(2)).

The deemer approach can apply in a variety of circumstances, not limited to emergencies or rescue efforts. For example, in an Illinois case, two high school students who were chosen to be unpaid teachers' assistants in a swimming class were found to qualify as "employees" under the immunity law, despite their student status:

> *[Under] Section 1-202 of the Tort Immunity Act ... '[e]mployee' includes a ... volunteer ... whether or not compensated ... [S]ection 3-108(a) grants absolute immunity to a public entity or a public employee. ...*
>
> *In this case, Styx and Krastin were ... student volunteers and the plain language of section 1-202 controls our decision. Styx and Krastin applied for the position of student guard to assist the freshman swimming class, were not compensated for their services, and were under the direct supervision of [the teacher]. ... Therefore, because of their status as volunteers, both Styx and Krastin qualify as public employees. Consistent with the language of the Tort Immunity Act and the clear intention of the legislature, we conclude that the actions of uncertified student guards under the supervision of a certified teacher are entitled to immunity ...*
>
> Trotter v. School District (2000)

A Maryland statute allows a volunteer to be considered "state personnel" for purposes of tort claims if the person provides a service without pay, and if the individual:

(a) Is performing services to or for a unit of State government, the employees of which are considered State personnel ...

(b) Is engaged in the actual performance of [State services] at the time of the incident giving rise to a claim; and

(c) In the performance of the services ...

(i) Is participating in a formal volunteer program, or

(ii) Before the beginning of those services, is formally recognized by the unit as a volunteer.

Code of Maryland Regulations 25.02.01.02(B)(8)

It is difficult to summarize state deemer laws because they vary enormously in the details of exactly who is covered and under which circumstances. In general, though, if persons who are not part of an agency's regular workforce – whether volunteers or government workers from another jurisdiction – are participating in that agency's disaster response or emergency effort, there is at least a strong possibility that those extra workers will be deemed to be temporary or special employees. One has to consult each state's law to determine its precise scope.

■ ■ Critical Thinking ■

The laws that deem a nonemployee to be an employee not only affect individual liability but also create an incentive for individual volunteers to accept the control and direction of rescue efforts by government agencies. Volunteers come from a wide variety of backgrounds, with many motivations, from religious to civic to selfish. What are the advantages and disadvantages of incorporating all these people as temporary government employees?

The Federal Volunteer Protection Act

In 1997, responding to a wave of state legislative efforts, Congress adopted the Volunteer Protection Act (VPA) to establish one uniform national law that would shield volunteers from personal liability in situations where they could not be deemed employees of a governmental body. One of the major concerns motivating Congress was that fear of liability would deter people from volunteering for charitable activities. Nonprofit organizations wanted to be able to assure volunteers that they need not worry about being sued for damages if they made honest mistakes. In addition, government entities also wanted to extend liability protection to volunteers even if their jurisdiction lacked an adequate deemer law.

The VPA defines a "volunteer" as a person who performs services for a nonprofit organization or a unit of government and who receives no compensation other than for expenses (42 U.S. Code § 14505(6)). It shields volunteers from liability for harm caused by that individual's act or failure to act, but *only if* four key criteria are met:

1. The volunteer was acting within the scope of his or her responsibilities in the nonprofit organization or governmental entity at the time of the act or omission.
2. If appropriate or required, the volunteer was properly licensed, certified, or authorized to engage in the particular action.
3. The harm was not caused by willful or criminal misconduct, gross negligence, reckless misconduct, or a conscious, flagrant indifference to the rights or safety of the individual harmed by the volunteer.
4. The harm was not caused by the volunteer operating a vehicle.

(42 U.S. Code § 14503(a)). Note that one consequence of the first condition is that the VPA does not extend to random individual volunteers but only to those who are working under the supervision of either a nonprofit organization or a government agency.

The VPA additionally provides that its immunities do not apply to actions by volunteers that constitute violent crimes, international terrorism, hate crimes, sexual offenses, violations of civil rights laws, or actions taken while the volunteer is intoxicated or under the influence of drugs (42 U.S. Code § 14503(f)).

Momans v. St. John's Northwestern Military Academy
U.S. District Court for the Northern District of Illinois, 2000

> *Plaintiffs [are] parents or guardians of current or former students at St. John's Northwestern Military Academy ("St. John's"). [They] instituted this state law fraud action against St. John's and certain members of its Board of Trustees ... alleg[ing] that they were persuaded to enroll their children or wards in St. John's based upon misrepresentations made by the Defendants. ... [Their complaint] alleges that the individual Defendants violated the Illinois ... Consumer Fraud Act and committed common law fraud by engaging in a course of action designed to mislead parents and guardians of students and potential students at St. John's. ...*

> *The Volunteer Act was enacted to "provide certain protections from liability abuses related to volunteers serving nonprofit organizations and governmental entities." The individual Defendants contend that they are volunteers within the meaning of the Act, which defines volunteers as individuals, including directors, who perform services for a non-profit organization and who do not receive compensation. ... As such, the individual Defendants are immunized from liability for harm caused by them in the scope of their responsibilities, if the harm is not caused by "willful or criminal misconduct, gross negligence, reckless misconduct or a conscious, flagrant indifference to the rights or safety of the individual harmed by the volunteer."*

> *Although the ... Complaint does not specifically allege what each individual Defendant said, it does allege generally that*

Defendants made certain representations that they knew were false. Plaintiffs also allege in their common law fraud claim that Defendants acted with the intent to induce reliance on the representations. The Volunteer Act does not define the term "willful." Nevertheless, the term has an established meaning: "[t]he usual meaning assigned to 'willful' ... is that the actor has intentionally done an act of an unreasonable character in disregard of a known or obvious risk that was so great as to make it highly probable that harm would follow[.]" In civil actions, the term is commonly used for an act which is intentional, knowing, or voluntary, as distinguished from accidental.

The court concludes that under these standards, Defendants have not met their heavy burden of establishing that this statute precludes recovery by Plaintiffs. Plaintiffs allege both intent to induce reliance and knowledge of the falsity of their representations. Construing the alleged facts in Plaintiffs' favor – e.g., that Defendants made fraudulent misrepresentations to promote and advertise St. John's – a fact-finder could reasonably conclude that the individual Defendants acted with sufficient intent and knowledge so as to be ineligible for immunity under the "willful misconduct" exception to the Volunteer Act. ...

To create more national consistency, the VPA preempts any state law that provides less protection to volunteers. If a state law offers more protection, then its terms will be applied rather than the VPA (42 U.S. Code § 14502).

■ ■ ■ ─────────────────────────────────

The VPA provides no protection from lawsuits for the charitable organization itself, only for individual volunteers (42 U.S. Code § 14503(c)).

───────────────────────────── ■ ■ ■

There are exceptions to preemption as well, however. Although Congress did not include these additional limitations in the federal law, it did provide that if states adopted them, they would not be preempted. As a result, the following provisions in state law, if they exist, will *not* be preempted:

- That the nonprofit organization where volunteer activities occur must adhere to risk management principles, including mandatory volunteer training
- That a nonprofit is liable for the acts or omissions of its volunteers to the same extent that an employer is liable for the acts or omissions of its employees
- That there is no immunity if the volunteer is a defendant in a civil action brought by a government official
- That the immunity applies only to volunteers working at nonprofits that provide a "financially secure source of recovery," such as insurance

(42 U.S. Code § 14503(d)). Another mechanism in the VPA for achieving greater consistency across states is that, even if immunity does not apply, only compensatory, and not punitive, damages may be awarded in a lawsuit against volunteers (42 U.S. Code § 14503(e)).

State Volunteer Protection Laws

Every state has some sort of volunteer protection or "good Samaritan" law, but, as indicated above, these laws vary widely. Many have the same or similar kinds of limitations as does the federal VPA: no immunity for acts that are reckless, willful, grossly negligent or unlawful, or for negligent acts committed while driving a motor vehicle. According to a report by the Nonprofit Risk Management Center, many state laws are specific to certain groups of volunteers, such as firefighters (Alabama), health care practitioners (many examples – see below), athletic coaches (Ohio), food donation volunteers (Texas), and even those who volunteer at libraries (Vermont) and bingo raffles (Colorado) (*State Liability Laws for Charitable Organizations and Volunteers*, updated 2006). Given such specificity of coverage, many states have multiple volunteer protection laws, with different rules for different occupational classifications. Again, one would have to consult each state's laws to determine exactly who and what is covered.

■ ■ Critical Thinking ■

One huge distinction between deemer laws and volunteer protection laws is how they affect the plaintiff in such lawsuits, i.e., the person injured by the actions of a volunteer. If the volunteer is treated under the law as a government employee, the plaintiff may well receive compensation from the government (assuming that all relevant criteria for a successful lawsuit have been met). If the volunteer is simply immunized, however, it is possible that the same plaintiff will receive no compensation at all. When would this occur? Is this outcome fair? How can or should the law try to avoid such situations?

Liability Issues for Health Practitioners

Laws applying to health practitioners are probably the largest single subset of state volunteer protection laws. The following case illustrates how one state's laws operate.

Frields v. St. Joseph's Hospital and Medical Center
New Jersey Superior Court, Appellate Division 1997

> *… At approximately 7 p.m. on September 15, 1990, William T. Frields (Billy) arrived at his father's residence in Paterson. Soon thereafter, Billy reported to his father that he felt dizzy and collapsed on the kitchen floor. His father noticed that his son's breathing was irregular and instructed one of his daughters to call an ambulance. Mr. Frields attempted to assist his son's breathing and massaged his back until emergency personnel arrived.*
>
> *A Mobile Intensive Care Unit (MICU) from the Hospital and an Emergency Medical Technician (EMT) team from the City arrived in response to Frields' call. The MICU team noted that Billy had vomited and was incontinent before their arrival. Believing that Billy exhibited signs of a drug overdose, the MICU personnel administered [a drug] to counteract the effect of any narcotic. Soon thereafter, Billy "woke up."*
>
> *It is undisputed that when Billy became responsive he resisted mightily the efforts of the emergency personnel to subdue him and to transfer him to an ambulance. Several men, including a police officer on the scene, were required to restrain him. Once restrained, the emergency personnel were able to transport him to the ambulance. Billy arrived at the Hospital between 7:50 and 7:55 p.m. He died at*

9:02 p.m. An autopsy revealed that he died from a subarachnoid hemorrhage.

Mr. Frields filed a wrongful death and survival action against the Hospital and the City based on the actions of the Hospital and City emergency personnel ... He complained that the emergency personnel used excessive force in their attempt to restrain his son. He also asserted that the actions by the Hospital and City personnel constituted negligent and intentional infliction of emotional distress.

Through several statutes, the Legislature has granted qualified immunity to a wide range of persons who provide medical assistance in emergency situations. ... [P]aid professionals who respond to a medical emergency and render treatment are immunized pursuant to ... the [New Jersey] Good Samaritan Act. It provides that any individual, including licensed health care professionals, ... who in good faith renders medical care at the scene of an accident or emergency to a victim is immune from damages in a civil action as a result of any act or omission by the person rendering the medical care.

[A similar law] provides ... good faith immunity to mobile intensive care [MICU] paramedics; [another] provides a good faith immunity to EMT-intermediates.

[The MICU law] provides:

No mobile intensive care paramedic, licensed physician, hospital or its board of trustees, officers and members of the medical staff, nurses or other employees of the hospital, first aid, ambulance or rescue squad, or officers and members of a rescue squad shall be liable for any civil damages as the result of an act or the omission of an act committed while in training for or in the rendering of advanced life support services in good faith and in accordance with this act.

[The EMT law] provides:

No EMT-intermediate, licensed physician, hospital or its board of trustees, officers and members of the medical staff, nurses or other employees of the hospital, or officers and members of a first aid, ambulance or rescue squad shall be liable for any civil damages as the result of an act or the omission of an act committed while in training for or in the rendering of intermediate life support services in good faith and in accordance with this act.

It is undisputed that the Hospital personnel were members of a mobile intensive care unit and that the City personnel qualify as EMT-intermediates. Therefore, the inquiry is whether they acted in good faith.

"Good faith" has been defined as honesty of purpose and integrity of conduct without knowledge, either actual or sufficient to demand inquiry, that the conduct is wrong. ... This test recognizes that even a person who acted negligently is entitled to a qualified immunity, if he acted in an objectively reasonable manner.

Applying these principles [here], we are satisfied that plaintiff presents proofs that the emergency personnel may have acted negligently; however, any negligence does not strip them of their immunity. Plaintiff contends that the emergency personnel used excessive force to restrain his son. He contends that his son could have been restrained sooner and with less force, if he had been sedated. ...

[However] Plaintiff's expert [conceded] that the emergency personnel could not be expected to diagnose a subarachnoid hemorrhage in the field[.] [P]laintiff has failed to present any facts which create a genuine issue of material fact that defendants' employees did not act in an objectively reasonable manner. Accordingly, the City personnel were immune pursuant to the immunity conferred by [the MICU law], and the Hospital employees were immune pursuant to the terms of [the EMT law] ...

The phrase "good Samaritan law" is applied to statutes that absolve physicians of liability for negligence when they volunteer to treat someone who is not their patient and who needs immediate care. In a number of states, the good Samaritan law is broader, covering anyone who stops to help someone in need of assistance.

Some states have adopted narrowly targeted health care provider immunity laws as well. In Maryland, "[a] health care provider is immune from civil or criminal liability if the health care provider acts in good faith and under a catastrophic health emergency proclamation" (Maryland Public Safety Code § 14-3A-06). Note how important it is to read the text of each statute carefully. Would this Maryland law protect a dentist who continues to see her patients after an earthquake strikes? What additional facts would you need to know to answer this question?

Licensure and Emergency Mobilization for Health Practitioners

Health care professionals who volunteer in emergency response efforts have concerns with licensure as well as liability. Physicians (and others) are licensed only by the state in which they practice, and they are not authorized to practice medicine beyond the borders of the states where they hold licenses. Obviously, in an emergency, there is no time for volunteers to go through the licensing process in the state where their services are needed. (This same issue arises for other licensed professionals as well, but health care presents the most frequent example.)

As we noted in Chapter 11, every state has become a party to the Emergency Management Assistance Compact (EMAC), a mutual aid agreement among states. One of EMAC's most important provisions allows out-of-state physicians to practice in the state requesting assistance. This temporary exemption from the requesting state's licensure laws applies only to physicians (and other licensed professionals) who provide aid as part of an organized effort overseen by officials of the responding state. It does not apply to individual doctors who travel to a disaster area on their own.

In recent years, the federal government has undertaken the development of systems to make emergency response by health care professionals faster and more efficient. Begun in the 1980s primarily to provide auxiliary services to military troops, the National Disaster Medical System (NDMS) has shifted its mission to that of backup for domestic disaster relief (Franco et al. 2007). NDMS has three functions:

- Deploying medical personnel, supplies, and equipment to a disaster area
- Transporting patients out of the disaster areas, by bringing them to staging areas where they can board military aircraft
- Providing medical care at participating hospitals in unaffected areas.

The DHHS Secretary can activate NDMS without issuing a declaration of public health emergency. (See Chapter 5.) The key to the system is a network of regionally organized groups of specially trained health professionals and support personnel who volunteer to provide assistance during disasters. Once deployed, they are federalized into temporary employee status and are paid by the federal government.

NDMS was part of the federal response to Hurricane Katrina. Although the use of NDMS succeeded in evacuating thousands of patients, a Senate report found that medical teams were overwhelmed by the number of patients and were unable to institute a reliable patient tracking system. In 2007, the White House ordered a review of NDMS capacities, which is ongoing.

In 2002, Congress directed the Secretary of Health and Human Services to establish an Emergency System for Advance Registration of Volunteer Health Professionals (ESAR-VHP). ESAR-VHP allows advance verification of the credentials, licenses, accreditations, and hospital privileges of those who register (42 U.S. Code § 247d-7b). Even if not covered under EMAC, a physician who is registered with ESAR-VHP can be cleared to travel independently to an emergency response zone and provide assistance.

The continuing ESAR-VHP system is a national network of state-based emergency volunteer registries. States are responsible for designing, developing, and administering their respective systems and databases. As one law review article noted:

> Ideally, these standardized systems allow states and territories to quickly identify and better utilize volunteer health professionals in emergencies and disasters. Ultimately, they may enable the development of an interoperable system that will allow aggregation of state registration systems for use at the regional or national level.
>
> Hodge et al. (2005)

Important Terms

- Emergency Management Assistance Compact
- Emergency System for Advance Registration of Volunteer Health Professionals
- "Federalized" volunteers
- Good Samaritan laws
- Indemnification
- National Disaster Medical System

- *Respondeat superior*
- Temporary government employees
- Volunteer Protection Act
- Willful conduct
- Worker compensation laws

Review Question

Underlying all the questions covered in this chapter are public policy concerns, such as the fear that risk of liability will deter people from volunteering, which would in turn weaken the nonprofit organizations that provide so much assistance during emergencies. What are some other important public policy issues that are relevant to the legal principles in this chapter?

Testing Your Knowledge

A Dirty Bomb Explodes in Washington, D.C.

Introduction

This chapter is designed to test your knowledge of the legal concepts that we have examined so far. Engaging with the exercise will give you a sense of your strengths and weaknesses in understanding the material and will be good preparation for a final examination.

The facts in the briefings and the scenario are grounded in science, but they are not intended to substitute for the most authoritative research. Obviously, the narrative and many of the details are invented. The exercise encompasses only a small number of the many issues that would arise should a real attack occur. As you read the scenario, note what some of the most important additional issues would be if the event actually occurred.

Background Briefing: Radiological Dispersion Bombs (RDBs)

A dirty bomb – more precisely, a radiological dispersion bomb (RDB) – is a relatively unsophisticated device that combines radioactive materials with conventional explosives. When exploded, such a device scatters radioactive particles into the environment. Anyone within the initial blast radius will probably be killed immediately, and more casualties could result from the long-term effects of the dispersed radioactive material. Almost all deaths and serious injuries would be confined to the immediate vicinity of the explosion.

Unlike with a true nuclear weapon, no nuclear-fission reaction takes place when a dirty bomb is detonated. The number of immediate fatalities from such a blast would not be increased by the presence of radioactive materials, unlike what would occur if even a crude nuclear device were detonated. However, widespread contamination exceeding Environmental Protection Agency (EPA) safety guidelines would be likely to result.

The dust and debris generated by a dirty bomb explosion would land on the skin of the people closest to the explosion and could then be inhaled, ingested, or absorbed through wounds. Radiation released by radioactive materials inside the body can damage the liver, thyroid, kidneys, and bones, as well as increase a victim's chances of getting cancer.

Victims might also be exposed to radiation from radioactive materials scattered nearby. An invisible radioactive plume could develop and carry small amounts of radioactive material to locations miles away; the direction that the plume would travel would depend on wind and weather conditions.

To stop the exposure to radiation, victims would need to be decontaminated by removing irradiated clothing, washing the skin, and purging inhaled or ingested materials from inside the body. Figure 15.1 illustrates a method for treating internal contamination. The surrounding area would also need to be decontaminated to remove radioactive material, prevent radioactive dust and debris from spreading, and protect food and water supplies. The effects would be most damaging to survivors who had been closest to the explosion: approximately 1 in 100 survivors in the area less than a half-block from the source would die of cancer. People a half-mile to a mile from the blast would be in contaminated areas but probably not seriously affected. Most experts say that except for people in the immediate area of the blast, the odds are against anyone absorbing enough radiation to suffer long-term effects, such as radiation poisoning or cancer.

Applying its safety guidelines, the EPA would probably recommend the long-term evacuation of the contaminated area, approximately half

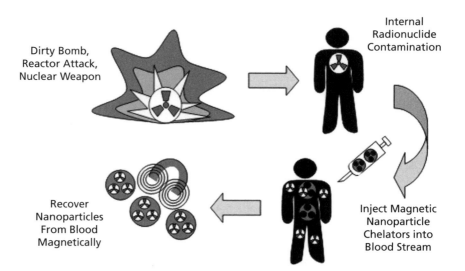

FIGURE 15.1 Cleansing the Body of Radioactive Materials
Source: U.S. Armed Forces Radiobiology Research Institute. Available At: www.anl.gov/Media_Center/News/2006/photo/061020_dirty_bomb_treatment-large.jpg

a mile to a mile from the blast. With urban areas especially difficult to decontaminate after a radiological attack, any abandonment could be permanent, potentially costing trillions of dollars.

In addition to this economic damage, a dirty bomb attack would also be likely to produce a psychological effect out of proportion to the actual physical damage it would achieve on its own. Experts who have run simulations of dirty bomb attacks have warned officials to expect large-scale panic reactions by the public.

THE GOIÂNIA, BRAZIL INCIDENT

On September 13, 1987, two scrap metal scavengers broke into an abandoned radiotherapy clinic in Goiânia (a large city in south central Brazil) and removed a source capsule containing radioactive material from the protective housing of a teletherapy machine. The International Atomic Energy Agency (IAEA) estimates that the source capsule contained 1375 Ci of cesium-137 chloride ($137CsCl$) in soluble form. The capsule had been abandoned when the clinic moved to a new location two years earlier. Both men became sick almost immediately. They assumed that the vomiting and diarrhea was caused by bad food they had eaten.

Five days later, one of the men punctured the window of the source capsule, allowing the powder to leak out. This was the critical event that sparked the most serious consequences. That same day the assembly was sold to a junkyard owner. That night the new owner saw that the powder glowed blue. Intrigued by the glowing blue material, he took the capsule into his house to show it to his family and friends. He gave fragments away, and several people sprinkled or rubbed the material on their bodies as they might have done with the glitter used for Carnival.

On approximately September 21, the wife of the junkyard owner became ill with symptoms of acute radiation sickness. Her mother nursed her for two days and then returned to her home outside Goiânia, taking a significant amount of contamination with her. Over the next few days, two employees at the junkyard disassembled the structure; both died. One of the thieves had become ill enough to be admitted to a local hospital. On September 24, a six-year-old girl played with the colorful source powder, painted it on her body, and ate a sandwich while her hands were contaminated. She was massively internally contaminated and died a month later.

The correct diagnosis of acute radiation sickness was made September 28 after the owner's wife and an employee at the junkyard took the remnants of the rotating assembly to a doctor's office at the clinic of the Vigilancia Sanitária. They carried the material in a plastic bag and took a public bus to the clinic, thus contaminating the bus and exposing other passengers to the cesium. The owner's wife later died of radioactive poisoning.

Acting on the diagnosis and in partnership with a team from the IAEA, Brazilian authorities monitored over 112,000 people in an Olympic-sized soccer stadium for radiation exposure and sickness. Radioactive contamination spread throughout Goiânia and even reached Rio de Janeiro, some 700 miles away. For several days, nobody remembered to decontaminate the ambulances used to transport some of the sickest victims from the Rio airport to the naval hospital there, which had the country's primary facility for the treatment of radiation sickness.

According to the IAEA report on the incident, a total of 249 people were identified as contaminated by the cesium-137, 151 people exhibited both internal and external contamination, and 49 people were admitted to hospitals. The internally contaminated patients were themselves radioactive, seriously complicating their treatment. In the end, 28 people suffered radiation burns and five people died. There was also a major economic impact: as a result of the incident, it became impossible for farmers in the region to sell their produce.

The Scenario Unfolds

It is lunchtime on a lovely spring Wednesday in Washington, D.C. As is always true in the spring in D.C., when hundreds of schools schedule class trips to the capital, a line of yellow school buses is parked near the National Mall. Nearby, members of Congress and their staffs are working. Across the street from the far side of the Capitol, the Supreme Court is in session. At 12:45 p.m., a school bus parked at the foot of Capitol Hill (see Figure 15.2), close to the National Gallery of Art, explodes with a deafening roar.

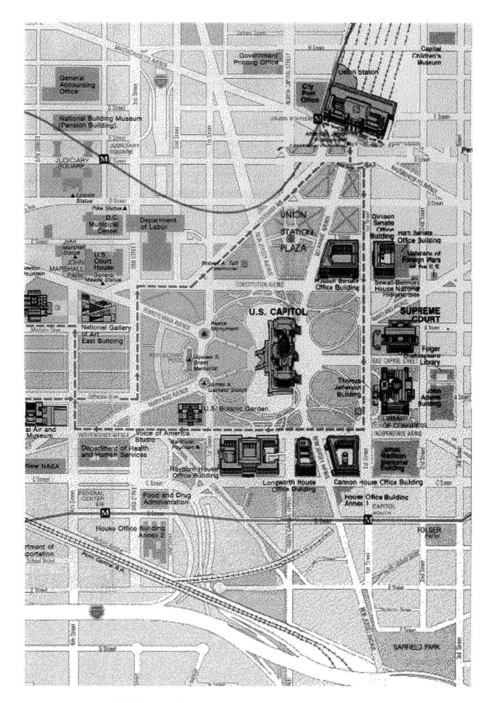

FIGURE 15.2 Capitol Hill in Washington, D.C.

The carnage is instant. Bodies and body parts are scattered on the ground near the detonation point. Some of the survivors are crying or screaming; others are dazed. The National Gallery of Art has collapsed, as has a portion of the west front of the Capitol. Several other buildings and vehicles are burning. In the surrounding blocks, thousands of people heard the blast and felt what seemed like an earthquake. Within a few minutes, the sound of sirens fills the air, as police, fire, and ambulance crews rush to the scene. Special security agents surround members of the Congressional leadership and the Justices of the Supreme Court. A dozen blocks away, the President and other high-ranking officials are whisked into a top-secret bunker. From a municipal building not far from the White House, the Mayor is also taken to a secure location.

Five minutes after the blast, a bulletin is broadcast on the emergency radio frequency shared by first responders: radiation sensors in the area of the explosion have spiked. Initial reports estimate that the bomb contained approximately 1,000 curies of cesium-137 (an amount sufficient to cause the damage described below). Responders are instructed to wear hazmat gear at the scene. Many responders rushing to the scene do not have such gear, however, so some turn back. As the crews start to arrive, the surviving victims see persons clad in "moon suits" emerging from ambulances and walking toward them. Many of those who can, begin to run.

Reports have come in from the scene that survivors with minor or no injuries are being told to wait for special decontamination tents, which contain mobile showers, to arrive. But many do not obey that instruction. The police department has just begun the process of closing off streets in a one-mile radius around the blast, but it lacks the necessary personnel to complete this assignment. The metropolitan transit authority has issued orders to close all subway stations in the downtown area and to direct all buses and subways that are now operating to transport passengers to locations at least two miles from the blast site. Some people are breaking through police lines, and police are unsure how much force they can use to stop those trying to escape the cordon.

You are a member of the incident command legal council, which includes representatives from multiple federal and local agencies. For purposes of this exercise, assume that the District of Columbia is the equivalent of a state and that the Mayor has the same powers that a governor would have. You can also assume that the Federal Bureau of Investigation will take the lead role in investigating the criminal aspects of what has occurred.

WHAT ACTIONS SHOULD THE MAYOR TAKE NOW?

Assume that Washington, D.C. has laws authorizing the Mayor to declare a state of emergency. What are the most important goals to be achieved now? What kinds of further action would a state of emergency declaration enable?

What other actions should the Mayor take?

Consider:

- Activating EMAC
- Calling out the state's National Guard units
- Requesting assistance from the federal government
- Are there legal issues that need to be addressed with any of these possible actions?

WHAT ACTIONS SHOULD FEDERAL OFFICIALS TAKE NOW?

What options does the President have for declaring different types of emergency? What are the differences between them? Into what category or categories of federal emergency does a dirty bomb attack fit?

Should the President deploy troops to the scene? *Can* he deploy troops?

Should martial law be declared? What criteria would you recommend that the President use in deciding when, if at all, to invoke martial law?

Can the Secretary of Health and Human Services declare a public health emergency? On what basis? Have the criteria for such a declaration been satisfied?

What about the Secretary of the Department of Homeland Security? What should his initial actions be?

For each decision, what legal consequences will ensue?

Meanwhile, the news media have broadcast the news that the blast was a dirty bomb and that the best thing that people in the "hot zone" in downtown Washington, D.C. can do is to go inside and shelter in place until they are directed through the decontamination process. Mobile decontamination units – in which people can undress, shower, and change into clean shirts, pants, and disposable shoes – are being set up at the exit points from the police cordon. Most people are obeying instructions.

Response units from Maryland and Virginia have begun to arrive. Several more workers whose units lacked protective equipment have refused to obey orders to go into the hot zone, and they have been fired. A special RDB (dirty bomb) Squad from a nearby Army base has brought additional decontamination equipment into the District and is operating several of the units through which people are being processed. Army personnel have also set up a checkpoint on the Mall, and are questioning certain people about what they know about the blast.

Outside the hot zone, traffic has overwhelmed many streets as thousands of people try to flee the area. Police have closed some streets to all but emergency traffic. Hospitals in the immediate area are struggling to accommodate casualties being brought in by ambulance or private car, as well as a number of people who are simply walking into the emergency room. One person who was driving two friends who had been injured in the blast to the hospital caused a multicar accident, in which two other people were killed.

Because the attack occurred so close to Congress and the Supreme Court, news media have begun speculating on what measures will be taken to protect those institutions. The Majority Leader of the Senate was giving a speech at an outdoor rally on Capitol grounds when the bomb exploded, and his death has been confirmed. The Capitol sustained structural damage from the attack but is still standing. Other buildings appear undamaged. No members of Congress or Justices have been seen since the attack.

The President has just addressed the nation and urged people to remain calm. No other attacks have occurred, and no one has claimed "credit" for this one.

CONTINUING QUESTIONS

A disagreement has arisen about the firing of the first responders who refused to enter the hot zone without protective equipment. Should they be quickly reinstated and furnished with equipment or should the firings stand? What legal issues might be implicated?

The situation at hospital emergency rooms is getting dangerous, in part because the hospitals do not have enough special equipment for treating persons suffering from radiation burns. They are also short on personnel, a situation made worse because some hospital workers are refusing to come into contact with these patients. What legal options could apply here? Can the hospitals close their emergency rooms to new patients? Can the government take over the hospitals, most of which are private? Can makeshift emergency treatment locations be set up, and where? How can additional medical staff be obtained? Can the workers who are refusing to participate in providing care be forced to do so? Already, some physicians and nurses from Delaware and Pennsylvania have started to appear at area hospitals, volunteering to assist. Is there any problem with this?

Can National Guard troops be used to guard the perimeter that has been set up around the hot zone? Should the President revisit the question of martial law?

Planes are arriving at Andrews Air Force Base near Washington, D.C. containing several thousand doses of "Radioburnase" that have been shipped from the Strategic National Stockpile. Radioburnase can be very effective in purging the body of cesium contamination, but only if it is administered within four hours of exposure. It is now 2:30 p.m. A decision must be made immediately about how and where the drugs are dispersed.

LAW AND ETHICS

Members of Congress have been gathered in a few locations in basements of the congressional office buildings and have gone through the showers-and-fresh clothes decontamination process; the same process has occurred with the Supreme Court Justices. Staff members have been processed separately. Approximately 550 doses of Radioburnase will be sufficient for members and Justices. (Everyone working at the White House is already being treated.)

Approximately 3,000 congressional and Supreme Court employees have also been told to wait for treatment. However, there are tens of thousands of other affected people, including some high-ranking government officials at other agencies. Hospitals within Washington, D.C. are in crisis mode, and some patients are starting to appear at suburban hospitals. Hundreds of first responders are at risk. These people, however, are geographically scattered.

What principles should govern the distribution of Radioburnase?

At the decontamination unit on the Mall being run by Army troops, certain "suspicious" persons are being detained for extensive questioning. It appears that only persons who cannot speak English and those with Arabic names are being held. The next day, a habeas corpus petition on their behalf is filed in local court.

Also on the next day, the scientific backup team has briefed the legal council with a map of the bomb's impact, given the weather conditions, measured in concentric circles out from the detonation point (see Figure 15.3). Virtually everyone who was in the small area closest to detonation is dead, as are many people in the second circle. The third circle represents the official contamination zone, where the buildings and grounds are assumed to require extensive "muck and truck" – digging and demolition followed by removal of the debris to a radioactive waste storage facility – if the area can ever be inhabited again. It is unclear whether that degree of physical rebuilding is feasible, despite the presence within the contaminated zone of the Capitol building, the Supreme Court, and the Library of Congress, as well as business and residential areas. The radioactive plume has drifted to the Maryland suburbs, a fact that the news media are highlighting.

EPA and health officials begin a search of every building in the contamination zone. In addition to corpses and stranded victims, they

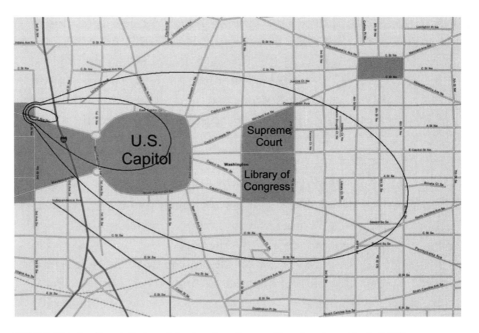

FIGURE 15.3 Predicted Circles of Destruction from a Dirty Bomb on Capitol Hill
Source: Congressional testimony of Prof. Michael Kelly, Federation of American Scientists.

report finding illegal drugs and other contraband, which they are seizing with the plan to turn the items over to local police.

Hospitals have been flooded with calls from people seeking news of loved ones who may have been injured or killed in the blast. DC Memorial Hospital released a list of all those whom it has treated for radiation burns. The first person on that list has already been notified that he is fired. Meanwhile, the press is reporting that the "good Samaritan" who caused yesterday's accident while driving people to the hospital could lose his home because of lawsuits.

NEXT DAY QUESTIONS

How should the habeas corpus petition be answered? Were the actions of the Army troops lawful?

If police later seek to prosecute someone for possession of illegal drugs based on the evidence seized during the rescue sweep, will that prosecution stand?

Should the hospital have released the names of its patients?

Does the man who was fired have legal grounds to regain his job?

What about the individual who caused an accident on the way to the hospital – does he have a legal defense if those who were hurt in the accident sue?

Maryland residents who live closest to the District are demanding that the Governor of Maryland declare a health emergency in that state. What would be the advantages and disadvantages of doing so? Draft a statement for the Governor explaining the reasons behind whichever decision you recommend.

As the District tries to recover, what will be some of the legal issues for the future?

Postscript: The Movie Version

As a way to enrich this exercise – and just have some fun – rent a copy of *Dirty War*, a British film made in 2004 in which the story centers on a dirty bomb explosion in central London. Although it is fiction, the 90-minute film is so well done that a number of first responder agencies have used it in training. Does it suggest other legal issues?

⁙ 16
A Pandemic Flu
Outbreak in New Jersey

Introduction

This chapter is designed to test your knowledge of the legal concepts that we have examined so far. Engaging with the exercise will give you a sense of your strengths and weaknesses in understanding the material and will be good preparation for a final examination.

The facts in the briefings and the scenario are grounded in science, but they are not intended to substitute for the most authoritative research. Obviously, the narrative and many of the details are invented. The exercise encompasses only a small number of the many issues that would arise should a real outbreak occur. As you read the scenario, note what some of the most important additional issues would be if the event actually occurred.

Background Briefing: Pandemic Influenza

A Potential Influenza Pandemic
Congressional Budget Office 2006

> Although a pandemic could be caused by any of several influenza strains, scientists are particularly worried about H5N1, a strain that has caused repeated epidemics with high mortality among poultry in Asia, has spread from Southeast Asia to flocks in Central Asia and Europe, and has made the jump from birds to humans, causing the deaths of over 60 people. Moreover, viruses of the H5 subtype are not known to have ever circulated among the human population, which means that there would be little immunity to it. To date, close contact with infected poultry is thought to be required for human infection, but the danger exists that the virus will evolve in a way that allows for efficient human-to-human transmission.

If the virus does acquire that capability, a worldwide epidemic, or pandemic, could occur. Depending on the virulence of the particular strain of flu, such an outbreak could have substantial consequences for people and economic activity around the world. ...

Avian influenza (or "bird flu") is a contagious animal disease that infects birds and some mammals. Scientists believe that all bird species are susceptible to infection but that some are more resistant than others. Wild waterfowl, especially ducks, are a so-called natural reservoir of influenza viruses, including the bird flu. The birds carry the virus without displaying any symptoms of the disease and can spread the virus over great distances while remaining healthy.

Poultry are quite susceptible to avian influenza, which can cause a wide range of symptoms, from mild (reduced egg production) to severe (rapid death). The severe form of the disease, which is known as "highly pathogenic avian influenza," is extremely contagious and has been the source of numerous epidemics among domesticated birds. It is also characterized by very high and rapid mortality, with rates approaching 100 percent and death sometimes occurring on the first day that symptoms appear.

Although frequently deadly for poultry, avian influenza viruses in the past have rarely caused severe disease in humans. However, in 1997, a highly pathogenic strain of bird flu known as H5N1 jumped from birds to humans during an outbreak among poultry in Hong Kong. The 1997 event was notable for two reasons. First, molecular studies indicated that the genetic makeup of the human and avian viruses were virtually identical, indicating direct transmission from birds to humans. Second, the H5N1 virus caused severe illness with extreme mortality among humans: of the 18 persons known to have been infected, six died. The outbreak ended after authorities slaughtered Hong Kong's entire stock of poultry (about 1.5 million birds).

The Hong Kong episode put world health officials on alert because the H5N1 strain had fulfilled two of the three prerequisites for a pandemic. First, the strain was a new virus subtype to which the population would have little or no immunity, and second, the virus had the ability to replicate in humans and cause serious illness. However, the virus still has not developed the ability to be transmitted efficiently from human to human. …

Since the 1997 episode in Hong Kong, there have been several outbreaks of the H5N1 influenza around the world, leading to tens of millions of infections among poultry and dozens of cases among humans. The first human infection occurred in Hong Kong in February 2003, when a nine-year-old boy and his father became sick after a trip to southern China. The man, who was 33, died, but his son recovered.

Then, in 2004, the H5N1 virus spread among poultry populations in Southeast Asia, with outbreaks of influenza reported in two separate waves. The first wave, in January and February, affected Vietnam, Japan, Korea, Thailand, Laos, Cambodia, Indonesia, and China. The second wave, which began in July and continued into 2005, included outbreaks in the same countries and in Malaysia as well. More recently, the virus has shown up in Russia, Kazakhstan, Turkey, and Romania. The scope of the outbreaks is historically unprecedented: a highly pathogenic strain of avian influenza has not been known before to spread so widely and so rapidly.

The number of human cases of the H5N1 virus has also grown. Between January 2004 and August 2005, there were 112 human cases of H5N1 avian flu (in Vietnam, Thailand, Cambodia, and Indonesia) that resulted in 57 deaths. The vast majority of those cases (and deaths) involved children and young adults. However, accurately computing the case fatality rate (the percentage of infected persons who eventually die from the disease or from its complications) is impossible because authorities do not know how many people had milder cases but did not seek medical care or how many received care that was not reported. Nearly all of the human cases resulted from close contact with infected birds. There is evidence, though, of at least one case of probable human-to-human transmission, and some experts suspect that a few other cases of human-to-human spread of the H5N1 virus have occurred.

Events since the beginning of 2004 have heightened concerns among public health officials. Not only has the H5N1 virus spread widely – expanding beyond Southeast Asia and China into Central Asia and Europe – but laboratory results indicate that the virus has evolved in ways that may make a pandemic more likely:

- It has found a permanent ecological niche, becoming entrenched among domestic ducks in rural areas of Asia.
- It has become more robust than the 1997 strain and is able to survive longer under a broad range of environmental conditions.
- It has become increasingly pathogenic in poultry and has increased the range of species it can infect, now including domestic cats (in laboratory experiments) and captive tigers (after being fed infected chicken carcasses in a zoo in Thailand).
- It has become resistant to one of the two classes of antiflu drugs.

Experts do not know if an avian influenza pandemic is likely to occur, largely because they cannot predict when, or even if, the H5N1 virus might acquire the ability to pass readily from human to human. But the wider presence of the avian strain raises the probability of a pandemic because it increases the likelihood that an individual will become infected with the human strain and the avian strain at the same time, thus opening up the possibility of a genetic reassortment that could improve transmissibility of the disease. Wider prevalence of the virus also increases the likelihood that a series of mutations will produce a pandemic strain, even without the virus's undergoing reassortment. ...

Although the dimensions of a future flu pandemic are unknowable, past outbreaks suggest the following pattern of events:

1. The virus would spread widely in a very short time. On the basis of experience with severe acute respiratory syndrome (SARS) in 2003, a pandemic influenza virus would be expected to cross national borders very rapidly.

2. A rapid surge in the number of cases in each affected area would occur very quickly, within weeks. The number of cases would vary with the severity of the outbreak, but there would be a sharp increase in demand for medical services.

3. The pandemic would probably spread across geographic areas and vulnerable populations in waves. In any given geographic region, each wave could last for three to five months, and a second wave could appear anywhere from one to three months after the first disappears. ...

WHO Global Pandemic Phases

The World Health Organization has developed the system shown in Table 16.1 for coding phases of a pandemic, in the same way that codes indicate the severity of a storm or hurricane:

Table 16.1   Phases of a Pandemic

Phase	Public Health Goals
Interpandemic Period Phase 1 – No new influenza subtypes have been detected in humans. If present in animals risk of human infection or disease is considered low.	Strengthen preparedness
Phase 2 – No new influenza subtypes have been detected in humans, but a circulating animal influenza virus subtype poses a substantial risk of human disease.	Minimize risk of transmission to humans; detect and report such transmission rapidly if it occurs.
Pandemic Alert Period Phase 3 – Human infections with a new subtype, but no human-to-human spread or, at most, rare instances and only to a close contact.	Ensure rapid characterization of the new virus subtype and early detection, notification and response.
Phase 4 – Small clusters with limited human-to-human transmission, but spread is highly localized.	Contain the new virus within limited foci or delay spread to gain time to implement preparedness measures, including vaccine development.
Phase 5 – Larger clusters but human-to-human spread still localized	Maximize efforts to contain or delay spread to possibly avert a pandemic and to gain time to implement pandemic response measures.
Pandemic Period Phase 6 – Pandemic – increased and sustained transmission in general population	Minimize the impact of the pandemic

Source: World Health Organization, Department of Communicable Disease

The Scenario Unfolds

Frank Wheeler's wife, Martha, picked him up at Newark International Airport, and they returned home to Montclair, NJ. Frank was exhausted. He had spent two weeks in Istanbul representing his client, a computer maker, in negotiations over business transactions throughout Eastern Europe and Western Asia. He had been sneezing throughout the long flight back to the United States and wanted nothing more than to sleep. He took one day to recover from jet lag but found that the sneezing had progressed to a cough, scratchy throat, runny nose, and muscle aches. On his second day back, believing that he had the flu but worried about the work that had accumulated during his absence at his law office in New York, he took the commuter train into the city.

By the time he got home from work that day, he felt much worse. Most alarmingly, he was starting to have difficulty breathing. At about 3 a.m., when he began gasping for breath, Martha drove him to Montclair Memorial Hospital. He was intubated (a plastic tube was inserted into the trachea to assist in breathing) and later put on a ventilator. The chief resident, who had been following news reports of increased incidence of avian influenza in humans elsewhere in the world, could hardly believe that a case might have come to her suburban New Jersey hospital. But it had. After extensive testing, Frank was diagnosed with a virus that had formed from the mixture of genetic material from two viruses: influenza A and H5N1 influenza. Because this was a new pathogen, Frank had no immunity to it.

Neither did Martha, who was an assistant district attorney for the county. By the time she took Frank to the hospital, she had already begun to display symptoms, and she too entered the hospital and was diagnosed with avian flu. One of their two children was also admitted and placed under observation. Their other child, Frances, had left on a Girl Scout weekend camping trip the same morning that Frank had gone to his office. When public health officials arrived at the camp, they found that Frances had begun sneezing and felt tired. The parents of the other children began to receive phone calls telling them that the camp was suddenly closing, that county physicians were examining the children, and that the parents' consent would be necessary for their children to receive antiviral drugs. It did not take long for the story to hit first the local, then the national, then the international news media: there was a bird flu outbreak in New Jersey. The next day, WHO raised the risk level from Phase 3 to Phase 4 in its coding system for pandemics.

FIRST DECISIONS

In Atlanta, the CDC receives reports of Frank's diagnosis, then of Martha's diagnosis, and of suspicious symptoms that have appeared among the children at Frances' camp and among some court staff in the county where Martha works. Reports of similar cases, although with no confirmed diagnosis yet, have come from New York and Los Angeles. State and local health departments reassure CDC that they are on top of the issue. Assume that the 2005 proposed regulations discussed in Chapter 5 are now in effect. What actions can federal officials legally take at this point?

The New Jersey Health Department begins a massive public education effort. Their central message is that avian flu is generally transmitted only when an individual comes into fairly close contact with an infected person – the ballpark estimate is three to six feet. People are encouraged to stay three to six feet away from other persons at all times, to the maximum extent possible.

Health departments in the three locations where the first cases have appeared also begin the process of tracking the contacts of each of those persons. Anyone who is found to be exhibiting the symptoms of avian flu is immediately placed in hospital isolation; those without symptoms are given antiviral medications (which may have some preventive effect) and asked to stay home for 72 hours to see if symptoms develop. Their household contacts are also given antiviral drugs and face masks.

Additional cases are confirmed as avian flu, including several among health care workers at Montclair Memorial, court staff, and children at Frances' camp. The number of cases is also growing in other areas in the United States, including a few outside New York and Los Angeles. All schools and day care centers in New Jersey are closed for two weeks. There is an immediate spike in absenteeism at work, as thousands of parents suddenly have to stay home. Servers crash as more people attempt to work from home. There is growing public debate over whether large-scale quarantine should be imposed. The WHO has announced that the disease is in the Phase 6 – pandemic – stage.

THE GOVERNOR'S POWERS

New Jersey officials are trying to steer a path between effectively responding to the growing crisis and not making it worse by overreacting. The debate centers on whether the Governor should declare a public health emergency under the New Jersey law described in Chapter 6. What actions would such a declaration enable? What would be the advantages and disadvantages of declaring an emergency?

Meanwhile, a strange set of circumstances has arisen. Many normally busy streets are empty, and restaurants and shopping malls are virtually deserted. On the other hand, grocery and drug stores have been overrun and are finding it difficult to restock, in part, because absenteeism is becoming widespread. Many small businesses do not want to close but have no choice because there are no customers. The unemployment rate is ratcheting up.

Hospitals are struggling to deal with an increasing number of avian flu patients with a decreasing number of staff. Fewer sick patients are discharged and all elective procedures are delayed. Even greater numbers of the "worried well" are coming to emergency rooms when they develop sneezes or coughing. There is a wait of several hours, during which the healthy and the sick alike sit in the same waiting rooms.

MEDICAL CARE

Because this is a new strain of influenza, there is no vaccine for it. Scientists began working to develop one, starting with some of the virus first found in Frank Wheeler. They estimate that it will be another five months before such a vaccine can be produced. In the meantime, the only medical intervention consists of antiviral drugs that can be helpful in warding off viral infections if administered within 48 hours of exposure. Supplies of those are now running out.

How should the remaining stock of antivirals be allocated? When the vaccine does arrive, in what order should people have access to it? What modifications if any would you suggest to the CDC proposal outlined in Chapter 7? Explain your reasoning.

Are there legal interventions that could mitigate the crisis situation at the hospitals? What are the advantages and disadvantages of various options?

Social and economic life continues to deteriorate. School closures have continued past the initial two-week period, and it now appears that eight weeks may be a more realistic estimate. Social service agencies and charities have run food distribution programs for those in voluntary home quarantine, but they are running out of volunteers. One charitable organization working with a county agency inadvertently distributed tainted food, probably because there was insufficient oversight by an overworked staff.

As public discontent has risen, automobile travel has increased sharply (air travel is heavily restricted). There are reports of many people from New Jersey renting temporary residences in Pennsylvania, where more restaurants and stores remain open.

CONDITIONS WORSEN

The Governor asks the President to declare an emergency under the Stafford Act so that unemployment benefits and other emergency financial aid can flow into the state. Are there any legal barriers to this declaration? Are there other federal powers that can be used?

One critical area is community policing, which is stretched to the breaking point. Can the Governor deploy National Guard troops to assist local law enforcement agencies?

The Governor declared a public health emergency almost 30 days ago, and now it must be renewed (see Chapter 6). Confidentially, she asks your advice on whether to announce that the renewal will remain in effect indefinitely. A member of the legislature from the opposition party has threatened to challenge the constitutionality of an indefinite declaration. What do you advise?

Historical Perspectives

In recent years, a number of books have been written about the worldwide influenza epidemic of 1918. Although medical care is much better now, mobility is also much greater, and thus there is the potential for infectious disease to spread much faster. Consider those factors as you read about the 1918 experience, in such books as *The Great Influenza, Flu: The Story of the Great Influenza Pandemic*, and *America's Forgotten Pandemic*. Do you think a 21st century avian flu pandemic would have greater or lesser social impact than the 1918 flu?

PANDEMIC DEFINITIONS

Antibiotic (also antimicrobial): A drug produced by bacteria or fungi that destroys or prevents the growth of other bacteria and fungi.

Antiviral: A drug that is used to prevent or cure a disease caused by a virus by interfering with the ability of the virus to multiply or spread from cell to cell.

Asymptomatic: Presenting no symptoms of disease.

Avian flu (also AI or bird flu): A highly contagious viral disease with up to 100% mortality in domestic fowl caused by influenza A virus subtypes H5 and H7. Low pathogenic AI causes few problems and is carried by many birds with no resulting problems. Highly pathogenic AI kills birds and can also be fatal if transmitted to humans. There is little or no human immunity, but humans are rarely affected.

Containment measures that apply to use of specific sites or buildings include cancellation of public events (e.g., concerts, sports events, and movies), closure of office buildings, apartment complexes, or schools, and closure of public transit systems. These measures may also involve restricting entrance to buildings or other sites (e.g., requiring fever screening or use of face masks before entry).

Community-based measures to increase social distance include measures applied to whole neighborhoods, towns, or cities (e.g., snow days, establishment of fever clinics, and community-wide quarantine).

Drift: The process in which influenza virus undergoes normal mutations. The amount of change can be subtle or dramatic, but eventually as drift occurs, a new variant strain becomes dominant.

This process allows influenza viruses to change and reinfect people repeatedly through their lifetime and is the reason influenza virus strains in vaccine must be updated each year. See also "Shift."

Epidemic: A disease occurring suddenly in humans in a community, region, or country in numbers clearly in excess of those that may be typical.

H5N1: A variant of avian influenza, which is a type of influenza virulent in birds. It was first identified in Italy in the early 1900s and is now known to exist worldwide. There are both low and highly pathogenic variants in different regions of the world.

HPAI: Highly pathogenic form of avian influenza. Avian flu viruses are classified based upon the severity of the illness, and HPAI is extremely infectious among humans. The rapid spread of HPAI, with outbreaks occurring at the same time, is of growing concern for human health as well as for animal health. See also "LPAI."

Hemagglutinin: An important surface structure protein of the influenza virus that is an essential gene for the spread of the virus throughout the respiratory tract. This enables the virus to attach itself to a cell in the respiratory system and penetrate it. It is referred to as the "H" in influenza viruses. See also "neuraminidase."

Influenza: A serious disease caused by viruses that infect the respiratory tract.

Isolation: A state of separation and restriction of movement between persons or groups to prevent the spread of disease. Isolation measures can be undertaken in hospitals or homes, as well as in alternative facilities.

LPAI: Low pathogenic form of avian influenza. Most avian flu strains are classified as LPAI and typically cause little or no clinical signs in infected birds. However, some LPAI virus strains are capable of mutating under field conditions into HPAI viruses. See "HPAI."

Mutation: Any alteration in a gene from its natural state. This change may be disease-causing or a benign, normal variant.

Neuraminidase: An important surface structure protein of the influenza virus that is an essential enzyme for the spread of the virus throughout the respiratory tract. It enables the virus to escape the host cell and infect new cells. It is referred to as the "N" in influenza viruses. See also "hemagglutinin."

Pandemic: The worldwide outbreak of a disease in humans in numbers clearly in excess of normal.

Pathogenic: Causing disease or capable of doing so.

Prepandemic vaccine: A vaccine created to protect against currently circulating H5N1 avian influenza virus strains with the expectation that it would provide at least some protection against new virus strains that might evolve.

Prophylactic: A pharmaceutical or a procedure that prevents or protects against a disease or condition (e.g., vaccines, antibiotics).

Quarantine: A time period of separation or restriction of movement decreed to control the spread of disease. Before the era of antibiotics, quarantine was one of the few available means of halting the spread of infectious disease. It is still employed today as needed. Individuals may be quarantined at home or in designated facilities.

Seasonal flu: A respiratory illness that can be transmitted person to person. Most people have some immunity, and a vaccine is available. This is also known as the common flu or winter flu.

Shift: The process in which the existing H (hemagglutinin) and N (neuraminidase) are replaced by significantly different Hs and Ns. These new H or H/N combinations are perceived by human immune systems as new, so most people do not have preexisting antibody protection to these novel viruses. This is one of the reasons that pandemic viruses can have such a severe impact on the health of populations. See also "Drift."

Snow days: Days on which offices, schools, and transportation systems are closed or cancelled, as if there were a major snowstorm. This approach may be recommended to reduce disease transmission.

Virus: Any of various simple submicroscopic parasites of plants, animals, and bacteria that often cause disease and that consist essentially of a core of RNA or DNA surrounded by a protein coat. Unable to replicate without a host cell, viruses are typically not considered living organisms.

Widespread or community-wide quarantine refers to the closing of community borders or the erection of a real or virtual barrier around a geographic area (a *cordon sanitaire*) with prohibition of travel into or out of the area.

Appendix
Case Study: The Spring 2009 Swine Influenza Outbreak

Introduction

In April 2009, doctors, first in Mexico and then in California, reported cases of a new influenza virus that scientists later identified as a type of swine flu and labeled H1N1. Reports of these atypical swine flu cases rapidly began to accumulate, and within days after the first case was confirmed, government officials activated the public health emergency apparatus described in Chapters 5 and 6. The U. S. Department of Health and Human Services (DHHS) declared a national public health emergency. The World Health Organization (WHO) elevated its levels of pandemic alert, first from 3 to 4 and then from 4 to 5 (see Chapter 16). Governors issued emergency declarations. On all-news television and radio channels, coverage of the "swine flu pandemic" was almost nonstop.

In less than a month, however, both the "pandemic" and the panic it generated began to subside. Health authorities in Mexico reported that the rate of new cases was diminishing, and in the United States most persons who had been diagnosed with this new strain of influenza recovered from what seemed to be a fairly mild illness, at least when treated. Many criticized the media for excessive coverage, in effect creating an "infodemic." Some scientists expressed apprehension, however, that a second wave could appear in future months. The bottom line remained that the infection could be easily transmitted from human to human.

This appendix draws together some of the key legal and policy documents generated by the outbreak through early May 2009, when this book when to press. If you read between the lines, you can see how officials sought to use some of the new (and old) legal powers that were adopted in the wake of anthrax (2001) and SARS (2003) for a new infectious disease. Consider for yourself how well you think those powers worked in the context of a swine flu episode that may not yet over.

What Is Swine Flu?

Swine influenza is a common respiratory disease of pigs caused by type A influenza viruses. These and other animal viruses are different from seasonal human influenza viruses. Laboratory analysis performed at the Centers for Disease Control and Prevention (CDC) determined that a novel 2009 H1N1 virus began circulating in the United States and Mexico, and that it contained genetic pieces from four different virus sources (see Figure A.1). According to the CDC, this particular genetic combination of H1N1 influenza virus is new and had not been recognized before in the United States or anywhere else. With additional testing, scientists hope to produce a complete genetic sequencing.

The new virus is contagious and spreads from human to human. Patients present with symptoms similar to those of seasonal influenza. Flu viruses are thought to spread between persons mainly by coughing or sneezing. People may also become infected by touching an object or surface with flu viruses on it and then touching their mouth or nose.

It Began in Mexico

Outbreak of Swine-Origin Influenza A (H1N1) Virus Infection – Mexico, March–April 2009
    Morbidity and Mortality Weekly Report (April 30, 2009)

In March and early April 2009, Mexico experienced outbreaks of respiratory illness and increased reports of patients with influenza-like illness (ILI) in several areas of the country. On April 12, the General Directorate of Epidemiology (DGE) reported an outbreak of ILI in a small community in the state of Veracruz to the Pan American Health Organization (PAHO) in accordance with International Health Regulations. On April 17, a case of atypical pneumonia in Oaxaca State prompted enhanced surveillance

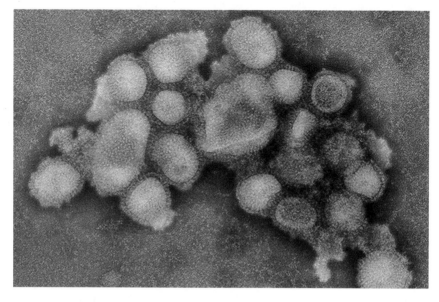

FIGURE A.1 The Swine Flu Virus

throughout Mexico. On April 23, several cases of severe respiratory illness laboratory confirmed as swine-origin influenza A (H1N1) virus (S-OIV) infection were communicated to the PAHO. Sequence analysis revealed that the patients were infected with the same S-OIV strain detected in two children residing in California. This report describes the initial and ongoing investigation of the S-OIV outbreak in Mexico.

Enhanced Surveillance

On April 17, in response to the increase in reports of respiratory illness, DGE issued a national epidemiologic alert to all influenza-monitoring units and hospitals. The alert asked hospitals to report all patients with severe respiratory illness and recommended collection of diagnostic respiratory specimens from these patients within 72 hours of illness onset. On April 18, DGE staff visited 21 hospitals throughout the country to confirm the apparent increase in illness incidence.

After laboratory confirmation of S-OIV infection on April 23, DGE developed case definitions. A suspected case was defined as severe respiratory illness with fever, cough, and difficulty breathing. A probable case was defined as a suspected case in a patient from whom a specimen had been collected and tested positive for influenza A. A confirmed case was defined as a probable case that tested positive for S-OIV by real-time reverse – transcription polymerase chain reaction (RT-PCR). Health-care officials were contacted and asked to provide retrospective and ongoing data for persons having illness consistent with these case definitions and seeking care on or after March 1.

During March 1 – April 30, a total of 1,918 suspected cases were reported, including 286 probable and 97 confirmed cases. A total of 84 deaths were reported. A majority of case-reports were for hospitalized patients, reflecting the concentration of surveillance efforts within hospitals. However, DGE also received reports from sites conducting routine seasonal influenza surveillance of patients with ILI. Of 1,069 patients with suspected and probable cases for whom information was available, 755 were hospitalized, and the remaining 314 were examined in outpatient settings or emergency departments. Suspected or probable cases were reported from all 31 states and from the Federal District of Mexico. The four areas with the most cases were Federal District [Mexico City] (213 cases), Guanajuato (141), Aguascalientes (93), and Durango (77). In other states, the number of suspected or probable cases ranged from two to 46. Suspected and probable cases were identified in all age groups. Mexico routinely monitors seasonal influenza in a network of outpatient facilities throughout the country. Fifty-one influenza A positive specimens from six states were collected during January 4 – March 11 in this surveillance network. All of these specimens tested negative for S-OIV at CDC.

Confirmed Cases of S-OIV Infection

As of April 30, DGE surveillance activities, focusing on patients with severe respiratory disease, had identified 97 patients with laboratory-confirmed S-OIV infection, including seven persons who had died. The first of the 97 patients reported onset of illness (any symptom) on March 17, and the most recent patients reported onset on April 26. Laboratory confirmation of S-OIV infection for the most recent 73 of these 97 cases was reported on the evening of April 29. Collection of additional information on these 73 cases is ongoing. Of the 24 patients for whom demographic and clinical information is available, 20 (83%) were hospitalized, three were examined in outpatient settings, and one had illness that was not medically attended. Patients ranged in age from <1 to 59 years, with 79% aged 5 to 59 years; 15 (62%) patients were female. Patients with confirmed S-OIV infection were identified in four states: Federal District (15 cases), Mexico State (seven), Veracruz (one), Oaxaca (one). Of the seven deaths, six occurred in Federal District, and one occurred in Oaxaca.

Among the 16 patients with complete clinical records, 15 reported fever, 13 reported cough, 10 reported tachypnea, and nine reported dyspnea. In addition, seven of 16 patients reported either vomiting or diarrhea. Of these seven patients, two reported vomiting only, two reported diarrhea only, and three reported both. Eight of 16 patients were admitted to intensive-care units; of these, seven required mechanical ventilation, and six subsequently died after developing acute respiratory distress syndrome. Twelve of 15 patients with radiography records available had confirmed pneumonia. Three of the 16 patients had underlying health conditions. Information on the duration of hospitalization before death was available for six patients and ranged from 1 to 18 days (median: 9 days).

Prevention and Control Measures

On April 24, the Council for General Hygiene convened with the President of the Mexican Republic and decreed the closure of all schools in the Federal District and metropolitan area of Mexico City. Incoming and outgoing airport passengers were informed of the outbreak and advised to seek care immediately should they experience symptoms of ILI. Other measures included 1) disseminating educational messages regarding respiratory hygiene through mass media; 2) distributing masks and alcohol hand-sanitizer to the public; and 3) discouraging large public gatherings, including church services, theater events, and soccer games. On April 25, a national decree allowed for house-isolation of any person with a suspected case, and on April 27, school closures were mandated throughout the country.

Editorial Note:

... Previous instances of human-to-human transmission of other swine viruses have been reported to result in small clusters of disease and limited generations of disease transmission. Several findings indicate that transmission in Mexico involves person-to-person spread with multiple generations of transmission. Patients with probable and laboratory-confirmed disease have presented over a period of 4 weeks. Limited contact tracing of patients with laboratory-confirmed disease also has identified secondary cases of ILI.

The clinical spectrum of S-OIV illness is not yet well characterized in Mexico. However, evidence suggests that S-OIV transmission is widespread and that less severe (uncomplicated) illness is common. Patients with confirmed disease have been identified in several states, and suspected cases have been identified in all states, which suggests that S-OIV transmission is widespread. In addition, several countries are reporting S-OIV infection among persons who have travel histories involving different parts of Mexico in the 7 days before illness onset. To date, case-finding in Mexico has focused on patients seeking care in hospitals, and the selection of cases for laboratory testing has focused on patients with more severe disease. Therefore, a large number of undetected cases of illness might exist in persons seeking care in primary-care settings or not seeking care at all. Additional investigations are needed urgently to evaluate the full clinical spectrum of disease in Mexico, the proportion of patients who have severe illness, and the extent of disease transmission. ...

The epidemiologic characteristics of this outbreak underscore the importance of monitoring the effectiveness of community mitigation efforts, non-pharmaceutical interventions, and clinical management practices in anticipation of a possible pandemic.

Figure A.2 shows the number of confirmed (N = 97) and probable (N = 260) cases of swine-origin influenza A (H1N1) virus (S-OIV) infection, by date of illness onset, in Mexico, during March 15 to April 26, 2009.

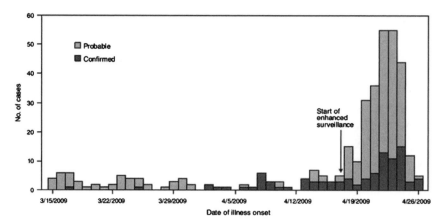

FIGURE A.2 Cases of Swine Flu in Mexico.
Source: Morbidity and Mortality Weekly Report. The U.S. Centers for Disease Control and Prevention, April 30, 2009.

The Outbreak in California

The 10-year-old boy who became "Patient A" in the United States was almost not diagnosed. With unremarkable symptoms of a cough and fever, he did not stand out among the patients seen at an outpatient clinic on a naval base in San Diego. But because the Naval Health Research Center was participating in a clinical trial of new flu tests, the staff took a nasal swab and tested it the same day. The results puzzled the virologists; they did not recognize the strain of virus.

The naval laboratory sent the sample to other laboratories for additional testing, and eventually it was sent to the CDC in Atlanta. The previous day, the CDC had received an e-mail from the Mexican Health Ministry describing an "unexplained respiratory illness." In the meantime, the naval facility got its second case of mysterious influenza, this time in a 9-year-old girl. Her nasal swab sample was sent immediately to the CDC, which found that it, too, was a previously unknown form of swine flu virus. In addition, two teenage boys in Guadalupe County, Texas had been diagnosed with an unrecognizable flu virus.

CDC staff scientists were unsure what they had on their hands, but they drafted the following bulletin to report the two California cases and to describe the epidemiological investigations that had begun:

Swine Influenza A (H1N1) Infection in Two Children – Southern California, March – April 2009

Morbidity and Mortality Weekly Report – Web site early release April 21, 2009

> On April 17, 2009, CDC determined that two cases of febrile respiratory illness occurring in children who resided in adjacent counties in southern California were caused by infection with a swine influenza A (H1N1) virus. The viruses from the two cases

are closely related genetically, resistant to amantadine and rimantadine, and contain a unique combination of gene segments that previously has not been reported among swine or human influenza viruses in the United States or elsewhere. Neither child had contact with pigs; the source of the infection is unknown. Investigations to identify the source of infection and to determine whether additional persons have been ill from infection with similar swine influenza viruses are ongoing. This report briefly describes the two cases and the investigations currently under way. Although this is not a new subtype of influenza A in humans, concern exists that this new strain of swine influenza A (H1N1) is substantially different from human influenza A (H1N1) viruses, that a large proportion of the population might be susceptible to infection, and that the seasonal influenza vaccine H1N1 strain might not provide protection. The lack of known exposure to pigs in the two cases increases the possibility that human-to-human transmission of this new influenza virus has occurred. Clinicians should consider animal as well as seasonal influenza virus infections in their differential diagnosis of patients who have febrile respiratory illness and who 1) live in San Diego and Imperial counties or 2) traveled to these counties or were in contact with ill persons from these counties in the 7 days preceding their illness onset, or 3) had recent exposure to pigs. Clinicians who suspect swine influenza virus infections in a patient should obtain a respiratory specimen and contact their state or local health department to facilitate testing at a state public health laboratory.

Case Reports

Patient A. On April 13, 2009, CDC was notified of a case of respiratory illness in a boy aged 10 years who lives in San Diego County, California. The patient had onset of fever, cough, and vomiting on March 30, 2009. He was taken to an outpatient clinic, and a nasopharyngeal swab was collected for testing as part of a clinical study. The boy received symptomatic treatment, and all his symptoms resolved uneventfully within approximately 1 week. The child had not received influenza vaccine during this influenza season. Initial testing at the clinic using an investigational diagnostic device identified an influenza A virus, but the test was negative for human influenza subtypes H1N1, H3N2, and H5N1. The San Diego County Health Department was notified, and per protocol, the specimen was sent for further confirmatory testing to reference laboratories, where the sample was verified to be an unsubtypable influenza A strain. On April 14, 2009, CDC received clinical specimens and determined that the virus was swine influenza A (H1N1). The boy and his family reported that the child had had no exposure to pigs. Investigation of potential animal exposures among the boy's contacts is continuing. The patient's mother had respiratory symptoms without fever in the first few days of April 2009, and a brother aged 8 years had a respiratory illness 2 weeks before illness onset in the patient and had a second illness with cough, fever, and rhinorrhea on April 11, 2009. However, no respiratory specimens were collected from either the mother or brother during their acute illnesses. Public health officials are conducting case and contact investigations to determine whether illness has occurred among other relatives and contacts in California, and during the family's travel to Texas on April 3, 2009.

Patient B. CDC received an influenza specimen on April 17, 2009, that had been forwarded as an unsubtypable influenza A virus from the Naval Health Research Center in San Diego, California. CDC identified this specimen as a swine influenza A (H1N1) virus on April 17, 2009, and notified the California Department of Public Health. The source of the specimen, patient B, is a girl aged 9 years who resides in Imperial County, California, adjacent to San Diego County. On March 28, 2009, she had onset of cough and fever (104.3°F [40.2°C]). She was taken to an outpatient facility that was participating in an influenza surveillance project, treated with amoxicillin/clavulanate potassium and an antihistamine, and has since recovered uneventfully. The child had not received influenza vaccine during this influenza season. The patient and her parents reported no exposure to pigs, although the girl did attend an agricultural fair where pigs were exhibited approximately 4 weeks before illness onset. She reported that she did not see pigs at the fair and went only to the amusement section of the fair. The Imperial County Public Health Department and the California Department of Public Health are now conducting an investigation to determine possible sources of infection and to identify any additional human cases. The patient's brother aged 13 years had influenza-like symptoms on April 1, 2009, and a male cousin aged 13 years living in the home had influenza-like symptoms on March 25, 2009, 3 days before onset of the patient's symptoms. The brother and cousin were not tested for influenza at the time of their illnesses.

Epidemiologic and Laboratory Investigations

… Preliminary genetic characterization of the influenza viruses has identified them as swine influenza A (H1N1) viruses. The viruses are similar to each other, and the majority of their genes, including the hemagglutinin (HA) gene, are similar to those of swine influenza viruses that have circulated among U.S. pigs since approximately 1999; however, two genes coding for the neuraminidase (NA) and matrix (M) proteins are similar to corresponding genes of swine influenza viruses of the Eurasian lineage (1). This particular genetic combination of swine influenza virus segments has not been recognized previously among swine or human isolates in the United States, or elsewhere based on analyses of influenza genomic sequences available on GenBank. Viruses with this combination of genes are not known to be circulating among swine in the United States; however, no formal national surveillance system exists to determine what viruses are prevalent in the U.S. swine population. ...

The viruses in these two patients demonstrate antiviral resistance to amantadine and rimantadine, and testing to determine susceptibility to the neuraminidase inhibitor drugs oseltamivir and zanamivir is under way. Because these viruses carry a unique combination of genes, no information currently is available regarding the efficiency of transmission in swine or in humans. Investigations to understand transmission of this virus are ongoing.

Federal and International Responses

On April 23, two days after the CDC's Morbidity and Mortality Weekly Report (MMWR) described the two California cases, the acting head of the CDC convened a teleconference with officials representing the 50 state public health laboratories and urged them to watch closely for a spike in diagnoses of flu and for reports of an unknown virus. American health officials also informed the WHO in Geneva of the developing outbreak.

The CDC had already begun to screen travelers entering the United States. Between April 19 and 27, health workers identified 15 persons with symptoms consistent with H1N1 virus infection who were entering the United States from Mexico. Of the 15, two were quickly confirmed as infected; nine were placed in isolation pending additional laboratory testing; and four were released after infection with the new virus was ruled out.

Media interest intensified each day. On April 25, the head of the WHO called a press conference to discuss the outbreak.

World Health Organization

Influenza-Like Illness Outbreak in The United States and Mexico

Transcript of
Global Telephone News Conference with Dr. Margaret Chan,
Director-General, World Health Organization
25 April 2009
Opening Statement by Dr. Margaret Chan

Good afternoon, thank you for coming. WHO is concerned about cases of swine flu ed States. A new virus is responsible for cases in both countries. The situation is evolving quickly. A new disease is, by definition, poorly understood.

We do not yet have a complete picture of the epidemiology or the risks, including possible spread beyond the currently affected areas. Nonetheless, in the assessment of WHO, this is a serious situation which must be watched very closely.

Yesterday, while in the United States, I was able to speak directly with health officials in the US and in Mexico. Both countries have expressed their concern, and I know they are taking the situation very seriously.

I thank them for their openness, transparency, and willingness to work with WHO to address this newly emerging infection.

Yesterday, I cancelled all planned meetings on other matters and cut short my trip to get back to Geneva.

Today, I spoke with WHO epidemiologists and infectious disease specialists in the different geographical offices of WHO. We do not, at present, have indications of similar outbreaks in other parts of the world.

Our vigilance will remain high. It would be prudent for health officials within countries to be alert to outbreaks of influenza-like illness or pneumonia especially if these occur in months outside the usual peak influenza season.

Another important signal is excess cases of severe or fatal flu-like illness in groups other than young children and the elderly, who are usually at highest risk during normal seasonal flu.

We are today convening a meeting of an Emergency Committee to evaluate the evidence and advise me on an appropriate course of action. The Committee will also advise me on whether WHO needs to introduce any temporary measures in the interest of protecting international health.

Influenza viruses are notoriously unpredictable and full of surprises, as we are seeing right now. The viruses causing cases in some parts of Mexico and the US are genetically the same. This is an animal strain of the H1N1 virus, and it has pandemic potential because it is infecting people.

However, we cannot say, on the basis of currently available laboratory, epidemiological, and clinical evidence, whether or not it will indeed cause a pandemic.

As a precautionary measure, I have instructed all regional offices in WHO to work closely with their countries to assess if indeed similar outbreaks or unusual patterns of flu-like illness and pneumonia have been observed. And we have also sent experts to Mexico at the request of the Government, to work with them to further analyze all the data and information, to answer some of the critical questions.

For example, how many of the 800 plus cases of severe pneumonia requiring hospitalization are indeed caused by this new virus or other causes? And in addition, we will work with US scientists and scientists from other countries to help us to assess other important dimensions. For example, we need to know how the virus is spread, and what is the transmission pattern, and whether or not it is going to cause severe disease and in what age group. Clearly, in the days and weeks ahead, we need to work very closely with the US authorities as well as with the Mexican authorities, bringing together the world's experts to bear on this very important issue.

Above all, it is important that we will keep you, the public and keep our countries, our Member States and our ministers of health informed as we move forward on these and other issues. All these issues are receiving my highest personal attention. I will stop here and will be happy to answer any questions that colleagues from the media community may have.

Journalist Associated Press. I wondered if you could talk first of all about what some of the other countries are doing, if other Member States are taking measures and also go through some of things WHO might consider, like about travel recommendations, or border closures, what are the things being considered? Are there recommendations for public health interventions, like stopping mass gatherings?

Dr. Chan: Thank you for that question. At this stage, the most important recommendation coming from WHO to other countries is to increase and enhance their surveillance. As I said, for unusual patterns of disease, whether or not there is an increase in pneumonia cases, whether or not there are outbreaks of flu-like illness outside of their seasonal flu peak season. So those are the most important. Without that kind of information, it is very difficult to realize – to know whether or not the situation is indeed confined to US and Mexico as we're seeing now. Now, as to your question about other border closures and travel advisories, I think it is too premature at this stage to make those announcements without, first and foremost having a better analysis, trying to understand the data that are coming from the Mexican authorities and help us to further understand exactly what is happening there. So for now, we will not issue those recommendations, but of course, of course, these will be questions to be addressed by the Emergency Committee that will be convened later today.

Journalist Canadian Press: Thanks very much for taking my question, Dr. Chan. I was wondering if you could tell us if you have any indication from the Mexican authorities about potential mild illness. We've been hearing about a death, and a death suspected to be associated with this virus, and lots of hospitalized cases. Given the pattern of infections in the United States, and given infectious diseases in general, you would expect, or at least hope, that there would be lots of mild cases, or that's what we are seeing is the tip of the iceberg, do you have any evidence for that?

Dr. Chan: Thank you for that question. Clearly, this is an important question. Based on the limited number of cases in the US, so far reported eight cases, all of them have recovered, and they are mild in terms of the severity of the disease. In Mexico, the picture, because of the size of the number of cases, we are seeing a range of severity, from mild to severe and to some deaths. So that is exactly what I was referring to in my earlier answer to Maria's question. We need to really comb through those data and get the granularities and understand exactly who is suffering and in which group the diseases are more severe than others and these are the work that the experts that we dispatch to the ground, they are already on the ground, working with the Mexican authorities, and hopefully, this will give us more information in the days ahead.

HB: Could I ask a follow-up question?

Dr. Chan: Yes, go ahead.

Journalist: If I hear you correctly, would you say that it would be premature to try to assess what the case fatality of the virus is and I'd also like to ask if WHO is thinking about asking vaccine manufacturers to potentially switch to production of swine flu vaccine?

Dr. Chan: Yes indeed. At this point in time, it is too premature to calculate the case fatality rate. Hopefully, you know, more evidence will emerge to give us a better sense. And your second question is again we will definitely discuss this with the emergency committee, but on the basis of information available now, I'm sure, you know, the experts will agree we need to wait for a few more days and perhaps, based on the final analysis we can have a better handle on which way to go, vis a vis, vaccine production.

Journalist at National Public Radio in the US: My first question is what, precisely is the Emergency Committee going to consider today? There's been a bit of confusion whether you're considering whether to raise the alert level or whether you're meeting to decide to declare a public health emergency of international concern. And then I have a follow-up.

Dr. Chan: Well, thank you for your question. I would expect the members of the Emergency Committee having heard the reports and representations by the two governments, namely the US and Mexico, and also the overall assessment by WHO, they may need to address those questions, indeed.

Journalist: So, the question of pandemic alert is on the table?

Dr. Chan: Yes, indeed.

Journalist: My follow-up is from my colleague Richard Knox. We've had a lot of trouble dialing into the conference today, here from the US. He wonders about the capacity of Mexico, especially Mexico City, to do the kind of flu virus typing that's needed in the kind of speed with which you need to come to decisions. Do they have the capacity there or will WHO somehow be helping them out with additional laboratory equipment or what?

Dr. Chan: Thank you for that question. I think that this is a very important question. Our experience is that with any new and emerging infection, no matter how good your existing laboratory capacity is, there would be requirement for additional research capacity in terms of having the right kind of methodology and the kind of skills to do those tests.

But I have to say the Mexican government has been very open, transparent, and they have shared virus samples with Health Canada and as well as with US Centers for Disease Control (CDC). Scientists from these two countries are working with them to do exactly the kind of work that you are talking about. And in fact, I actually met the US authorities and I talked to the Minister of Health in Mexico. We also talked about providing WHO additional expert support in laboratory science to the Mexican authority. So I just want to say, yes, we are gearing up on our side and so is the Mexican authority and I would like to thank the international community who come to assist in this assessment. It is important that we get to the bottom of the matter as soon as possible. Speed is important. Capacity is important, and we are addressing both.

Journalist from Reuters in Geneva: Are you satisfied that the Mexican authorities have enough antivirals to address this outbreak and whether you feel that Tamiflu is going to be the answer to this and whether you have any indication that there is resistance to it among any population or any certain groups affected.

Dr. Chan: At this point time, the resistance test that has been done by scientists demonstrated that this new virus is sensitive also to Tamiflu. I also had a discussion with the Minister of Health on the issue of medicine. They do have a sizeable supply themselves but of course depending on how the outbreak evolves, WHO stands ready along with international partners to support the government if it is required to acquire additional supply.

Journalist from NHK, Japan: Want to confirm with Dr Chan, can we regard this virus as a pandemic potential virus and what kind of decisions do you think you can make in this Emergency Committee?

Dr. Chan: As I mentioned in my statement earlier, this is clearly an animal strain of the H1N1 virus and it has pandemic potential because it is infecting people. The emergency committee that is convened under the authority of the International Health Regulations 2005 will examine a range of questions including whether or not based on the information available so far, what kind of recommendations they make.

But perhaps, let me take this opportunity to qualify. As I said, there are a lot of information gaps still because of the size of the outbreak, we need to really work in the days and weeks ahead with the Mexican authorities to find answers to some of the critical questions. Depending on the strength of evidence available today, we may have some answers to the kind of recommendations or questions you have raised and we may need perhaps a few more days to get further evidence to answer other questions. So in a nut shell, the experts would be examining a range of issues and we will do our best working with the two governments to present the available evidence, and based on that evidence, we will make appropriate temporary measures.

Washington Post: Timing of the meeting today and if you will be making a decision today and if so, what time and if you could explain, if you do raise the pandemic alert as a result of this meeting, what will be the impact of that.

Dr. Chan: The Expert Committee will be convened today at about 16:00 h Geneva time. Based on the whether the information as I said, whether we are going to announce this, confirm this, this is going to be a public health emergency of international concern – it has a set of implications and experts will need to look at what kind of temporary recommendations they can make. Some examples have been given – in the International Health Regulations 2005, article 18, some suggestions have been given for the consideration of the Emergency Committee.

Bloomberg News in Paris: What explanation do you have for the epidemiology in Mexico indicating disproportionate numbers of otherwise healthy young people coming to the illness and what parallels if any can we draw between this and the 1918 Spanish flu?

Dr. Chan: Can we draw any parallel to the 1918 Spanish flu – it is too premature to say. Having said that I suspect the reason you raise this question is because reports say a rather high proportion of young adults suffer from severe disease. This is one feature we were observing in the 1918 outbreak. Now, to answer your question whether or not we are indeed seeing that picture, that is one question we would like to have an answer and we need to look at whether or not the big number of cases reported are genuinely infections due to this new H1N1 or it is due to other viruses or other causes of pneumonia, so don't have those data now and we will be happy to provide those date as and when they are available.

Journalist from Japanese Newspaper: Reported that many patients in Mexico are workers at hospitals and I would like to know why so many people in the medical field are infected by the virus?

Dr. Chan: I would like to put on the record – it is not correct to say that there are "many" health care workers affected or infected, it is true that we have information that two health care workers were affected so we need to understand – that's the epidemiology and the history we need together, under what circumstances are the possible reasons for those infections to occur. It would be premature to jump to conclusions because they are health care workers that automatically the infection is from the health care setting – it could be or it could be due to other reasons. That is exactly the kind of analysis WHO experts are working with Mexican authorities to find out and report back to all my Member States and of course to the media and through the media to the general public.

Following this press conference, the Emergency Committee of the WHO met and issued a determination that the outbreak constituted a "public health emergency of international concern," the phrase used in the WHO's International Health Regulations (IHR). With this declaration, WHO asked nations to increase their surveillance activities, and CDC began to conduct additional screening for international flights. CDC also recommended that Americans avoid nonessential travel to Mexico.

Emergency Declarations in the United States

On April 26, the Acting DHHS Secretary issued the following statement:

> As a consequence of confirmed cases of Swine Influenza A (swH1N1) in California, Texas, Kansas, and New York, on this date and after consultation with public health officials as necessary, I, Charles E. Johnson, Acting Secretary of the U.S. Department of Health and Human Services, pursuant to the authority vested in me under section 319 of the Public Health Service Act, 42 U.S.C. § 247d, do hereby determine that a public health emergency exists nationwide involving Swine Influenza A that affects or has significant potential to affect national security.

Note that the DHHS Declaration references "national security." The reason for that is the relationship with another law.

The Project Bioshield Act of 2004 allows the Food and Drug Administration (FDA) to issue Emergency Use Authorizations (EUAs) during a declared emergency involving "a significant potential to affect national security." Using that precise language, the lawyers who drafted the Declaration gave a green light for the FDA to begin its own internal procedures for EUAs. EUAs authorize physicians to prescribe unapproved medical products or to prescribe approved products for unapproved uses because of the exigencies of an emergency.

The FDA issued several EUAs on April 27. The most significant EUA allowed for Tamiflu (oseltamivir) and Relenza (zanamivir) to be distributed to large segments of the population without having to comply with federal labeling requirements. Another EUA allowed for Tamiflu to be prescribed to infants under one year of age, a group for whom the FDA has not approved use of the drug under normal conditions.

In addition to the actions by the HHS and the FDA, several governors also issued declarations of emergency, including Governor Schwarzenegger of California:

WHEREAS the World Health Organization has reported an outbreak of hundreds of cases of non-seasonal influenza, including the H1N1 Swine Flu, in the Federal District of Mexico City and the surrounding Mexican states, causing multiple deaths; and

WHEREAS the first potential case of H1N1 Swine Flu was detected in California on April 18, 2009, and was subsequently confirmed; and

WHEREAS additional cases of the H1N1 Swine Flu have been detected in California, and have now been found in several other states; and

WHEREAS the evidence to date from reported human infections in Mexico indicates that the H1N1 Swine Flu Virus has adapted itself to humans so that it can emerge and spread from one person to another; and

WHEREAS the World Health Organization has raised its pandemic alert for the H1N1 Swine Flu Virus to phase four, two steps short of a full pandemic; and

WHEREAS the United States Department of Health and Human Services has declared a public health emergency, and President Obama has explained that the declaration was needed as a precautionary tool to make sure that the federal government has appropriate resources to combat the spread of the virus; and

WHEREAS the spread of the virus poses a threat to property in the state due to illness-related absenteeism, particularly among public safety and law enforcement personnel and persons engaged in activities and businesses critical to the economy and infrastructure of the state; and

WHEREAS state and local health departments must use all preventive measures, which will require access to available services, personnel, equipment, and facilities, to respond to the H1N1 Swine Flu; and

WHEREAS the H1N1 Swine Flu constitutes a potential epidemic under section 8558(b) of the Government Code that, by reason of its magnitude, is beyond the control of the services, personnel, equipment and facilities of any single county, city and county, or city and require the combined forces of a mutual aid region or regions to combat.

NOW, THEREFORE, I, ARNOLD SCHWARZENEGGER, Governor of the State of California, in accordance with the authority vested in me by the California Constitution and the California Emergency Services Act, and in particular California Government Code sections 8558(b) and 8625, find that conditions of extreme peril to the safety of person and property exists within the State of California and HEREBY PROCLAIM A STATE OF EMERGENCY in California.

Pursuant to this Proclamation, I issue the following orders to be effective immediately:

IT IS HEREBY ORDERED that all agencies and departments of state government utilize and employ state personnel, equipment, and facilities as necessary to assist the California Department of Public Health and the Emergency Medical Services Authority in immediately performing any and all activities designed to prevent or alleviate illness and death due to the emergency, consistent with the State Emergency Plan as coordinated by the California Emergency Management Agency.

IT IS FURTHER ORDERED that the Department of Public Health and the Emergency Medical Services Authority enter into such contracts as it deems appropriate to provide services, material, personnel and equipment to supplement the extraordinary preventive measures implemented by local jurisdictions, if needed.

IT IS FURTHER ORDERED that, pursuant to Government Code sections 8567 and 8571, the provisions of the Government Code, the Public Contract Code, the State Contracting Manual and Management Memo 03-10, and all policies applicable to state contracts for all agencies and departments of state government, including, but not limited to, advertising and competitive bidding requirements and approvals for non-competitively bid contracts, are hereby temporarily suspended with respect to contracts to provide services, material, personnel and equipment to respond to the emergency to the extent that such laws would prevent, hinder, or delay prompt mitigation of the effects of this emergency.

IT IS FURTHER ORDERED that, pursuant to Government Code section 8567 to ensure adequate availability of technical personnel, I am invoking Standby Order Number 1, which waives the period of time permissible for emergency appointments for the hiring of necessary emergency personnel.

IT IS FURTHER ORDERED THAT pursuant to section 8571 of the Government Code, the certification requirement of section 1079 of title 17 of the California Code of Regulations is suspended as to all persons who meet the requirements under the Clinical Laboratory Improvement Amendments of section 353 of the Public Health Service Act for high complexity testing and who are performing analysis of samples to detect H1N1 Swine Flu in any certified public health laboratory.

I FURTHER DIRECT that as soon as hereafter possible, this proclamation be filed in the Office of the Secretary of State and that widespread publicity and notice be given to this proclamation.

IN WITNESS WHEREOF I have hereunto set my hand and caused the Great Seal of the State of California to be affixed this the 28th Day of April 2009.

ARNOLD SCHWARZENEGGER
Governor of California

Altogether, however, only a small number of governors declared an emergency in their states (see Figure A.3). What kinds of considerations do you think explain the different decisions?

Congressional Engagement

With the sense of national emergency building, Congress sought to be formally briefed on how the agencies of the Executive Branch were responding. Numerous officials testified before several different congressional committees during the week of April 27. With DHHS Secretary Kathleen Sebelius not confirmed until a Senate vote on April 28, Secretary of Homeland Security Janet Napolitano took the lead in providing information to Congress and the public.

Testimony by Secretary Napolitano to the Senate Committee on Homeland Security and Governmental Affairs on Federal Coordination in Response to the H1N1 Flu Outbreak.
April 29, 2009

Secretary Napolitano: Thank you, Mr. Chairman [Senator Joe Lieberman], Senator [Susan] Collins [the ranking minority member], members of the committee. Thank you for the opportunity to testify on the national response to the H1N1 flu outbreak. This is, as you have noted, a serious situation that we are treating aggressively.

As President Obama said yesterday it is a cause for concern but not for alarm. There is a lot we don't yet know about this outbreak, but we have been preparing, as if we are facing a true pandemic, even though we don't know the ultimate scope of what will occur. We also have been preparing with the understanding that this will be a marathon and not a sprint. We are going to be at this for a while.

Mr. Chairman, as you noted, the Secretary of Homeland Security is the principal federal officer for domestic incident management, including outbreaks like this one. Under that role, we have been leading a true collaborative effort. HHS and the CDC also have lead roles on the health and science aspects of this outbreak, but every department of the federal government, or virtually every one, has a role to play.

For example, the Department of Education already has a conference call with 1,400 participants on how to report, identify and prevent H1N1 in school facilities. The United States Department of Agriculture has been working to reassure people of the safety of our pork and pork products, and to work with other countries with respect to the import of our pork products. The United States Trade Representative [is] doing the same. ...

[O]ur state, local and tribal partners are absolutely indispensable, because on many questions they actually have the lead role. They are the first responders. We are now at the Department of Homeland Security conducting daily conference calls with these partners. Some days we've had as many as 48 states participating. We have 40-plus states participating on a regular basis. ... [T]he public has a role to play here and a responsibility – responsibility to cover our mouths when we cough and responsibility to wash our hands regularly; if you are sick not to go to work; not to get on a plane

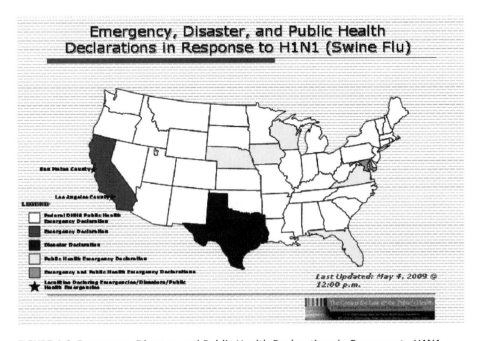

FIGURE A.3 Emergency, Disaster, and Public Health Declarations in Response to H1N1 (Swine Flu).

or a bus. [And] [i]f your child is sick, [a responsibility] not to send them to school [so as] to avoid infecting others. ...

Indiana, Nevada, Kansas, Kentucky and Ohio have received antivirals from the stockpile [Strategic National Stockpile] today. Antivirals are on their way to Arizona, California, Texas and Utah, and I'd be happy to supply the other schedule for the delivery, but that's the status as of this morning. We have placed priority on states with confirmed cases of H1N1 and, of course, with the Southwest border. But all states will ultimately get resources and we intend to have complete delivery by the third of May. ...

The State Department also has been involved with the CDC. We have issued travel health alerts and travel warnings for non essential travel to Mexico, and I anticipate those warnings and alerts will be up until the public health officials tell us they no longer need to be. Our actions are being guided by science and by what the public health community is telling us.

In addition, with respect to the Department of Homeland Security, we are moving forward in accord with planning and frameworks that had been worked on for several years. At the land ports and at the airports, CBP (Customs and Border Protection) is monitoring incoming travelers for possible H1N1 flu symptoms. Those who appear sick are put in separate rooms to be evaluated by health officials.

The TSA [Transportation Security Administration] also has similar protocols, for air travelers who appear ill, and the Coast Guard is working with shipping companies with respect to possibly ill crew members.

The travelers health advisory notices made by the CDC tell travelers about the H1N1 flu, what to do if they have symptoms, and CBP is distributing tear sheets, cards, at the land ports and to those coming in on planes from Canada and Mexico.

We're also distributing materials to passengers on cruises that stopped in Mexico; and, of course, TSA is posting all of this information at airport checkpoints. The actions at the border are consistent with and match the recommendations of the CDC and the World Health Organization.

There has been some question raised about closing the borders. ... [F]irst, the actual statutory authority is not with respect to closing an entire border. It's with respect to closing a particular port or series of ports. ... [M]aking such a closure right now has not been merited by the facts. [It] would have very, very little marginal benefit in terms of containing the actual outbreak of virus within our own country.

... [O]ur coordination with state [and] local partners is very robust. We are also coordinating with our international partners and with the private sector. I have been in phone contact with the governors of many of the states and I'll be making another series of calls this afternoon. I have spoken with my direct counterparts in Mexico and Canada.

We have adopted, in many respects, a tri-national approach to this because the virus itself doesn't know when to stop at a border. ...The private sector office and the infrastructure protection offices of the department are working with the private sector and informing them that it's time to dust off their pandemic flu plans, ... and to focus on business continuity planning as we move forward. ...

Coercive Measures and Overreaction

Several countries instituted stringent requirements for passengers arriving on international flights, especially those coming from North America. In Japan, health inspectors carrying thermographic sensors that can detect fevers walked through aircraft arriving from Canada, Mexico, and the United States. They screened 6,000 passengers a day, in a process that took an hour on large planes. Hong Kong authorities announced that any traveler arriving from a country that had reported a confirmed case of swine influenza and who had a fever or respiratory symptoms would be sent to a hospital until his or her health status could be verified by laboratory testing, a process that would take two or three days.

It should come as no surprise that the reactions to a scary new infectious disease included examples of unnecessary restrictions on individual liberty and excessive interventions directed at persons based on their nationality. By far, the most flagrant example to date has been a series of decisions by Chinese authorities, who confined dozens of Mexican tourists despite their exhibiting no signs of infection. China also placed a group of 25 Canadian exchange students in quarantine.

China's reaction came after an infected man arrived in Shanghai on a flight from Mexico City. Chinese health officials traced his whereabouts and also began rounding up the other passengers who had arrived on the same flight, as well as Mexican tourists who had arrived on other flights. The detention of Mexican nationals included some who had not been home in months. After China canceled all flights to and from Mexico, the Mexican government chartered a plane to bring the quarantined persons home, as well as any other Mexican citizens who were seeking to return.

Meanwhile the infected man whose arrival triggered the subsequent events was found in Hong Kong, where he had registered at the Metropole Hotel. The Hong Kong health authority quarantined more than 300 people in the hotel, including guests and employees, for a week.

President Felipe Calderon of Mexico condemned nations that he said were "acting out of ignorance and disinformation" and taking "repressive, discriminatory measures."

If these events had occurred in the United States, what laws would apply?

■ ■ Conflicting Views ■

Fighting the Flu With One Hand Tied
By Lawrence Gostin

> The World Health Organization and the Centers for Disease Control and Prevention are responsible for containing swine flu – a critical job that could affect tens of thousands of people in the United States and perhaps millions worldwide. But the public health agencies that are suddenly so much in the public eye lack key powers and resources. In fact, successive U.S. administrations have marginalized both, essentially rendering them less effective in times such as these.

> The outbreak of severe acute respiratory syndrome (SARS) a few years ago helped to prepare the world for today's pandemic threat because it galvanized the revision of the badly antiquated International Health Regulations in 2005. The new regulations require countries to notify the WHO of all events that may constitute a public health emergency of international concern; they grant the WHO authority to issue temporary and standing recommendations such as travel advisories and restrictions and to regulate invasive medical exams and vaccinations as a condition of entry for travelers. Yet while all other major countries with federal systems signed on without reservation, the United States gave notice that it might not comply with the regulations under principles of federalism if a public health power belonged to the states rather than the federal government.

> During the SARS outbreak, China's failure to report cases in a timely manner seriously hindered the international response. It's not clear whether the more expansive International Health Regulations will curtail the widespread noncompliance that undermined past efforts to protect public health globally. Health experts are already concerned about delays in the Mexican government's response to swine flu. The WHO is empowered to use "unofficial" sources of information, but nothing substitutes for the rapid action of countries. And the frightening truth is that the WHO has no

real power. It lacks an effective mechanism for monitoring and enforcing national reporting. Its recommendations to countries are expressly "non-binding." Countries do not even have to share virus samples with it. ...

... The CDC's legal authority to prevent the introduction, transmission or spread of communicable diseases into or within the United States dates to 1944, but its critical powers – to quarantine, inspect, disinfect and even destroy animals that are sources of dangerous infection to humans – have limited applicability to a few diseases. If the CDC did try to exercise power in response to swine flu, its legal authority would surely be challenged, causing needless delays and uncertainty – and its actions might be ruled unconstitutional. To its credit, the CDC has tried for more than a decade to modernize its legal authority. But its proposed fundamental revision was submitted more than three years ago, and regulations have yet to be finalized.

Public Safety v. Civil Liberties: Health Crisis Leads to New Case
By Amir Efrati

When a potentially deadly epidemic threatens a population, should the government be able to suspend individuals' rights if it is deemed to be in the public's interest? ...

"The history of public-health responses and the abuse of civil liberties is horrifying," says Wendy E. Parmet, a law professor at Northeastern University. Ms. Parmet says that abuses occur even though in every era, public-health officials "always believe they're doing the right thing and acting in good faith."

In the early 20th century, for instance, the federal government locked up suspected prostitutes for long periods in an effort to stem the spread of sexually transmitted disease. Officials haven't had to consider such steps in recent years, largely because there hasn't been a pandemic like the flu that killed half a million people in the U.S. in 1918–1919. But the plans exist for more drastic measures. During the Severe Acute Respiratory Syndrome and Avian Flu outbreaks of the past decade, President George W. Bush warned of possible military quarantines of U.S. populations if conditions worsened. ...

Critics say [such] provisions take a law-enforcement approach to outbreaks and treat people, not the disease, as the enemy. The new laws "assume that people will not take care of themselves and ... seem to assume the government should have power to force people to do whatever it wants them to do," says Wendy Mariner, a professor of public health at Boston University. Ms. Mariner says such laws are unnecessary; during prior outbreaks, Americans showed a willingness to comply with requests to be vaccinated or stay home.

Other detractors cite examples of how law-enforcement tactics can lead to abuses: In 2006, a tuberculosis patient in Phoenix named Robert Daniels was forced to stay in a jail for about a year after he disobeyed an order by county health officials to wear a face mask in public. ...

Conclusion or Midpoint?

As this book goes to press in early May, the CDC has reported 896 confirmed cases of swine flu in the United States and almost 1,000 more "probable cases." The WHO reported a worldwide total of 2,099 confirmed cases, including 1,112 in Mexico. The death toll in Mexico to date is 44 and in the United States is two.

Even though the acting CDC Director told the press that he expected the number of cases to keep climbing, the CDC lifted a recommendation that schools and daycare centers close if an employee or child had been diagnosed with the new virus. Also in the first week of May, Mexico lifted a number of restrictions on gathering places. High schools and universities were allowed to reopen after two weeks of having been closed, although all students were checked for flu symptoms. Primary schools were expected to reopen soon after. Restaurants were allowed to reopen with employees wearing surgical masks, and other public facilities such as movie theaters and sports events also returned to a normal schedule.

Opinions about what to expect next varied. The Mexican Minister of Health declared that the epidemic was waning in that country. In contrast, the head of the WHO section on influenza told a conference of Asian health ministers that swine flu H1N1 had the potential to infect one-third of the world's population in coming months.

Whatever the next phase of this outbreak brings, we can be sure that the powers and complexity associated with law will continue to reverberate at the heart of society's response.

References

Judicial Decisions

Adkins v. California, 50 Cal. App.4th 1802 (1996).

American Federation of Teachers v. Kanawha County Board of Education, 592 F.Supp.2d 883 (S.D.W.Va. 2009).

Aslakson v. United States, 790 F.2d 688 (8th Cir. 1986).

Berkovitz v. United States, 486 U.S. 531 (1988).

Bernal v. Fainter, 467 U.S. 216 (1984).

Bissonette v. Haig, 776 F.2d 1384 (8th Cir. 1985).

Boumediene v. Bush, 553 U.S. ___, 128 S. Ct. 2229 (2008).

Briscoe v. Potter, 355 F.Supp.2d 30 (D.D.C. 2004).

California-Nevada Methodist Homes, Inc. v. FEMA, 152 F. Supp.2d 1202 (N.D. Cal. 2001).

Camara v. Municipal Court of City and County of San Francisco, 387 U.S. 523 (1989).

Chisholm v. Georgia, 2 U.S. 419 (1793).

City of Cleburne v. Cleburne Living Center, 473 U.S. 432 (1985).

Cougar Business Owners Ass'n v. State, 647 P.2d 481 (Wash. 1982).

Cruzan v. Director, Missouri Department of Health, 497 U.S. 261 (1990).

Customer Company v. City of Sacramento, 895 P.2d 900 (Cal. 1995).

Davidson v. Commonwealth, 395 N.E.2d 1314 (Mass. App. Ct. 1979).

DeShaney v. Winnebago County, 489 U.S. 189 (1989).

Duncan v. Kahanamoku, 327 U.S. 304 (1946).

Ex parte Young, 209 U.S. 123 (1908).

Fairfield v. Occupational Safety & Health Review Commission, 285 F.3d 499 (6th Cir. 2002).

Florida Department of Agriculture v. Haire, 836 So.2d 1040 (Fla. 2003).

Franco-Italian Packing Co. v. United States, 130 Ct. Cl. 736 (1955).

Frazer v. City of Chicago, 57 N.E. 1055 (Ill. 1900).

Freeman v. United States, 556 F.3d 326 (5th Cir. 2009).

Frields v. St. Joseph's Hospital and Medical Center, 702 A.2d 353 (N.J. Super. Ct. App. Div. 1997).

Greene v. Edwards, 263 S.E.2d 661 (W.Va. 1980).

Harlow v. Fitzgerald, 457 U.S. 800 (1982).

House v. Los Angeles County Flood Control District, 153 P.2d 950 (Cal. 1944).

Housing Authority of City of Carrollton v. Ayers, 88 S.E.2d 368 (Ga. 1955).

In re Antoinette R., 630 N.Y.S.2d 1008 (Sup. Ct. NY 1995).

In re World Trade Center Disaster Site Litigation, 456 F.Supp.2d 520 (S.D.N.Y. 2006).

Jacobson v. Massachusetts, 197 U.S. 11 (1905).

Jew Ho v. Williamson, 103 F. 10 (C.C. N.D. Cal. 1900).

Lawrence v. Texas, 539 U.S. 558 (2003).

Marbury v. Madison, 5 U.S. 137 (1803).

Mathews v. Diaz, 426 U.S. 67 (1976).

McWaters v. FEMA I, 408 F.Supp.2d 221 (E.D.La. 2005).

McWaters v. FEMA II, 436 F. Supp.2d 802 (E.D.La. 2006).

Miami Area Local, American Postal Workers Union v. U.S. Postal Service, 173 F.Supp.2d 1322 (S.D. Fl. 2001).

Michigan v. Clifford, 464 U.S. 287 (1984).

Michigan v. Tyler, 436 U.S. 499 (1978).

Momans v. St. John's Northwestern Military Academy, Inc., 2000 WL 33976543 (N.D. Ill. 2000).

Motor Vehicle Manufacturers Ass'n v. State Farm Mutual Insur. Co., 463 U.S. 29 (1983).

New Jersey v. T.L.O., 469 U.S. 325 (1985).

New York State Elec. & Gas Corp. v. Secretary of Labor, 88 F.3d 98 (2d Cir. 1996).

Odello Brothers v. County of Monterey, 63 Ca.App.4th 778 (Cal. Ct. App. 1998).

Oklahoma City v. Vetter, 179 P. 473 (Okla. 1919).

People v. Clements, 661 P.2d 267 (Colo. 1983).

People v. Molnar, 774 N.E.2d 738 (N.Y. 2002).

Poe v. Ullman, 367 U.S. 497 (1961).

Romer v. Evans, 517 U.S. 620 (1996).

Sabine Pilot Service v. Hauck, 687 S.W.2d 733 (Tex. 1985).

Safeway Inc. v. Occupational Safety & Health Review Commission, 382 F.3d 1189 (10th Cir. 2004).

South Dakota Department of Health v. Heim, 357 N.W.2d 522 (S.D. 1984).

South Dakota v. Dole, 483 U.S. 203 (1987).

Souvannarath v. Hadden, 95 Cal. App. 4th 1115 (5th Dist. Cal. 2002).

State of Kansas v. United States, 748 F. Supp. 797 (D. Kan. 1990).

State of Missouri v. Pruneau, 652 S.W.2d 281 (Mo. Ct. App. 1983).

The National Tax-Litigation Committee v. Schwarzenegger, 8 Cal. Rptr.3d 4 (Ct. App. Dist. 3 2004).

Trotter v. School District 218, 733 N.E.2d 363 (Ill. 2000).

United States v. Caltex, Inc., 344 U.S. 149 (1952).

United States v. Carroll Towing Co., 159 F.2d 169 (2d Cir. 1947).

United States v. Pacific Rail Road, 120 U.S. 227 (1887).

Washington v. Glucksberg, 521 U.S. 702 (1997).

Wilson v. Layne, 526 U.S. 603 (1999).

Wong Wai v. Williamson, 103 F. 1 (C.C.N.D. Cal. 1900).

Worthington v. Fauver, 440 A.2d 1128 (N.J. 1982).

Youngstown Sheet & Tube Co. v. Sawyer, 343 U.S. 579 (1952).

Statutes

Administrative Procedures Act, 5 U. S. Code §§ 500 et seq.

Americans with Disabilities Act, 42 U.S. Code § 12101 et seq.

Emergency Management Assistance Compact, Public Law 104–321.

Emergency Medical Treatment and Active Labor Act, 42 U.S. Code §§ 1395dd.

Emergency System for Advance Registration of Volunteer Health Professionals, 42 U.S. Code § 247d–7b.

Family Medical Leave Act, 29 U.S. Code § 2601 et seq.

Federal Labor-Management Relations Act, 29 U.S. Code §§ 141 et seq.

Federal Tort Claims Act, 28 U.S. Code § 1346(b)(1).

Homeland Security Act, Public Law 107–296.

Insurrection Act, 10 U.S. Code §§ 331–334.

International Emergency Economic Powers Act, 50 U.S. Code §§ 1701–1706.

Maryland Emergency Management Act, Md. Public Safety Code §§ 14-101–14-115.

Model State Emergency Health Powers Act, Retrieved May 7, 2009, from http://turningpointprogram.org/Pages/ph_stat_mod.html.

National Emergencies Act, 50 U.S. Code §§ 1601–1605.

New Jersey Emergency Health Powers Act, N.J. Statutes, Title 26, Section 13.

New Mexico Statutes § 12-10A-16.

North Carolina General Statutes § 14-288.12.

Occupational Safety and Health Act, 29 US. Code § 651 et seq.

Pandemic and All-Hazards Preparedness Act, Public Law 109–417.

Posse Comitatus Act, 18 U.S. Code § 1385.

Project Bioshield Act, Public Law 108–276.

Public Health Security and Bioterrorism Preparedness and Response Act, Public Law 107–188.

Public Health Service Act, 42 U.S. Code §§ 243–271.

Robert T. Stafford Disaster Relief and Emergency Assistance Act, 42 U.S. Code §§ 5121 et seq.

The Military Commissions Act, 10 U.S. Code §§ 948 et seq.

The War Powers Resolution, 50 U.S. Code §§ 1541–1548.

USA Patriot Act, Public Law 107–56.

Volunteer Protection Act, 42 U.S. Code §§ 14500 et seq.

Books

Barry, J. M. (1997). *Rising Tide: The great Mississippi flood of 1927 and how it changed America*. New York: Simon & Schuster.

Barry, J. M. (2004). *The great influenza: The epic story of the deadliest plague in history*. New York: Penguin.

Crosby, A.W. (2003). *America's forgotten pandemic: The influenza of 1918*. New York: Cambridge University Press.

Goodman, R. A., Rothstein, M. A., Hoffman, R. E., Lopez, W., & Matthews, G. W. (2003). *Law in public health practice*. New York: Oxford.

Gostin, L. O. (2008). *Public health law: Power, duty, restraint*. Berkeley: University of California Press.

Heinzerling, L., & Tushnet, M. (2006). *The regulatory and administrative state: Materials, cases, comments*. New York: Oxford.

Kolata, G. B. (1999). *Flu: The story of the great influenza pandemic of 1918 and the search for the virus that caused it*. New York: Touchstone.

Markel, H. (1997). *Quarantine! East European Jewish immigrants and the New York City epidemics of 1892*. Baltimore: Johns Hopkins Press.

Novak, W. J. (1996). *The people's welfare: Law & regulation in nineteenth-century America*. Chapel Hill: University of North Carolina Press.

Articles and Other Materials

Abbott, E. B. (2005). Representing local governments in catastrophic events: DHS/FEMA response and recovery issues. *Urban Lawyer, 37*, 467–468.

Ackerman, B. (2006). Terrorism and the constitutional order. *Fordham Law Review, 75*, 475–488.

Annas, G. J. (2003). Puppy love: Bioterrorism, civil rights, and the public's health. *Florida Law Review, 55*, 1171–1190.

Arras, J. D. (2005). Rationing vaccine during an avian influenza pandemic: Why it won't be easy. *Yale Journal of Biology and Medicine, 78*, 283–296.

Barbera, J., Macintyre, A., Gostin, L., Inglesby, T., O'Toole, T., DeAtley, C., et al. (2001). Large-scale quarantine following biological terrorism in the United States. *Journal of the American Medical Association, 286,* 2711–2717.

Batlan, F. (2007). Law in the time of cholera: Disease, state power, and quarantine past and future. *Temple Law Review, 80,* 53–121.

Binder, D. (2002). Emergency action plans: A legal and practical blueprint: 'Failing to plan is planning to fail'. *University of Pittsburgh Law Review, 63,* 791–814.

Center for Counterproliferation Research, National Defense University. Anthrax in America: A chronology and analysis of the fall 2001 anthrax attacks (2002) (available at http://www.ndu.edu/centercounter/prolif_publications.htm), (last visited June 5, 2009).

Cohn, A. D. (2005). Mutual aid: Intergovernmental agreements for emergency preparedness and response. *Urban Lawyer, 37,* 1–52.

Cole, D. (2004). The priority of morality: The emergency constitution's blind spot. *Yale Law Journal, 113,* 1753–1800.

Congressional Budget Office. (2006). *A potential influenza pandemic.* Retrieved May 7, 2009, from http://cbo.gov/publications/collections/influenza.cfm.

Cooper, S. (2006). Test case: A preview of disruption. *Harvard Business Review, 84,* 36–40.

Cutter, S. (2006). The geography of social vulnerability: Race, class and catastrophe. Retrieved May 7, 2009, from http://understandingkatrina.ssrc.org/Cutter/.

Dana, C. L. (1916, January 2). Urges state to turn over quarantine to U.S. *New York Times.*

Decker, J. F. (1999). Emergency circumstances, police responses, and Fourth Amendment restrictions. *Journal of Criminal Law & Criminology, 89,* 433–534.

Efriat, A. (2009, May 7). Public safety v. civil liberties: Health crisis leads to new case. *Wall Street Journal,* A-13.

Enarson E. (2006). Women and girls last?: Averting the second post-Katrina disaster. Retrieved May 7, 2009, from http://understandingkatrina.ssrc.org/Enarson/.

Executive Order No. 12,866 (1993), printed at 58 Federal Register 51735.

Executive Order No. 13,295 (2003), printed at 68 Federal Register 17255.

Executive Order No. 13,375 (2005), printed at 70 Federal Register 12579.

Feinberg, D. L. (2006). Hurricane Katrina and the public health-based argument for greater federal involvement in disaster preparedness and response. *Virginia Journal of Social Policy & Law, 13,* 596–636.

Fidler, D. P. (2001). Legal issues surrounding public health emergencies. *Public Health Reports, 116* (Suppl. 2), 79–86.

Franco, C., Toner, E., Waldhorn, R., Inglesby, T. V., & O'Toole, T. (2007). The National Disaster Medical System: Past, present and suggestions for the future. *Biosecurity and Bioterrorism, 5*, 319–326.

Goodman, R. A., et al. (2003). Forensic epidemiology: Law at the intersection of public health and criminal investigations. *Journal of Law, Medicine, & Ethics, 31*, 684–700.

Gostin, L. (2009, May 1). Fighting the flu with one hand tied. *Washington Post.*

Gostin, L. O. (2003). When terrorism threatens health: How far are limitations on personal and economic liberties justified? *Florida Law Review, 55*, 1105–1170.

Gostin, L. O., Sapsin, J. W., Teret, S. P., Burris, S., Mair, J. S., Hodge, J. G., Jr., et al. (2002). The Model State Emergency Health Powers Act: Planning for and response to bioterrorism and naturally occurring infectious diseases. *Journal of the American Medical Association, 288*, 622–628.

Gould, R. M., & Stern, S. (2004). Catastrophic threats and the Fourth Amendment. *Southern California Law Review, 77*, 777–834.

Greenberger, M. (2006). The Alphonse and Gaston of governmental response to national public health emergencies: Lessons learned from Hurricane Katrina for the federal government and the states. *Administrative Law Review, 58*, 611–626.

Hodge, J. G. (2008). Principles and practice of legal triage, during public health emergencies. *NYU Annual Survey of American Law, 64*, 249–291.

Hodge, J. G., Jr., Gable, L. A., & Cálves, S. H. (2005). The legal framework for meeting surge capacity through the use of volunteer health professionals during public health emergencies and other disasters. *Journal of Contemporary Health Law & Policy, 22*, 5–71.

Hoffman, S. (2009). Preparing for disaster: Protecting the most vulnerable in emergencies. *University of California-Davis Law Review* (forthcoming).

International Labour Organisation. (1969). Medical care and sickness benefits recommendation, No. 134.

Kinlaw, K., & Levine, R. (2007). Ethical guidelines in pandemic influenza. Retrieved May 7, 2009, from http://www.cdc.gov/od/science/phethics/guidelinesPanFlu.htm.

Kosar, K. R. (2005). *Disaster response and appointment of a recovery czar: The executive branch's response to the flood of 1927.* Congressional Research Service (RL33126), Washington, D.C.

Lerner, K. (1991). Government negligence liability exposure in disaster management. *Urban Lawyer, 23*, 333–354.

Leroy, M. H. (2004). From docks to doctor office after 9/11: Refusing to work under "abnormally dangerous conditions," *Administrative Law Review, 56*, 585–656.

Maiello, M. (2003, May). Aftershock. *Forbes Magazine.*

National Defense University. (2002). *Anthrax in America*. Center for Counterproliferation Research. Retrieved May 7, 2009, from http://www.ndu.edu/centercounter/prolif_publications.htm.

National Emergency Management, The Emergency Management Assistance Compact: An Overview (available at http://emacweb.org/) (last visited June 5, 2009).

National Institutes of Health, National Institute of Allergy and Infectious Diseases. Emerging and re-emerging infectious diseases (available at http://www.niaid.nih.gov/topics/emerging/introduction.htm) (last visited June 5, 2007).

Nonprofit Risk Management Center. (2001–updated 2006). *State liability laws for charitable organizations and volunteers*. Retrieved May 7, 2009, from http://nonprofitrisk.org/store/state-liability.shtml.

Nowadzky, R. A. (1995). Lawyering your municipality through a natural disaster or emergency. *Urban Lawyer, 27*, 9–28.

Relyea, H. C. (2006). *National emergency powers*. Washington, D.C. Congressional Research Service (updated 2006) (98-505 GOV).

Rossi J. (2006). State executive lawmaking in crisis. *Duke Law Journal, 56*, 237–278.

Rothstein, M. A., Alcalde, M. G., Elster, N. R., Majumder, M. A., Palmer, L. I., Stone, T. H., et al. (2003). Atlanta, GA *Quarantine and isolation: lessons learned from SARS: A report to the Centers for Disease Control and Prevention*.

Rothstein, M. A., & Talbott, M. K. (2007). Job security and income repacement for individuals in quarantine: The need for legislation. *Journal of Health Care Law and Policy, 10*, 239–258.

Salzberg, K. (2006). The dog that didn't bark: Assessing damages for valid regulatory takings. *Natural Resources Journal, 46*, 131–156.

Sar, D. W. (1995–1996). Helping hands: Aid for natural disaster homeless vs. aid for "ordinary homeless". *Stanford Law and Policy Review, 7*, 129–150.

Schuck, P., & Park, J. (2000). The discretionary function exception in the second circuit. *Quinnipiac Law Review, 20*, 55–73.

Segal, M., & Hearne, S. A. (2005). Protecting corporate America from bioterrorism and epidemics after the sunset of the terrorism risk insurance act. *Biosecurity and Bioterrorism, 3*, 148–153.

Swanson, H. D. (2000). The delicate art of practicing municipal law under conditions of hell and high water. *North Dakota Law Review, 76*, 487–510.

Tandy, E. C. (1923). Local quarantine and inoculation for smallpox in the American colonies. *American Journal of Public Health, 13*, 203–207.

The White House. (2003, February 28). *Homeland Security Presidential Directive (HSPD) 5* Retrieved May 7, 2009, from http://www.dhs.gov/xabout/laws/gc_1214592333605.shtm.

Townsend, F. F. (2006). *The federal response to Hurricane Katrina: Lessons learned*. Retrieved May 7, 2009, from http://georgewbush-whitehouse. archives.gov/reports/katrina-lessons-learned/.

U.S. Centers for Disease Control and Prevention. Interstate quarantine, 42 Code of Federal Regulations Part 70.

U.S. Centers for Disease Control and Prevention. Foreign quarantine, 42 Code of Federal Regulations Part 71.

U.S. Department of Health and Human Services. (2005, November 30). Control of communicable Diseases: Proposed rule. *Federal Register, 70,* 71871.

U.S. Department of Health and Human Services. *Pandemic Influenza Plan*. Retrieved May 7, 2009, from http://www.hhs.gov/pandemicflu/plan/.

U.S. Department of Homeland Security. *National response framework*. Retrieved May 7, 2009, from http://www.fema.gov/emergency/nrf/.

Weida, J. C. (2004). A republic of emergencies: Martial law in American jurisprudence. *Connecticut Law Review, 36,* 1397–1438.

Williams, V. J. (2006). Fluconomics: Preserving our hospital infrastructure during and after a pandemic. *Yale Journal of Health Policy, Law & Ethics,* Vol 7.

Index

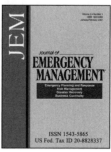